Beauty of the City

A. E. Doyle (RC)

Beauty of the City

A. E. DOYLE, PORTLAND'S ARCHITECT

BY

PHILIP NILES

Oregon State University Press
Corvallis

The front cover photograph was taken late in the summer of 1915 on SW 5th Avenue near Morrison when A. E. Doyle's Meier & Frank Building, on the right, was completed. Behind it are three of his other early tall buildings. Left to right, the Northwestern National Bank Building (now the American Bank Building), the Selling Building (now the Oregon National Building) and the Meier & Frank Annex (now part of Macy's) dwarf three early Victorians of which only Pioneer Courthouse survives. The Portland Hotel is now Pioneer Square and the four-story Stearns Building was razed in the 1930s to complete the Meier & Frank block to Doyle's plan. (PCA A2004-002.1441)

The paper in this book meets the guidelines for permanence and durability of the Committee on Production Guidelines for Book Longevity of the Council on Library Resources and the minimum requirements of the American National Standard for Permanence of Paper for Printed Library Materials Z39.48-1984.

Library of Congress Cataloging-in-Publication Data
Niles, Philip.
Beauty of the city : A.E. Doyle, Portland's architect / by Philip Niles.
p. cm.
Includes bibliographical references and index.
ISBN-13: 978-0-87071-298-2 (alk. paper)
1. Doyle, A. E. (Albert Ernest), 1877-1928. 2. Architects--United States--Biography. 3. Architecture--Oregon--Portland--20th century. I. Title.
NA737.D68N55 2008
720.92--dc22

2008020944

Printed in the United States of America

Oregon State University Press
121 The Valley Library
Corvallis OR 97331-4501
541-737-3166 • fax 541-737-3170
http://oregonstate.edu/dept/press

"All new things built with the idea of preserving the beauty of the city and adding to it."

A. E. Doyle, September 16, 1906

Contents

Preface

A. E. Doyle and Portland grew up together. As a boy he came with his mother and father to the small river town in a sparsely populated and distant American state. Within a few years in his childhood, railroads connected it to the East and to California and brought people and shipped out lumber, grain, flour, and salmon. He was a youth during the depression of the nineties and a student in New York during the recovery in the early 1900s. He opened his office in January 1907 at the beginning of a long period of growth and development, sometimes called "Portland's Golden Age," when tall buildings, public libraries, Reed College, the Art Museum, department stores, all institutions of twentieth-century urban life, appeared. Portland was becoming urban, even cosmopolitan, by copying New York and emulating Europe. Its architecture was to express accomplishments and aspirations and erase traces of the frontier. A notable group of architects with training in the East and Europe assembled. They formed a local architectural club, received recognition from the Beaux Arts Society, founded an Oregon chapter of the American Institute of Architects, and helped to develop a school of architecture at the University of Oregon in Eugene. It was a propitious time, which lasted from the Lewis and Clark Exposition which closed October 15, 1905, until the Great Depression. A. E. Doyle's career nearly filled that period. He began his practice just over a year after the end of the fair and he died January 23, 1928. For nearly all of that time he was Portland's most important architect.

He designed seven office buildings, three banks, two hotels, the Central Library, Reed College, Multnomah Stadium, and one of the city's three settlement houses. It was the heyday of the department store, and Portland had four. Three were completely his. For the fourth he was the local consulting architect; he designed the interior and planned a five-story extension, which was never built.

Arguably, he did more for Portland as it is today than any architect before or since. For example, when his career began, Pioneer Courthouse, for over a century the reputed center of the city, was already in a well-developed urban neighborhood. Today Pioneer Courthouse is the sole Victorian vestige in the area; and

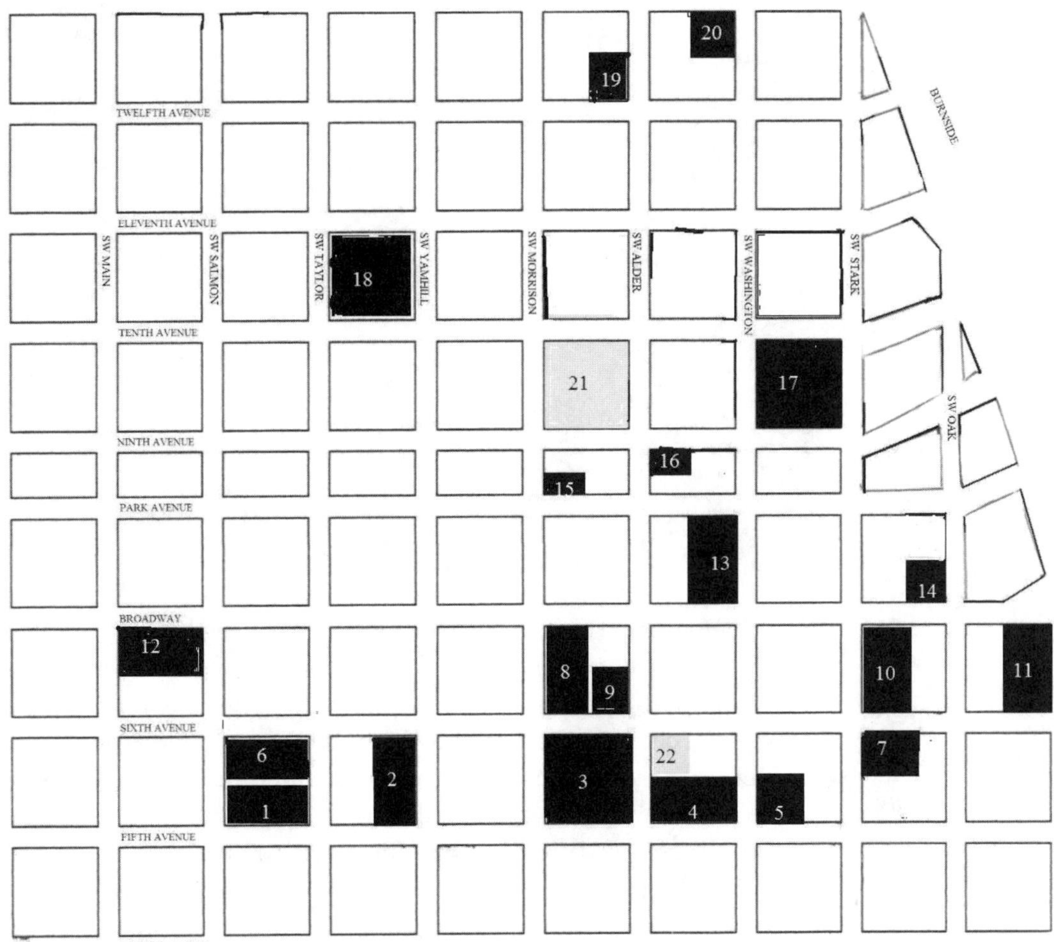

Doyle's Downtown Portland

1. Metropolitan Garage; 2. Pacific Building; 3. Macy's (Meier & Frank); 4. Hotel Monaco; 5. Mead Building; 6. Public Service Building; 7. Bidwell & Co. (Bank of California); 8. American Bank Building; 9. Oregon National Building; 10. U. S. Bank; 11. Broadway Garage; 12. Broadway Theater (gone); 13. Morgan Building; 14. Benson Hotel; 15. Whitmarsh Building; 16. Woodlark Building; 17. Pittock Block; 18. Central Library; 19. Terminal Sales Building; 20. First Presbyterian Church Parish House; in association with other architects: 21. Galleria; 22. Cascade Building

Central Portland was a well-established urban neighborhood of Victorian buildings when Doyle began. This photograph was taken at SW 5th and Morrison in 1907, the year Doyle opened his office. The Post Office (now Pioneer Courthouse) is the only building seen here that survives today. Whidden & Lewis' Meier & Frank is on the right. West of it is the four-story Stearns Building, which in 1932 was

it is dwarfed by two Doyle buildings. The Pacific Building, to the south, is a replica of an Italian Renaissance palace, and Macy's, to the north, is a white, terra-cotta, classic department store.[1] North of Macy's, on the west side of SW 5th Avenue, are two more Doyle buildings: Hotel Monaco and the Mead Building. One block west at SW 6th and Morrison is another Doyle street. On the west side of SW 6th are two buildings by him: south to north, the American Bank Building and the Oregon National Building. He was even the local associated architect for the Cascade Building on the northeast corner of SW 6th and Alder; while the design was not his, it adapts well to its neighbors and complements his idea for the area.

Most of his buildings continue to serve, if not the firms or institutions for which he designed them, in the same or a similar function as do all seven of his office buildings. His Multnomah Stadium has been restored, remodeled, and refashioned as PGE Park. His U.S. National Bank is the main Portland branch, now of U.S. Bank and his Women's Union, a home for young, single, working women, is now Montgomery Court, a Portland State University dormitory. The building he designed as the Central Library is the main branch of the Multnomah Library system. The Benson Hotel is still one of Portland's important hotels. Macy's is still a department store, although it is being renovated to house, in addition to the store on the bottom five floors, a boutique hotel above at considerable expense to the city because the building is an important part of the city's heritage. Other buildings have found new functions. Olds, Wortman, & King, now the Galleria, houses a few stores and restaurants as well as the Western Culinary Institute. The Holtz Department Store and the Woodlark Building have become office buildings. Lipman Wolfe is Hotel Monaco. His Neighborhood House was recently sold to Cedarwood School, which is now raising money for seismic upgrades to continue a tradition of education and neighborhood service. Sometimes changes say more about social attitudes than about buildings. His Henry Wemme Home for Wayward and Difficult Girls is today the Salvation Army's White Shield Center for "the needs of pregnant and parenting clients between the ages of twelve and eighteen."

replaced by the final section of the Meier & Frank building to match Doyle's design. Across SW 6th Avenue is the Marquam Building. West of the Courthouse is the Portland Hotel. Compare this photograph to the cover illustration, which was taken from the same position just eight years later to see how quickly and how much he changed Portland. (PCA A2004-002.741)

While many of his buildings have been in use for nearly a century and all are over seventy-five years old, only two have been demolished. The Cromwell Apartment House (1912) was where the Wells Fargo Center is now, at SW 5th and Jefferson, and the Broadway Theater was at SW Broadway and Salmon, where the 1000 Broadway Building now stands; his theater is recalled in a marquee at the base of the modern skyscraper where there is today a modern multiplex, also called Broadway.

Some of his buildings have become so closely associated with the institutions they house that his designs seem to signify the institutions themselves—like Macy's, the U.S. Bank, the Central Library, the Benson Hotel, and Reed College. On February 14, 1959, one hundred years to the day since Oregon became a state, a banquet commemorated the centennial in his soaring lobby of the U.S. National Bank.

One of his designs is an especially forceful icon of the city. His Benson Bubblers, the four-spigoted bronze fountains on many downtown streets, are as much about Portland as any of his designs of terra-cotta and brick. They also say a lot about A. E. Doyle himself, "an epitome in miniature" of his talent, "wholly practical" yet "a balanced, tasteful work of art."[2] They are "bubblers" because they bubble persistently except in droughts and cold weather, and they are named after Simon Benson, a timber baron, who paid to have them designed, manufactured, and installed. In the 1960s a zealous manager of the Benson Hotel (also named

Doyle designed his drinking fountains, affectionately known as Benson Bubblers, in 1912. The city has retained the mold and manufactures copies for street corners throughout the city. (Author's photograph)

For his large, expensive, and growing library, A. E. Doyle designed his own book plate, appropriate to his architecture and his interests. It was printed in about 1909 by Scribner & Sons in New York and again fifteen years later. A good supply of the plates remains today with his collection at Reed. (RC)

for Simon Benson because he commissioned Doyle to design it) decided the Benson Bubbler outside the hotel needed cleaning. The city thought otherwise, because there is a difference between tarnish and patina, and some symbols are too important to be polished. The city engineering department dismantled the shiny fountain, applied chemicals to oxidize the bronze, reassembled it, and billed the hotel $600.

In addition to his many downtown buildings A. E. Doyle designed a number of houses in Portland, especially in the West Hills. He designed banks and other buildings in other Northwest communities, including Oregon City, Salem, Albany, Eugene, Hood River, and Seattle. He worked for Monmouth College, now Western Oregon University; Albany College, now Lewis and Clark College; and Linfield College, as well as Reed. He designed country houses for clients in the Tualatin Valley, on the coast, and in the Columbia River Gorge. In his last year he even arranged for a bank and a department store in Boise, which he did not live to see completed. Because he and some of his friends vacationed at Neahkahnie on the Oregon coast, he designed four cottages there and some schools in nearby Wheeler, Mohler, Nehalem, and Tillamook.

For twenty-one years he was responsible for all the designs that came out of the firms he was part of. In 1907 he was in partnership with William Patterson, who was an engineer and supervised construction. In 1911 James George Beach, an engineer, joined the company; he left in 1913. Doyle and Patterson dissolved their partnership in 1915. In 1919 Doyle established a satellite office, Doyle & Merriam, in Seattle and in 1920 another in Pendleton, Doyle & Reese, which lasted just one year. Doyle & Merriam was dissolved in 1926. H. C. Reese and C. A. Merriam were both engineers and in matters of design they deferred to Doyle. Talented designers worked for Doyle, such as C. K. Greene and P. Belluschi, but even when Doyle was terminally ill, he maintained control.

In sum, he was the principal designer in the most important architectural firm during Portland's great building boom. What he built has been so well preserved that he has left an indelible mark on his city. It is evident on many streets in buildings of brick and terra-cotta with porticoes, pillars, pilasters, capitals, and loggias. They convey an impression of other times and places and intimate ancient temples and palaces. Doyle was a classicist; he emulated ancient Greece and those periods of the European past which returned for inspiration to Greece: especially Rome and the Renaissance in Italy, England, and France; his buildings show the influence of classical principles of balance and proportion, of "restraint" and "good taste," he said.

Acknowledgments and Sources

I would like to thank the members of A. E. Doyle's family who have assisted this project: the late George McMath, Marjorie Newhouse, and Ruth Ulvog (Doyle's grandchildren), and Lisa Holzgang (George McMath's daughter). They were born after Doyle died and never knew him. Marjorie Newhouse spent formative years in the Doyle home, where Lucie Godley (Mrs. A. E.) Doyle lived until she died. George McMath was early encouraged to become an architect. Strongly influenced by modernists, he was not interested in his grandfather's work until he was fifty, when he began writing on Doyle and other early Portland architects. McMath's many publications have defined the study of Portland and Northwest architecture. His knowledge of architecture, his relationship with the family, and his collection of materials early identified him as the authority on Doyle; he had intended to write the book on his grandfather in his retirement, but illness intervened. Lisa Holzgang has some of her father's collection—some has been lost—including a scrapbook, which McMath made from the pictures, plans, and family mementos that he inherited from his grandfather. It includes Doyle's last report card and newspaper articles that Doyle clipped himself, as well as drawings and plans. An invaluable job list of all Doyle's projects, prepared by George McMath, is included as an appendix in a Reed B. A. thesis.[3] Marjorie Newhouse is the unofficial and modest family historian with an indefatigable memory of family lore and a wonderful collection of Doyle memorabilia: the diary from his student's tour of Europe, letters he wrote his fiancée, Lucie Godley, their wedding invitation and wedding program, family photographs, newspaper clippings, and some of his sketches. Her home delightfully displays family keepsakes, portraits, and drawings. It is a wonderful testimonial to the grandfather she never met.

A. E. Doyle's business records, specifications for construction, correspondence, shop drawings, sketches, and plans, all the records of his firm, after his death, passed to his successor Pietro Belluschi, who kept them together with his own; when Belluschi retired, he gave his and Doyle's papers to the University of Syracuse Library. The collection is massive, covering nearly three-quarters of a century of Portland architecture and social history. It fills 455 feet of shelf space. I cite them throughout as the Belluschi Papers because that is how the University of Syracuse Library has catalogued even Doyle's papers. I am grateful to Diane Cooter and Bill Lee for the assistance they provided in using this collection. The Doyle records are best for the years 1926 to 1928 when Doyle was often absent from the office because of travel and illness, so he wrote instructions to and received reports from the firm. The papers for the period from about 1920 through 1926 are nearly as good; Doyle was usually in Portland, and his office staff preserved and classified the papers. For the period 1907-1920 the files are thinner.

A. E. Doyle's widow bequeathed his books to her grandson, George McMath, the only member of the family to become an architect. He kept and treasured them until he became ill. In 1994 they were placed on the market. Reed College bought them out of respect for the man who had designed its campus and principal buildings. They are catalogued and in the college's Special Collections, but after three quarters of a century, some have disappeared and others have crept in. I have compared the present collection to the catalogue of his library, which was prepared by his office staff in 1927, the year before his death. By my count there were 344 titles in 488 volumes in 1927; of these, 81 titles in 103 volumes are no longer found in the collection. Usually Doyle signed his books. Often he dated them. And occasionally he made marginal notations. The earliest books that he acquired in his youth were elementary textbooks and exhibition catalogues. As he prospered his acquisitions reflected his success. He collected books on European architecture especially of Greece, Rome, the Renaissance, and the Middle Ages. I want to thank Gay Walker and Mark Kuestner for their assistance with this library and with preparation of the illustrations for this book.

There are some other Doyle materials. The Oregon Historical Society has plans for many of his most important projects and photographs of some of his buildings. The Portland Art Museum has a correspondence between him and Anna Belle Crocker, a lifelong friend and the curator of the Art Museum. The Museum also has art he donated and a variety of papers by and about him, since he was a lifetime member, officer, and patron. Reed College has, in addition to his library, his large post card collection as well as letters and papers by and about him because he was the architect and a regent for a decade and a half.

I would especially like to thank Ann who has tirelessly toiled with me on this book and given me much good advice.

⇠

For convenience and brevity, I have adopted the following abbreviations for the various manuscript collections.

McMath	The Collection of George McMath
Newhouse	The Collection of Marjorie Newhouse
OHS	Oregon Historical Society
PAM	The Anne and James Crumpacker Family Library in the Portland Art Museum
SUPBP	The George Arendt Research Library in the E. S. Bird Library of Syracuse University Pietro Belluschi Papers
RC	Reed College Special Collection, Eric V. Hauser Memorial Library

I have also used:

Jour.	*The Journal*
HRI	Historic Resource Inventory, City of Portland, Bureau of Planning, 1984
NRHP	National Register of Historic Places, The Nomination Forms of Doyle buildings are at Oregon Parks and Recreation Department, State of Oregon Preservation Office, Salem, and at the OHS
Oreg.	*The Oregonian*
OHQ	*The Oregon Historical Quarterly*
PCA	City of Portland Archives
SB	Scrapbook

A Note on Addresses and Names

Street names and house numbers changed during A. E. Doyle's life. In 1931, nearly four years after his death, a wholly new system was adopted, establishing one hundred numbers for each block and five geographic divisions for the city: N, NE, SE, NW, and SW.[4] For clarity, unless I indicate otherwise in the text, I give the modern address.

Here in the preface I have discussed his legacy by identifying buildings with their modern names. Elsewhere in the text I identify buildings with the names he and his contemporaries used. In the appendix I list buildings and houses with their modern addresses and with both modern and original names.

CHAPTER 1

Growing Up

Albert Doyle was no more than five when he came to Portland. His arrival was unrecorded except for the appearance of his father's name in the City Directory of 1882.[1] James Doyle was born in 1840 in Louisville, Kentucky, and he served with the Confederacy during the Civil War. His wife, Mary Oakey Doyle, was born in England January 17, 1847, but she grew up in Memphis. The couple came west in 1868. He was a carpenter, and they tried Portland briefly in the 1870s, but on July 27, 1877, when Albert Ernest Doyle was born they were living in Santa Cruz, California. They were there still in 1880 for the U.S. Census.[2]

Portland was a provincial river town, an American outpost with regular boat service to San Francisco. Steamers announced themselves by firing a gun, and a crowd gathered. The first transcontinental train arrived on September 10, 1883. The night before, Thomas Lamb Eliot, the pastor of the Unitarian Church, spoke at Evensong about the significance of regular train service with the East. As a fifteen-year resident he knew Portland's isolation. He had come to be Portland's first Unitarian minister in 1867, two years before the transcontinental railroad reached San Francisco. He and his family left St. Louis November 11, 1867, and traveled by way of New York. A steamer took them to the Isthmus of Panama. Another on the Pacific side brought them to San Francisco and a six-day wait for the boat to Portland. They arrived in Portland the day before Christmas after a transit of forty-four days; Mrs. Eliot was seasick for most of them.[3] The arriving train, he said, would do more than move people and goods; it would end an era when "Isolation became a habit of mind. Our thoughts have so long gone around by San Francisco." *The Oregonian* agreed. Portland would be jolted into a new relationship with the outside world. "The Northern Pacific line is destined to greatly accelerate its (Portland's) already rapid rate of growth and to yield incalculable advantages to all its interests." There would be new industries and new products like fresh salmon in refrigerator cars and fresh and dried fruits. Land values soared in the early 1880s.

People were pouring into Portland, twelve hundred a month by one estimate. Portland developed rapidly into a small city. In 1880 the population was 17,577. By 1890 it had nearly tripled to 46,385. There was work for carpenters like James Doyle.[4]

A brief account of A. E. Doyle's childhood and training was written in 1922 at the height of his career for a collection of short biographies of Oregon worthies, more flattering than correct. He was said to have come from a prominent family, which prepared him for success, for his father was an important Portland contractor of "many of the most substantial structures during the early period in the development of this city" in "partnership with Mr. Porter," who was "one of the pioneer builders of the city." From their work together Porter & Doyle "became known as leading contractors of Portland, the excellence of their work securing for them many important contracts."[5] This information has been repeated in obituaries, in biographical dictionaries of American architects, and in the nomination forms for the National Register of Historic Places.

In fact there was no Porter & Doyle firm; James Doyle was for two years a carpenter working for Robert Porter, contractor. The city directories have a classified section with lists of the members of each profession. As Portland grew so did the list of carpenters and contractors. Yet on those lists between 1882 and 1904, when James Doyle died, his name appears only eight times.[6] His career, such as it was, languished between odd jobs and wage work. In the 1880s and 1890s carpenters had low wages and difficulty finding work; there was a recession in the middle of the eighties and in the 1890s there were bank failures and a depression. Regular train service brought job seekers who, whatever their skills, infiltrated the building trades because carpentry was a job more than a profession.[7]

By the time A. E. Doyle was prominent, James had been long enough dead after an obscure life that no one outside the family knew anything about him. The family had one fixed memory of him, a simple summation of one man's life and struggles: James was an alcoholic. His alcoholism made an impression on his son: A. E. Doyle kept his household abstemious except for wine at Christmas. His childhood was difficult. His formal education ended at the eighth grade, and he went to work early.[8] These were facts known to the family and perhaps to members of his firm; but no one wanted to write them in his prime or after his death.

The family grew quickly. His brother Arthur was born in 1880, Edward in 1882, and Daisy in 1885. Despite their numbers they lived in small houses in working-class neighborhoods. They moved often, seven times in their first thirteen years in Portland, but their houses did not become bigger or better.[9] They were small frame structures with sheds attached, probably for a carpenter's workshop. In 1882 their first Portland house was on SW 9th between Yamhill and Taylor, approximately where the Guild Theater is today. They moved first to SW 5th near Burnside, then to Slabtown, to NW 23rd, then to NW Savier between 17th and 18th, in a neighborhood that was obliterated by the freeway approaches of I405 and US30 and the Fremont Bridge. From there they went to South Portland and houses successively on SW Corbett, on 3rd, on Woods, and on Curry. Today these streets, or what remains of them, are surrounded by the main arteries that connect central Portland to Lake Oswego, Milwaukie, and Tigard. In the 1960s the neighborhood was truncated by urban renewal, which did not reach far enough south to blot out completely the neighborhood of small late nineteenth- and early twentieth-century working-class cottages. Already at the end of the nineteenth century, the neighborhood was absorbing immigrants and developing an ethnic character it would retain for three quarters of a century. Increasingly east European Jews and Italians with some Irish,

In the backyard of A. E. Doyle's home on NE 8th Avenue, the Doyle family gathered for a picnic in about 1915. Mary Doyle is at the head of the table. Near her are two of her children, A. E. Doyle's siblings. To her left is her youngest child and only daughter Daisy. The young man second on Daisy's left is Edward Doyle, her youngest son. (Newhouse)

Scandinavians, Asians, and Blacks moved there for affordable housing and proximity to the city. South Portland felt a bit like Eastern Europe, New York, or Chicago. There were Jewish peddlers "with horses and carts to sell their wares ... kosher markets, drugstores, delicatessens, [and] bakeries."[10]

I don't know who owned the houses the Doyles occupied, but I am fairly sure James Doyle did not. I have looked in vain for his name in the Multnomah County Books of Deeds. Workers usually rented. From 1895 to 1900 the Doyles had a small house on the corner of 2nd and Curry. It was not a very desirable property. Curry was at the southern edge of Portland's ghetto. The house was small even by the neighborhood standards; it was set back a few feet from the streets and well within earshot of the railroad and the streetcar line on SW 1st.[11]

When they left Curry Street, Mary and James separated. According to the 1900 U.S. Census, which was taken in June 1900, Mary Doyle, a divorcee, was the owner and head of the household at what is now 5717 NE 9th Avenue (the house is still there), where she lived with her four children. They stopped moving; their house remained in the family for the next thirty years. The family had found some prosperity, even without James, perhaps because of his absence. There were three wage earners. Albert was a draftsman, Arthur was an assistant shipping clerk, and Edward was a stenographer. When Mary paid off her mortgage on March 2, 1904, two days before James died, she said she was unmarried.[12]

In about 1900, SW Meade and Corbett had a collection of nearly identical workers cottages, probably all rentals. I suspect this is not Meade and Corbett, as the OHS photograph says, but SW 2nd near Meade. Whichever the photograph shows, this street was near and like the neighborhoods in South Portland where the James Doyle family had four different houses. The family moved from South Portland to Albina in 1900. (OHS 91601)

The 1900 Census has James living in a boarding house, the Trans-Continental House, above a saloon on Savier between NW 23rd and 24th across from a streetcar barn. It could not have been a pleasant accommodation. He lived in a house with nineteen other men. Twelve worked at the streetcar barn. Six were motormen. Four were streetcar conductors. And two were car carpenters. The other seven were workmen: a few laborers, a lumberman, a painter, and a sawmill engineer. Eight were immigrants. Only one other besides James had been married, and he was widowed. A few were young. Seven were in their twenties, nine were in their thirties, three in their forties. James was reported incorrectly to be sixty-eight. In 1900 he was not quite sixty-one and even at that he was four years older than the next oldest man.[13] By 1903, when he next appeared in a City Directory, he lived above small shops on SW 3rd between Yamhill and Taylor in a collection of mostly windowless rooms. He died there March 4, 1904, of cancer and exhaustion.[14]

The Doyle boys left school early. None of them went on to high school, which was for college-bound students. By my calculation about one Portland child in fourteen attended high school.[15]

Albert finished the eighth grade at Park School at fourteen. His report card was remarkable more for his reliability than for his scholarship. He was not tardy or absent his final term, yet his grades are unexceptional. His highest mark was in mental arithmetic; he got a 94 out of 100.[16]

He was the oldest of four children and the first to work outside the home.[17] According to family memory, he worked for his father. He appeared for the first time in the 1892 City Directory, which meant, according to Polk Company policy, that he was employed.[18] The following year he was an apprentice with the architectural firm Whidden & Lewis. By 1895 he was a draftsman as he was each year through 1905, except in 1902 and 1903, when he was omitted from the directories because he was working in New York. William Whidden and Ion Lewis were Portland's only architects with national standing. They had been classmates at MIT. After graduating Whidden studied in Paris at the Ecole des Beaux Arts. Back in the States he briefly practiced in a small firm in Boston and went on to New York and McKim, Mead, & White, America's most important architectural firm, which in 1881 was hired by Henry Villard, then the president of Northern Pacific Railroad, to design the Portland Hotel. Whidden went to Portland to supervise construction but was recalled to New York when Villard's financial schemes failed and he was removed from the company. After

The Concord Building, which Whidden & Lewis designed in 1891 and where their offices were when A. E. Doyle worked for them, is still at the southwest corner of SW 2nd and Stark. (Author's photograph)

The Portland Library was on the south side of SW Stark between Broadway and Park. Whidden & Lewis did it in 1893, and Doyle may have had some small part in it. He began his apprenticeship with them that year. (PCA A2004-002.668)

a few years a group of Portland investors bought out Villard's interest to finish the hotel, but McKim, Mead, & White, were no longer interested. In 1888, Whidden, on his own, took the job, and returned to Portland. He stayed on. The following year, Ion Lewis, who was working for the prestigious firm Peabody & Stearns, visited, and the two decided to practice together.

They brought to Portland the historicism respected in Boston and New York and were immediately successful. In their first years they completed a number of large houses in the elegant new neighborhood developing in Northwest Portland, the Arlington Club's first clubhouse (gone), the Concord Building, Portland's largest and, at the time, most up-to-date office building (it is still at the corner of SW 2nd and Stark), and the Portland Hotel, Portland's largest and the city's most significant commercial establishment (gone). In the next decade, they completed the Portland Library (gone), the (present) City Hall, and the Meier & Frank building, Portland's largest department store (gone).

At the end of Doyle's second year with Whidden & Lewis, on July 17, 1895, the members of the firm were photographed in their office in the Concord Building. Doyle, just ten days shy of eighteen years, is at the back slightly right of center. Left to right are his mentors. Ion Lewis is intently studying a book or a plan. William Whidden is looking at Doyle with his hand raised as if he has been caught mid sentence in an instruction. At Doyle's

The Whidden & Lewis staff were photographed July 17, 1895, in their offices in the Concord Building. Doyle had been with them for two years when this photograph was taken. Left to right are Ion Lewis, William Whidden, A. E. Doyle, and Seth Catlin. (OHS 46752)

left, hunched over work, is Seth Catlin, Whidden & Lewis' other and senior draftsman. While Doyle is the youngest person in the photograph, the photographer seems to have been studying this earnest, adolescent draftsman, neatly dressed with tie, white shirt, and vest, beardless, his hair short, clean, and shining. He faces the camera. His head is turned slightly in Whidden's direction. He looms above his mentors and the senior draftsman. His arms are slightly outstretched as if youthful energy has been arrested as much by the camera shutter as by his concentration on what Whidden is saying.

Years later Doyle recalled how he got "his training in the building business." He learned early that "it was a tough business" with "a lot of toughs in it," who "could go on a job, spit a wad of tobacco that would split a two inch plank, and let out the proper accompanying language, which I could understand, in fact, I could use some of it in a mild manner." Whidden, with a gruff exterior, Parisian education, and New York experience, was the dominant member of the partnership. There were no telephones, and Doyle was the messenger. When Whidden needed to talk to one of the builders, Doyle tracked him down. He explained: "All I had to do was to start in any time after three o'clock in the afternoon at the old Fountain Saloon on 2nd and Washington Streets and take in about six or eight of them (saloons), winding up in the Quelle at 6th and Stark." Eventually he found "the victim" and dragged "him trembling to see the boss." On the way, "I would have one or two schooners of beer and a free lunch" and "a lot of good accidental education." He was, he concluded, "perfectly at home with the bunch of toughs on Burnside. In fact, that is where I belonged."[19]

Albert Doyle learned to be an architect on the job. There was no architectural school in Oregon until 1914, no professional organization for architects until 1906, no art school until 1909, no Beaux Arts Society competition until 1910, and no American Institute of Architects chapter until 1911. Portland architects developed an educational program in 1911 when Doyle was four years into his practice and a member of the Portland Architectural Club's Education Committee. In his youth, there was also very little opportunity to see or study art. The Portland Art Museum did not open until 1895, when he was seventeen. Some of the Oregon colleges had introduced art courses, principally for women undergraduates. Willamette University began offering art in 1860 and Pacific University, in 1883. Portland public schools had begun some art instruction in 1877, and Doyle received a grade for drawing on his report card.[20]

In 1912, when he was a successful architect, Doyle spoke to a group of draftsmen about their responsibility for educating themselves. He advised them to read the many books on architecture in the Portland Library.[21] As a youth he bought books, and in a practice he followed throughout his life, he dated them with the year of the purchase. His lifetime of reading and study are evident in his library, now in the Reed College Special Collections. His first two books were *Pen Drawing an Illustrated Treatise*, by Charles D. Maginnis, "formerly instructor" at Cowles Art School in Boston, and *The Building Trades Pocketbook a Handy Manual of Reference on Building Construction*, a textbook for a correspondence school with instructors who are "men of education . . . selected on account of their special fitness for teaching students who know nothing [and] must obtain an education or be left far behind in the rush of modern progress." Any young man has an hour each working day or 313 hours each year or "62 school days." Staying home nights, saving money, and learning "will prove the making of any young man and fit him for a successful career" and will give him "a technical education with spare money, in spare moments, in time usually thrown away." There are testimonials to the program. One successful architect wrote that he left school at sixteen. He went to work as a carpenter and did the course for two and one half years to become an architect. There are also two other small, inexpensive, self-help books: J. V. Van Pelt's *A Discussion of Composition Especially as Applied to Architecture* and John C. Trautwine's *The Civil Engineers Pocket-Book*, which, according to the preface, "elucidates, in plain English, a few important elementary principles which the savants have enveloped in such a haze of mystery as to render pursuit hopeless to any but a confirmed mathematician."

He and some other young men interested in art and drawing met together evenings and weekends. Harry Wentz, who was A. E. Doyle's lifetime best friend and who went on to become Portland's foremost art teacher and an important local artist, was in the group. Two years older than Doyle, Wentz was born in The Dalles in 1875 into a large family. His father was a cabinet maker. As a youngster Harry Wentz was sickly, and his parents were told he would not survive childhood. His family moved to Portland about 1890 when he was fifteen. In 1892 he was a clerk at Buckingham & Hecht, wholesalers of boots and shoes. Through the 1890s until he was at least twenty-five, he lived with his parents and his siblings. both he and his brothers and sisters had jobs early and presumably helped to support their family when their father retired from carpentry and cabinetmaking.

Wentz recalled the formation of the Portland Sketch Club in an interview in 1957, when he was eighty-two. A group of enthusiastic young men, he said, "interested in drawing" and between fifteen and twenty-one years old held evening and holiday meetings for discussion and sketching "on the sixth floor of the Worcester Building" (now gone) on Third and Oak. They "put on the walls small exhibitions of their work," and they sometimes invited the public.[22] Doyle did much of the work of organizing the Sketch Club. He was one of the founders. He and Seth Catlin, five years older and the senior draftsman at Whidden & Lewis, were the club's president and secretary, respectively, from 1896 through 1901, when Doyle left Portland to work in New York for two years. When he returned from New York, in early 1904, he was again secretary.[23]

In 1895 the Sketch Club was well enough established for *The Oregonian* to announce that the young men would create a formal organization and invite others to join. At an evening meeting May 28, 1895, they would adopt a constitution and bylaws. They expected to have twenty members, for "A great deal of interest has been awakened among the lovers of sketching in this city over the formation of the club, and it seems sure to be very successful, if enthusiasm can make it so." There was disagreement about admitting "ladies." Some men opposed women "as tending to make it more of a social organization than would be compatible with earnest work, such as a thorough sketch club should do to be of benefit to its members." Yet an agreement was forming "that it would be a mistake for the club to exclude ladies."[24] Harry Wentz recalled the disagreement and how the group of men had met for several years without women. When women joined, he said, "This added strength."[25]

One of the women admitted was Anna Belle Crocker, who years later was the director (the curator as the Portland Art Association then designated its executive) of the Portland Art Museum. Born in 1868, she moved to Portland with her family when she was eleven. Her father died in 1882 or 1883 when she was fourteen or fifteen. She and her sister Florence lived with their mother in South Portland. By 1893 the Crocker sisters were stenographers at the Ladd & Tilton Bank. Anna Belle was one of the first typists in Portland. So unusual was typing and so accomplished was she that

The Portland Art Museum was on the second floor of the Portland Library. These cast copies of Greek and Roman statues lined the walls. The Portland Sketch Club met here Wednesday evenings and Saturday afternoons to sketch the statues, or as it was said at the time when copies of ancient sculpture were used as models, "to sketch from the antique." (PCA A2004-002.672)

people would "stand there with their noses against the window (of the bank) to watch a woman running a typewriter."[26] She wrote an autobiography after she retired in 1936. She remembered the comradeship of the young people in the club who, like herself, were "interested from the art students' point of view." A few were older; some had even been to Europe. There were "architects' assistants, teachers, and clerks, all longing to try what the brush could be made to do in their hands and to bathe their minds in knowledge of artists' ways and thoughts." They "nervously attacked" their drawings. They used all the leisure they could "squeeze from" their jobs to work in "this extemporized art school." There were "classes in the evening in composition and cast drawing, on Saturday afternoons, life drawing and paintings from the head and on Sundays, all day, out of door sketching." There was an art teacher, "a well known New York instructor who had been engaged to criticize" the students' work. They "ate and drank the words of the teacher just back from a year's holiday in France."[27]

Architectural educators emphasized sketching. Richard Morris Hunt, the preeminent late nineteenth-century American architect and architectural educator, advised students to "draw, draw, draw, sketch, sketch, sketch … it doesn't matter (what), it will ultimately give you a control of your pencil that you can the more readily express on paper your thoughts in designing."[28] A surviving catalog for a Portland Sketch Club exhibit in November 1900 lists twelve members and one hundred eleven separate pieces of their work. Four were Doyle's and only one was of an architectural subject: "The Old Carter House." The other three were various natural and local scenes: "On the Cowlitz," "Guild's Lake," and "Oneonta Gorge."[29] Years later he reflected on the value of learning to draw: "it helps in training your observation and appreciation. You will be observing all kinds of things and wondering how you would draw them."[30]

The Portland Sketch Club met Wednesday evenings in the Portland Library, the city's most significant cultural institution. In 1893, Whidden & Lewis, completed the Romanesque brick and stone two-storied building with a basement and a slate roof, on the south side of Stark between SW Broadway and Park. The Library had twenty-one thousand volumes and each year added a thousand. Its building was strikingly similar to the Boston Public Library. Books, periodicals, and newspapers were on the first floor. On the second floor was an art museum. This was a private subscription library, yet it was committed to making its growing collection available as widely as possible yet an annual student membership cost a dollar, not a negligible sum since that was the cost of pair of shoes or forty pounds of flour.[31]

The Sketch Club met upstairs in the Art Museum for the "splendid collection of specimens of antique sculpture," cast copies of major Greek and Roman statues. The museum had an enviable collection of art reproductions. Plans were being made for its own building for collection and for an art school. The second major acquisition, after the casts of ancient statues, was a "collection of fifteen thousand photographs of works of the old masters."[32] For thirteen years there was a museum but no original art. The museum acquired its first painting, *Afternoon Sky, Harney Desert*, by Childe Hassam in 1908.

The Portland Library and the Art Museum grew from legacies and gifts. The largest was in 1889, $125,000, the bulk of the estate of Ella M. Smith, "one of the wealthiest single ladies in Oregon," an heiress of a riverboat fortune.[33] The room for the Art Museum's collection was a memorial in her honor. Other founders included Henry Failing and Thomas Lamb Eliot. Henry W. Corbett paid for the plaster casts and bequeathed $50,000 and a lot near SW 5th and Yamhill. William S. Ladd died in 1892, leaving a bequest. His widow gave money to buy a collection of photographs of European art and to help build the Art Museum. Their son, William M. Ladd, was for years the president of the Portland Art Association. A niece of Henry Failing, Henrietta Failing, was appointed the first "curator" of the Museum.

Henry W. Corbett, Henry Failing, and William S. Ladd were young merchant adventurers when they arrived in Portland in the spring of 1851, a few months after Portland was incorporated, when it was a few wooden buildings on the bank of the Willamette with about a thousand people, almost all men. In time Corbett, Failing, and Ladd became bankers, real estate speculators, mill owners, wholesalers, and retailers. They invested in river boats, railroads, streetcars, and real estate. Within a generation they built Second Empire mansions that formed an imposing neighborhood on what was the western edge of the city. Corbett's was on the block bounded by SW 5th, 6th, Yamhill, and Taylor. Failing's was across Taylor surrounded by SW 5th, 6th, Taylor, and Salmon. Ladd's was a few blocks south between SW 6th and Broadway and Jefferson and Columbia. The Oregonian Building now occupies the site.[34] More than proximity and fashion joined these families. They created an interlocking dynasty. Failing married Corbett's sister. And Corbett's son married Ladd's daughter.

They had many qualities, but connoisseurship was not one of them. According to Crocker, Corbett was "not without traditions," but he was "quite lacking in esthetic feeling or understanding." He and the other founders had "pioneers' nostalgia for things of the civilization" they had left behind in the East. Their parlor walls were hung "symmetrically with large steel engravings framed in gold with wide white mats" and in other rooms there were "old fashioned water-colors." Some even had "ancestral portraits in darkening oils."[35]

The William S. Ladd mansion was on the block now occupied by the Oregonian Building at SW 6th and Broadway. Ladd built it in 1869 and lived here until his death in 1893. His widow survived him here and his daughter, Helen Ladd Corbett, lived here after she was widowed in 1894. She moved to Riverwood in 1927 when this house was razed. (PCA A2004-002.538)

A New Yorker was even less impressed. Gretchen Hoyt Corbett was the wife of Henry Ladd Corbett, Henry W. Corbett's grandson. She was a New York debutante from an affluent, traveled, and cultivated family who arrived in Portland in 1908 as a young bride, unimpressed with the sophistication of her husband's family and friends. Their art was, she said, "pretty dreadful," like paintings "of the school where you had Arabs on horseback and you had sheep in fields. They were not good."[36]

Mrs. Corbett must have been refreshing. When she came to Portland in 1908 as a young wife, she brought with her refinement and elegance. She attended ladies' luncheons and teas. She served in various charitable organizations. She helped found the Junior League, the Oregon Symphony, and the League of Women Voters. In 1967 when the Oregon Historical Society interviewed her about her early days in Portland, she was widowed and eighty-one, but she still spoke with clarity in a clipped and cultivated accent as arresting today as it must have been when she arrived in Portland.

She was both amused and impressed by Portland's pioneer merchants. They were, she said, "a very remarkable group . . . the first pioneers who set up a certain standard for their city. They were very city minded." She explained the founding of the Art Museum. She had heard the story from Winslow B. Ayer, who was from a lumbering family in Bangor, Maine. At age twenty-three, in 1883, the year after he graduated from MIT in civil engineering, he came west and first worked for J. K. Gill before starting a cordage company. He prospered and married in 1892; and in the fashion of the Portland class which he had achieved, he and his new wife planned a grand tour. Henry W. Corbett heard of their plans and approached Ayer with a proposal: "It is time we had a museum in this town, and I think we had better start one. I think you are the one to find out. Here are $10,000 take that and learn how to start a museum." Ayer was reluctant. He demurred; "But, Mr. Corbett, I can't. I don't know anything." Corbett insisted: "I've thought about it, and I think you are the one. Go and ask authorities. Go to museums and ask them." Ayer explained: "No one ever said no to H. W. Corbett. I went off with my $10,000 in my hand, and I asked them all the same question: 'If you were a small town on the Pacific Coast as far as possible from any access to artistic things, how would you begin a museum?'" Everyone gave the same answer: "The Greek is the beginning of all that is art and so . . . they made for him casts that could be made and it was the beginning of the collection of Greek casts." Then Mrs. Ladd, Mrs. Corbett's husband's maternal grandmother, sent more money because "the family had got thoroughly into this thing." Ayer asked the great art museums how he should spend it. They said, "Well you are so far away you must have reproductions of all the great works of art." And so the museum gathered a collection of reproductions: "You can find a reproduction of any painting in the world." Mrs. Corbett delighted in the details of this story; she giggled about imperious Henry W. Corbett, about everyone's naiveté, and about the shipment of plaster casts that became the Portland Art Museum.

These reproductions were not much to a sophisticated New Yorker, but they inspired the Portland Sketch Club. In 1936 when Crocker wrote her memoirs after a distinguished career as director of the museum, she recalled her wonder of them. "In the early years," she wrote, "the upper floor" of the library "was unusually beautiful" with "reliefs around the walls" and "figures standing in clear light." There on Wednesdays after work, the members of the Sketch Club gathered "to draw in the evening from the antique." They "entered the sparsely lit, silent halls—often cold." They would "drag out easels" and with charcoal "try to get something of the life-blood of art from the white plaster images of Greek gods and goddesses" that opened their minds "to a certain type of calm but vivid order and to an old and faraway world of thought and feeling."[37]

In 1901, Doyle went to New York. He sent his portfolio ahead to William Rutherford Mead of McKim, Mead, & White, who placed him with Henry Bacon, an important New York architect.[38] His relationship with William Whidden must have eased his way in New York. Bacon had started his career with Whidden in Boston; when that office closed, both Bacon and Whidden went to New York to work for McKim, Mead, & White and remained friends. Henry Bacon made a profound impression on Doyle, and their relationship continued until Bacon died in 1924 at the top of his profession and a few years after completing his greatest achievement, in the opinion of Doyle and many others, the Lincoln Memorial in Washington D. C.

In New York and then in other American cities, there were ateliers (*atelier* is French for workshop or studio) modeled on the system of training architects in Paris, where students worked in groups under the supervision of an established architect. Doyle

While working and studying in New York, Doyle had an opportunity to see examples of Colonial architecture, then thought to be the only style of truly American architecture. This is a sketch he did on a visit to Boston, June 4, 1902, in his first year in the East. (Portland Architectural Club, Yearbook, 1908, p. 59)

attended the atelier of Donn Barber, a New York architect who had studied in Paris. He could also attend lectures at Columbia University and use the library as one of a number of "special students," draftsmen employed in offices who were permitted to participate in the Columbia architecture program even when they had no high school or college. The theory at the time was that they brought the working-world experience to college students enrolled in the program.

Doyle was in New York for about two years;[39] he returned to Portland at the end of 1903 or in early 1904 and again roomed with his mother. He was changed, marked by New York. He later described his attitude at the time: "I suppose my New York experience made me absorb a lot of ambition, greed and desire for speed as is the thing there, then I came home rather egotistical and bragging a good deal."

In later life, fondly remembering his time with Whidden & Lewis, he said that he had been wrong to go out on his own. He was happier, he said, before he assumed the responsibility for his own business. He "always loved to draw." It was what he "always liked the best." When he had the responsibilities of his own firm, he was not able "to do very much of it because the business end took so much time." He "would have been happier" to have had a studio with Whidden & Lewis and to have left the business end to them.[40]

Doyle's father died on March 4, 1904. A. E. provided information for the death certificate and arranged for the burial. *The Oregonian* listed James among the deceased the next day, but there was no obituary. Indeed there was no family present for the internment.[41] His grave is in River View Cemetery, where Portland's first families have their family plots and mausoleums. A. E. designed a simple stone. He copied it in 1917 for his mother and his father-in-law.

James died too soon to see his son's accomplishments, and even in death he does not share in his son's reputation, for up the hill in the cemetery there is a family plot for everyone else: A. E., his wife, his mother, and his wife's parents but not James.

Whidden & Lewis were busy. Preparations for the Lewis and Clark Exposition occupied Ion Lewis, who was Director of Architecture for the fair. Whidden & Lewis needed help. Doyle, who had worked ten years with them and two years in a major New York firm, was the firm's designer even though he was still called a draftsman.[42] He was doubtless paid well.

On August 19, 1904, Doyle purchased for $2000 the house still at 2136 NE 8th Ave,[43] where he would live with his family for thirteen years from his marriage in 1907 until 1920.

His future wife, Lucie Godley, was his age. She was born June 3, 1877, in Albany, Oregon, where her parents were married in 1864.[44] From 1889 they lived in Chehalis, Washington, where her father was a plumber. Albert Doyle and Lucie Godley had a long courtship. It may have begun before November 1900, when one of his sketches in the Portland Sketch Club Exhibition was "On the Cowlitz," which is a river running near Chehalis and the Godley home. Their courting was limited. He was in New York for two years and in Europe for six months. Even when he was in Portland they were eighty-five miles apart. The Doyle family has among its keepsakes a rumpled greeting card, a cut-out of a smiling cat, and a story about her impatience: he sent it to her, to mollify or to amuse her with a message: "Be happy, Lucie."[45]

Doyle was given major responsibility for one Whidden & Lewis project, the Forestry Building for the fair. How independent he was in designing it has been debated; the building has been attributed

The buildings for the Lewis and Clark Exposition in the summer of 1905 were temporary structures of wood frame and plaster built to appear to be stately masonry edifices in the Spanish Renaissance style. This view is across Guild's Lake (now gone) to the European and Agricultural buildings. (PCA A2004-002.781)

There was one exception to the plaster structures of the Lewis and Clark Exposition. A. E. Doyle designed the Forestry Building to represent the Pacific Northwest's important industry. The logs used for it were cut from Simon Benson's forests on the Columbia and floated to the site. The Forestry Building, seen here in a photograph taken for a publicity brochure, was the fair's most popular edifice, and it was the only building to survive long after the fair closed. It burned in 1964. (PCA A2004-002.778)

to both Lewis and to Doyle. Both signed the plans. There was no question about Doyle's responsibility for it among people who knew him well: "According to the family and to friends ... full responsibility for the structure was given to him."[46] That was the opinion of Harry Wentz, his lifetime best friend.[47]

The Forestry Building was immediately popular. Dubbed the "Log Parthenon," it was constructed of massive and modestly dressed logs and was very different from the assembly of temporary wood and plaster exposition buildings in the common style, Renaissance Spanish, because of early Spanish exploration of the West Coast. The Forestry Building was at once the world's largest log cabin, a Greek temple, or even a cathedral with a massive crossing of transept and nave. A few days after the Forestry Building was completed and over two months before the fair opened, *The Oregonian* praised it: "The Forestry Building ... is to attract more attention than any other of the structures at the fair . ... Since its completion it has consistently been the center of an admiring crowd ... There are few visitors that do not immediately inquire of the whereabouts of the building."[48] The *Pacific Monthly*, a Portland publication and one of the precursors of *Sunset Magazine*, previewed the Exposition in May, and singled out the Forestry Building, which is "an architectural wonder and which is itself a convincing exhibit of the forestry wealth of the Pacific Northwest."[49] In the autumn, after the fair closed, a New York group tried to buy it for $200,000 to ship it piece by piece around the Horn. The State of Oregon, reflecting the pride taken in this product of native talent and materials, decided not to sell it but to give it to the city for the price of the land. For nearly sixty years until it burned, it was a Portland treasure, a permanent museum for Oregon's forestry industry.

⋄⋄⋄

Doyle was in Portland through the summer of 1905, when he participated in the Sketch Club classes during the fair[50] and he was probably in Portland through the winter. He was in New York in February 1906, and he sailed from New York for Europe in April.

When he returned, he married. Yet he remained involved with his birth family. He had title to his mother's house, probably because he supported her. In 1909, as soon as his own firm was established, he hired his sister Daisy as his stenographer and his brother Arthur as his bookkeeper. Arthur lived with his mother until 1911, when he was thirty-one, and Daisy lived in that house until 1932, well after her mother's death. In 1913 she married Jason T. Edgerton, a timberman, who came to live with Daisy and her mother. He died before 1923, and Daisy lived on in Mary Doyle's house alone for another decade. Edward, the youngest brother, apparently never married. He lived in the family home until Mary died, when he was thirty-six.

A. E. Doyle, Anna Belle Crocker, and Harry Wentz were lifelong friends and colleagues. They were leaders of the Portland art community in the early twentieth century. A. E. Doyle became president of the Portland Art Association when Anna Belle Crocker was curator of the Art Museum and Harry Wentz taught in the Museum School. All three had Doyle-designed summer houses at Neahkahnie. The Doyle children were close to their father's friends. And Harry Wentz had an active part in the design and furnishing of some of Doyle's buildings. All three treasured the memory of the Portland Sketch Club. When A. E. Doyle wrote his daughter Kathleen in the last months of his life, he said, "It was more fun than anything else."[51] And in 1957, a half a century after it disbanded, Harry Wentz, who was eighty-two and retired from a celebrated career of teaching and painting, recalled it and the time with warmth, perhaps even excitement: "These were wonderful years."[52]

CHAPTER 2

Preparation

At the beginning of the twentieth century Portland was remote, certainly provincial, and probably philistine. Anna Belle Crocker thought it had no more than a "sight past the marshes of regressive superficial regionalism into the faraway world of history and thought, a glimpse ...to peaks with larger perspectives." There were a few original works of art in a "number of the best homes" that she was sometimes permitted to see. She enjoyed them but could not appreciate them fully because "I hadn't enough acquaintance with painting to follow their implications and missed much that was in them."

She went to New York twice, in 1904 and in 1908, to see and study art at her own expense and without any prospect of earning a living in art. On her first trip in Chicago, between trains, she visited the Chicago Art Institute, where she "at last had a deep experience of what painting could be." She was thrilled:

> *I stood before Rembrandt's Girl at a Window taking the living order of the masses and the color—the whole so clear and honest, opening a gateway to that strange stuff we are immersed in—life; and through this mountain pass I caught a glimpse into a realm, fresh, deep, transparent.*

On Crocker's second visit to New York in 1908, she was unexpectedly appointed curator of the Portland Museum "with the requirement that I visit some of the galleries of Europe before my return," because "there was then no course in America in museum administration nor in any sort of connoisseurship." She "haunted" the Metropolitan and the lectures of one "scholarly" docent before sailing for Europe to tour museums in England, France, Italy, and Greece.[1]

Travel and study in Europe more than university at home completed the training of many young American artists and architects of the late nineteenth and early twentieth centuries. They went to see buildings and paintings to learn about colors, textures, materials, and proportions. They were not so much acquiring information as developing "good taste." They "flock[ed] in ever larger numbers to Paris, Munich and Florence." American schools of architecture like Berkeley's, which was founded in 1902 and which was the school nearest Portland, assumed at the core of the curriculum that "American architecture could flower by tapping into the still-vital European classical tradition." Lectures were on "ancient, early Christian, medieval and Renaissance architecture, but little else." The only American buildings discussed were Georgian and classical revival.[2] University-trained architects upon graduation went to Europe for additional study, sometimes to the Ecole des Beaux Arts in Paris and increasingly to two American schools, the American Academy in Rome and the American School of Classical Studies in Athens.

Student architects from wealthy families went for long periods, sometimes for years. Increasingly college graduates could get scholarships for travel in Europe and study in Athens and Rome. When Doyle returned to Portland from New York, he worked for Whidden & Lewis, lived with his mother, and saved for Europe. The family tells a story that Henry Bacon assisted him, as Doyle, when he was established, helped his draftsmen, Charles Greene and Donald Stewart, who had scrimped for years when they went. We do not know what Doyle spent on his trip because, while he carefully recorded what he saw, he said little about what he ate, where or how he slept, or how cheaply and uncomfortably he traveled. Impecunious students struggled with finances, suffered in steerage over and back, and survived in Europe in cheap rooms on bread, cheese, and beer. When Doyle returned to Europe in 1926 after twenty years of success in Portland, he traveled with his family in style in chauffeur-driven cars and stayed in good hotels. On one leg of that trip, when he and his family were driven from Paris to Florence with two days in Nice, he reflected on how much his world had changed: "This ten day auto trip would cost more than my entire European trip 20 years ago including my steamer passage both ways. It is almost incredible yet true and is [the] most astounding observation of 'twenty years after.'"[3]

For travel in Europe there were invaluable aids: the guidebooks of the John Murray and Karl Baedeker firms, which had been published for three quarters of century when Doyle went. They permitted efficient observation of art and architecture. They listed all the important museums and sites, directions to them, hours of opening, fees, floor plans, and lists of exhibits. They also reminded poor students how poor they were. The guidebooks openly betrayed the prejudices of the traveling classes and said almost nothing about the people in the countries visited, their cultures, or even their food. The natives who happened to live where tourists went were, in the language of the guidebooks, the "others." They were to serve and so "dishonest, dirty and rapacious and generally so class peevish as to be kept from open insult only by fear of the law or the sack."[4] Italians were especially bothersome: "The traveler who has some knowledge of Italian will soon learn to adapt himself to the methods practiced by cab-drivers, gondoliers, guides, porters etc. in Northern Italy. In the south especially in Naples ... the insolence and rapacity of the lower classes has attained an almost incredible pitch."[5]

Doyle always had a guidebook. On the continent they were Baedekers. In Turkey he had an old Murray. In England he had one written for Americans. They dictated what he saw, what he experienced, sometimes even what he thought. Only one of his Baedekers has survived in the Doyle library at Reed. He wrote often in it. Lines and checks in the margin mark sites of interest, many of which he listed with brief comments in his diary. His timetable is on the flyleaf. On the diagrams of some buildings, he wrote the dimensions in feet which he had established by pacing them off.

While he traveled, his fiancée, Lucie Godley, lived with her parents. The Chehalis newspaper occasionally mentioned the family because in the small town of five thousand there was a column about the coming and going of visitors and residents, and Henry Godley was working at Aberdeen, fifty-five miles west of Chehalis. Mrs. Godley sometimes went to visit him, and he came home for the occasional weekend and holidays. While Doyle saw Europe, Lucie taught piano in her parents' home to the children of Chehalis, and waited for daily letters about travel and architecture which ended: "your own Bert."

There is a photograph of each of them before they married. His was taken in Rome the day before his twenty-ninth birthday. He sent it to his daughter Kathleen, in the fall of 1927, commenting "Notice the sensitive nose as in big nose just like a race horse, nervous pawing the ground and just rarin to go."[6] His nose is large; it was mentioned in the physical description given on his passport. There is certainly an intensity in his demeanor which his stature belied; he was short, five feet seven inches. A thin, dark face and square jaw emphasize his energy.[7] He seems directed by a purpose as if the photograph is delaying and inconveniencing him.

left: Albert Doyle was on his student tour of Europe when his picture was taken July 26, 1906, the day before his twenty-ninth birthday. The autumn before he died he sent a copy of it to his daughter Kathleen. It was a very small photograph, probably taken for identification, perhaps for an entry pass or a visa. (Newhouse)

right: Lucie Godley before her marriage to A. E. Doyle. (Newhouse)

Her portrait is otherwise; she is a nubile, pretty young woman, composed, diffident, retiring, and private. Probably too much can be made of posed photographs which are probably as much about portrait convention as about character. Yet each is consistent with the personalities and their lives. He was as ambitious and professional as she was private and housewifely.

His letters to her were a complete account of his trip, he said. He was dutiful about them; he wrote late into the night sometimes to be sure he could mail one in the morning. He described what he did and saw. Unfortunately only a few have survived. For the whole trip there is his diary where he listed what he saw and what he thought. Often his diary is a continuation of Baedeker as if his experiences were footnotes to the guidebooks, and he refers to Baedeker for a complete description or for a full list of what is in a museum or an exhibit. Sometimes he lifts his descriptions from Baedeker. He collected post cards because he could not afford photographs. After six weeks he had "several hundred." They were bulky and heavy. He bundled them up and sent them to Lucie and then worried: "I hope the package of cards arrives o.k. I have been wondering if it is safe to send them this way."[8] They are today in the Archive of Reed College. On most cards he wrote the date of his visit; and after his return, he filed them by country and subject.[9]

⋘

He left New York, April 21, 1906, on the steamship *Republic* of the White Star Line for the Mediterranean. Three years later, the vessel sank after a collision. The ship was new when he sailed on it. The crossing was ten days; he arrived at 8:00 a.m. May 1 in Gibraltar, which received ships of "all important harbours of the world."[10] Large ships anchored in the bay and landed their passengers "in tenders." Customs were brief; questioning was "usually limited to tobacco, spirits, and firearms." He wrote nothing about his visit. It was a fortification; visitors could not "make either drawings or notes." He left the Colony at 3:00 p.m. for Algeciras, then "a pleasant country town with 13,300 inhabitants," where he boarded a train to begin a circuit of several cities in southern Spain: Ronda, Granada, and Seville. He sketched stonework and iron railings and visited cathedrals, Alhambra, and Generalife.

He arrived in Naples May 10th. The city was "full of dust and ashes and very windy and disagreeable," because a month before, Mount Vesuvius had erupted. There was much "of interest architecturally," in the National Archaeological Museum: "great collections from Pompeii and Hereculaneum."[11]

Sunday, May 13, he took a steamer for the short ride to see the Villa of Tiberius on Capri: "an island of goats," a stark landscape above the sea. It was "very picturesque [with] huge cliffs." He walked the island to the small village of Anacapri, its "grand view" and a "quaint flower festival." He declined the horsecarts, which reduced the forty-five-minute walk to a half hour ride (Baedeker).

He was back on the mainland, May 15, in Sorrento. There were steamers from Capri to Sorrento, but row boats and oarsmen could be found to make the trip in two to two and a half hours. He walked from Sorrento through Amalfi to Salerno, about eleven and a half miles, carrying "a small pack with sketching outfit." Carriage drivers cursed him for preferring his feet to their carts.[12] The small villages clinging to the hillsides had been maritime trading cities in the Middle Ages rivaling Venice and Genoa. Amalfi had a population of fifty thousand at its height; in 1904 according to Baedeker it was 5,165. It was still undiscovered by artists and tourists.

May 17 he was in Pompeii, which got one of his few marks of great enthusiasm: three stars followed by a fervent "Great." Yet he chose to write not about the architecture but about the recent eruption of Mount Vesuvius. The vineyards were "in ruins" and "thousands of houses destroyed;" with "lava and ashes 12 to 18 feet deep in places." The next day he sailed to Sicily.[13] He had two days in Palermo for the Palazzo Reale which contained the Capella Palatina,"a perfect gem of medieval art," according to Baedeker, but Doyle was indifferent; he recorded simply that it was built by the Normans in 1132 and there were mosaics. He also saw a "good collection of architecture fragments and statues" in the National Museum, the cathedral, and the large modern theater, Teatro Massimo Vitorio Emanuele, with thirty-two hundred seats, completed in 1897 then "the largest in Italy."

Monday May 21, he sailed around the north side of Sicily through the straits of Messina. Taormina had "the greatest view imaginable" over the "ancient Greek Theater" to the sea "500 feet below and Mt. Etna in the distance." The theater seats were "hewn out of solid rock."

He was in Catania May 23 for a boat to Greece. The three-day voyage was interrupted on Friday at Canea, Crete, a "very picturesque," and "interesting oriental town" with "Turks, Arabs, Egyptians, Greeks and English, French, Austrian, Russian and Greek Soldiers" and "minarets, towers and domes of the Turkish Mosques."

Saturday May 26, he arrived in Athens.[14] Elsewhere on his trip, especially toward the end of it, his diary entries were little more than the names of buildings, artists, architects, and museums with terse summations of his impression: "good" or "great" or "very interesting." If especially moved he wrote "corking." But in Athens, he sketched, measured, and listed. A diagram of the theater of Dionysus includes a drawing of one of the seats; it was "extremely comfortable." There are sketches of a vase from the ancient cemetery on the Acropolis, a modern bandstand in a park, and ornaments on the Erectheum. He diagramed a column and listed the "offset measurements from a standard wire," to show the curve in the column. And he included a table of the "curvature of the horizontal lines in different temples." These pages must have been notes on reading at the American School of Classical Studies on the Greeks' concern for visual perfection and the need to correct for optical illusion. He copied out a long passage from the nineteenth-century treatise by Francis Cramer Penrose on Greek architecture, which is "humanly speaking perfect" in "the studied harmony of the proportions, the delicacy of feeling, ... the exquisite taste shown in the selection of the mouldings, [the) coloured ornaments so far as they are preserved to us; and above all, the unrivalled sculpture."[15] Years later he acquired his own copy of Penrose, which is now at Reed College. In it there is a long, dark pencil mark in the margin next to this passage.

The Parthenon impressed him for its "mathematical precision." After "careful measurements" he could find no more variation than one thirty-second of an inch even on "the courses of large stones." He was awed by the craftsmanship:

> *The stones are enormous and [the] workmanship so good that you cannot see the joints except in cases where earthquakes have shifted the stones and opened the joints. Some of the stones of the steps are just grown together. It is most difficult to discover the joints. You can't do it by passing your fingers over it. It is so perfect. It is a mystery to me how they ever did such work. When you do find a joint, it looks just like a faint scratch of a penknife. When you think that some of these stones are over 20 feet long and 4 to 5 and 6 ft high. It is appalling. If they were small stones we could see how they might be ground against each other until a perfect joint was effected, but I don't believe it was possible in these large stones. … They corrected optical illusions … there is hardly a straight line or a plumb line in the building. Everything curves which again makes the wonderful jointing appear much more marvelous.*

He trailed off; he realized his enthusiasm was less than infectious across the world to someone who had never been to Greece: "I'll not write any more of this. [I] will go into it sometime when I get home if it is interesting to you."[16]

The Parthenon was very important to Doyle as to many architects of his generation, who viewed it with reverence as an ancient perfection. He toiled to capture it first in water colors. When he could not get the colors, he did this sketch. His family has had a special affection for it. (McMath SB)

He tried to do a watercolor of the Parthenon, but the light changed while he worked; "the sun got behind the clouds and all the color changed." The color variations were great. The marble as it came from the quarry was "dazzling white" but in time and "with age it turns creamy and golden." It was "not paintable," because "where the marble has been broken or chipped," colors vary "from the original pure white to the dark gold almost brown in places," because of moss and weather stains. He gave up on color for a pencil sketch. He was pleased with the result because his drawing captured the Parthenon's size, which was elusive "because there is nothing to give big scale." The steps were oversized, twenty-one inches high "three times ordinary height," and do not therefore provide, as they should, a standard against which to "unconsciously judge other sizes in comparison." At first, his sketch "looked just like a little wooden temple." After he "struggled with it for hours … a feeling of bigness appeared."

June 8, after two weeks, Doyle left Athens for a three-day trip to Delphi, the spiritual center of Ancient Greece, to see the sanctuary and temple of Apollo. He went by boat from the Piraeus through the canal of Corinth into the Gulf of Corinth to Itea, and then up the mountain on "mule back" to Delphi, 1880 feet above sea level, "beautifully situated on the side of Mountains [among] immense cliffs and gorges." Two days after he returned from Delphi he visited the second most-important spiritual center of ancient Greece, the Sanctuary at Eleusis, an easy day trip from Athens. A week later he did a three-day tour of the Argive Plain to see Mycenaean relics in Mycenae, Tiryns, and Argos. He concluded his tour at Epidaurus for the "best preserved theater in Greece."

He wanted to go to Turkey, to see Troy and some of the Ionian sites on the west coast of Asia Minor. With a companion, he thought he could. He made a friend in Athens, a student at the American School. Martin (Doyle does not give his surname) was a "Harvard man," who had done some postgraduate work in Europe. He was "making a specialty of deciphering inscriptions." He had been abroad for four years. Doyle wrote, "I could never stand it that long. [I] think 6 months of it is going to be a great sufficiency for me." Martin knew Greek, German, and some Turkish and he had a Baedeker for Turkey that was available only in German. Doyle had an old copy of Murray's guidebook for Constantinople. It cautioned travelers about venturing outside the major cities: "The roads are indifferent, hotels almost unknown, and accommodation for travelers where it exists at all, wretched."

Travelers should "be prepared to rough it and to encounter at the same time some discomfort and occasionally a little risk" like brigands and malaria in summer and autumn.[17] Martin wanted to make the trip, but he was reluctant: "it is the middle of summer" and he "is afraid of the heat over there." When the weather cooled, Doyle persuaded him "that the heat won't hurt him."[18] They set out for Turkey on Saturday June 23, the day after Doyle had arrived back in Athens from Epidaurus.

At the border crossing, they were prepared for some unpleasantness. Murray recommended a bribe. Doyle wrote Lucie what happened: "Everything is examined with a microscope" and even so some possessions might be lost. He traveled light, just a comb, a brush, and a shirt, "which I did not think they would confiscate." Yet they suspected his guidebook and notebook; "they are death on books or any printed matter." So "I just put a 5 piastre piece (somewhat less than 25 cents U.S.) in the official's hand and he let me go." Martin did not "fare so well." He "was determined not to tip." They took his Baedeker and his tobacco. So the two friends were compelled to rely on the Murray, "which only takes in Constantinople and the plain of Troy" and "was no good for Smyrna (now Izmir) or Ephesus." Martin was "sore and disagreeable." They found a guide to take them through Smyrna, or at least its "principal streets and bazaars" but he was a poor substitute for Baedeker. He was "in cahoots with the shop keepers and at several places tried to get us to buy oriental things at fabulous prices." Even so Doyle found it all very interesting, and he "could have spent hours at it" but they went on to Ephesus, which was two hours by train. It was very hot and without a guide they could not accomplish much; yet they saw the Temple of Diana and the theatre. They decided to cut short their tour when they were told tourists needed an armed escort. Back in Smyrna Martin cursed "the arbitrary despotism of Turkey in general and the customs official that lifted his guide book in particular,"[19] and they set out for Pergamum (Bergame). Martin decided to return to Athens without seeing Troy. "He was dead tired." There was a Rumanian steamer at anchor in the harbor but no one would row him out to it because of a boycott until Doyle found "a dandy big Turk" to take him.

He went to the Dardanelles and looked up the American Consul, Frank Calvert, who was the uncle of Henry Bacon's wife, who was visiting when Doyle arrived. Bacon had written her to expect Doyle and to help him. Calvert owned a large farm, which contained part of the remains of Troy; he had begun the excavations there before Heinrich Schlieman. The Calverts housed, fed, and transported Doyle in "a very peculiar looking covered spring wagon something like our prairie schooner." For all his effort, according to Murray, there was little to see: "the scenery is wanting in grandeur" and all interesting artifacts were "at museums at Berlin, Athens, and Constantinople." Doyle, however, marveled at the view: "the mountains, sea, and islands in the distance." It was "magnificent;" he mused, "One could almost see in imagination the landing of the Greeks and the battles which followed."[20]

He spent the evening of June 30 with the Calverts, Mrs. Bacon, and her sister-in-law, listening to recordings of opera from New York's previous season on a "talking machine" which cost "$500" and a collection of records "at $5.00 per each." There were even performances by Caruso, "and they can have opera here to their hearts content. ... It is really very fine even if it is mechanical music." They listened and talked late into the night. He did not retire until he had finished his letter to Lucie at three o'clock in the morning.

Sunday, July 1, he caught a train for Constantinople, the Hagia Sophia, the principal mosques, the museums, "a Grand Bazaar," and a trip up the Bosporus. He would have liked another day, but he had seen "the most interesting things for me."

He was back in Athens the evening of July 5, 1906. He went up to the Acropolis "to have [a] last fond look by moonlight." It was "a grand sight." He "felt very sorry to have to leave the old place which I had learned to love. There is only one Athens."

The next day, he left Athens, and two days later he was in Corinth, in the old section of the city, where he read Paul's Epistles to the Corinthians. The next day there was an earthquake that shook plaster free and "one large hunk caught" him over the eye drawing blood. "The people were in great excitement." In Patras he got a train south to Olympia, where ancient athletic competitions were held.

This was uncomfortable, sometimes primitive travel. Trains and boats were slow and infrequent. The journey to Olympia, about a hundred kilometers southwest from Patras, which could today be done in hours, consumed two days and required, according to Baedeker, over ten hours of train travel. He complained, although not often. The food was disagreeable: "I got so sick of everything being served in black olive oil, that one day when I saw 'B-if-teki' on the bill of fare. I thought 'Oh boy a beefsteak' and ordered it, and to my disgust it was served swimming in black over ripe olive oil."[21] There were insects and heat: "Had a good sleep last night. Was so good and tired that I didn't notice the sand flees or mosquitoes or hear any noise."[22] Twice in Greece he was attacked by dogs. On the way to Delphi, he said, there was "no harm done," but a few days later when it happened again near Eleusis he was more concerned. He reported the dogs and "had them arrested and examined."

He was bitterly homesick. He went days without news. He suspected letters had been lost. On June 14 he wrote Lucie: "No letters. No letters. Have come to the conclusion that you have sent them to Rome and I have just written to have them forwarded." He had received one letter from his mother and one from his sister Daisy; probably they too had written to Rome. "I can't understand why they should, for I told them distinctly that I would be in Athens at least 6 weeks." Probably his letters would be in Paris when he reached Rome. He was deeply disappointed: "If you only knew how I enjoy getting a letter you would know what that means. Have only had one letter each from Mother and Daisy since I landed in Europe 6 weeks ago, and I think it is kind of shabby and I'm going to tell them so. I tell you what; it is a blamed lonesome pleasure excursion that I am on and letters help a whole lot."[23]

The next day, June 15, there was still nothing.

> *I feel just that I will have no letters for a week now, until they can be sent from Rome; and I could cry about it. It will mean almost 3 weeks without a letter from you. I wrote yesterday to have letters forwarded but it will be Monday before the letter is delivered in Rome and probably Thursday at the earliest before I receive an answer, but I do hope they will come before Saturday when I leave for Smyrna to be gone perhaps 10 days, for it would be awful not to have a letter until I return from Asia minor.*

He ended: "I'm so lonely Lucie, dear, just a wearying for you and wishin for you and I don't get no letter er nothin."[24] Finally two days later, on June 17, a letter came. "I was very delightfully surprised last evening to find a dear letter here from you. It was 5 days late." The letter had sat in the Chehalis post office two days, and it was another three days in some European post office. With twenty-one days in transit, twenty-six days had passed before he received it. Lucie promised to send a gift for his birthday on July 27 and a copy of *The Oregonian*. He thought the gift was "too much trouble and expense." He just wanted letters: "I do enjoy your letters. I was about starved." But he liked the idea of *The Oregonian*. "I shall surely be delighted to see the home paper again."[25]

Wednesday, July 11, he left Greece for Italy with a stop in Corfu, a "very beautiful town and a very beautiful island." From Brindisi there was a ten-hour train ride to Naples where, the following Sunday, he revisited the National Archaeological Museum for some "quiet time" and in the afternoon took streetcars to different

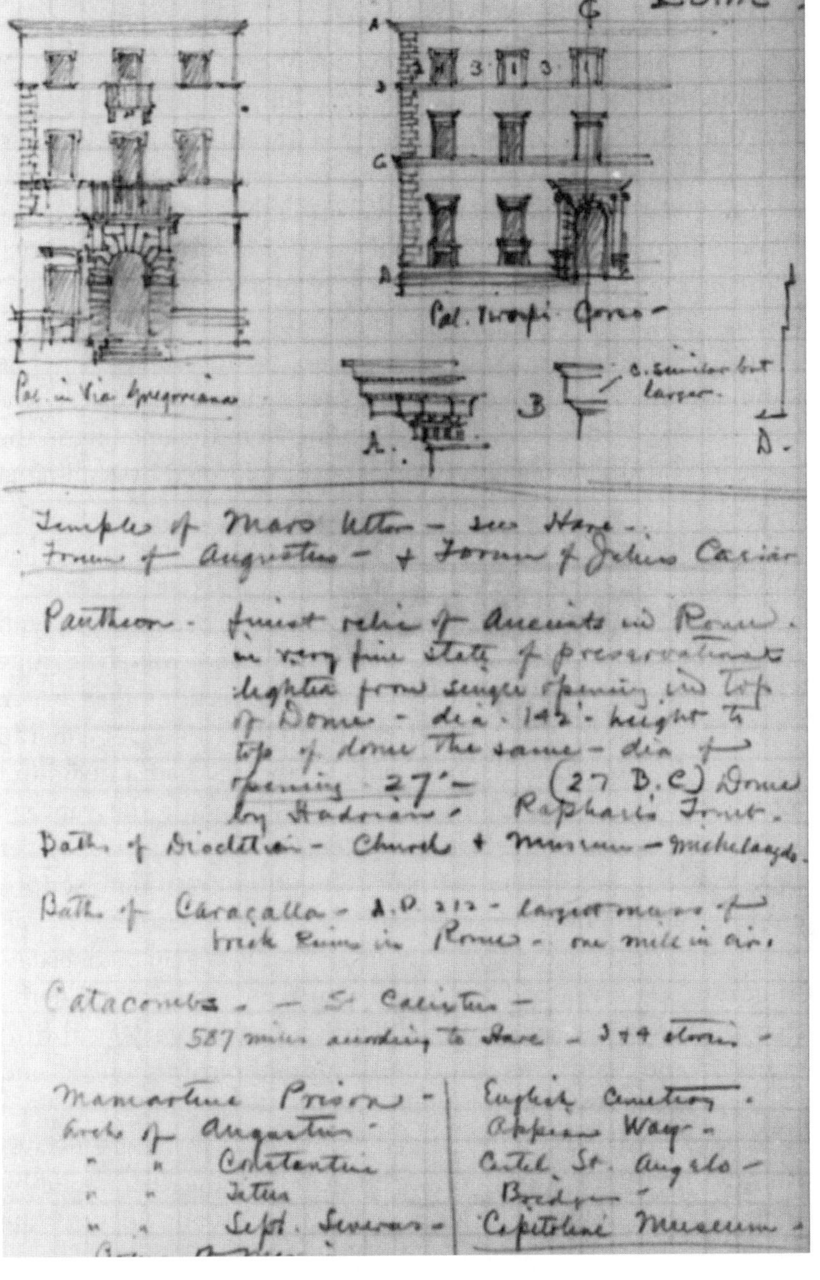
Rome

Pal. in Via Gregoriana

C. similar but larger.

Temple of Mars Ultor – see Hare –
Forum of Augustus – + Forum of Julius Caesar

Pantheon – finest relic of Ancients in Rome.
in very fine state of preservation –
lighted from single opening in top
of Dome – dia. 142' – height to
top of dome the same – dia of
opening 27' – (27 B.C.) Domed
by Hadrian – Raphael's Tomb.
Bath of Diocletian – Church + Museum – Michelangelo.

Bath of Caracalla – A.D. 212 – largest mass of
brick Ruins in Rome – one mile in cir.

Catacombs – St. Calixtus –
587 miles according to Hare – 3 + 4 stories –

Mamertine Prison –	English Cemetery.
Arch of Augustus –	Appian Way –
" " Constantine	Castel St. Angelo –
" " Titus	Bridge –
" " Sept. Severus –	Capitoline Museum –

In addition to his formal drawings, Doyle also diagramed and sketched in his small travel diary, a leather-bound book. This is one page from his entries on Rome. At the top of the page are two unnamed palaces that attracted his attention. The rest of the page, like the diary as a whole, contains brief descriptions of what he saw. (Newhouse) parts of the city and to St. Elmo above it. The day was "lovely" and the view was "magnificent."

Monday, July 16, in Rome, he began with the Palatine, the ancient seat of the kings and emperors of Rome and where in the time of the Republic senators had resided. He described the masonry: the "large huge blocks of tufa similar to the beehive tombs of Mycenae." The house of Livia had paintings and "very fine mosaic floors" which, because they were so intricate, "looked like rich rugs." He saw the Domus Augustania especially the "entrance hall, library [and] corking fine fountain in [the] court." In the Roman forum, he "worked out the different periods of construction" beginning with the early kings, a period that was identified by "large hewn blocks [like that of the] Greeks and Etruscans." The Republican period had "small stones [placed] diagonally upright for facing" over "rough stone and concrete work with big stones," while during the Empire, there was brick and concrete. The Coliseum was "very much restored in brick" because "it was used as a stone quarry for centuries." Travertine from its walls went for "many palaces and churches." The Pantheon was "the finest relic" of the ancients because it was well preserved and because of its lighting from the opening in the dome. As in Athens his observations seem informed by reading at the American Academy.

He emphasized the Rome of the Caesars and Renaissance Rome, not medieval Catholic Rome. He said nothing about the center of medieval Christianity, the Lateran Palace, except as a museum with statues, paintings, and mosaics. At the Vatican it was the Sistine Chapel and the ancient and Renaissance collections that struck him. In the Vatican picture gallery he listed the works of Leonardo da Vinci, Fra Angelico, Raphael, and Titian. He "had a delightful morning" in the Vatican Library, the "finest room in the Vatican" with "a fine view of the Pope's garden." The Library was "over 1000 feet long [and] filled with priceless treasures, manuscripts, bronzes, early paintings, jewels, and gifts to the popes."

After a little more than three weeks, he left Rome on Wednesday, August 8, on the railroad north along the Tiber, stopping at Viterbo and at Orvieto, a "charming hill town with a very beautiful cathedral and many interesting buildings and picturesque bits and details." He was in Siena on Friday and in Pisa on Sunday.

Monday, August 13, he arrived in Florence for sixteen days. He saw the important buildings: the Duomo, the Campanile by Giotto, and the Baptistery with its "beautiful bronze doors," the

Piazza della Signoria, and the Palazzo Vecchio, which was "bully." In the Cathedral Museum, he liked the Renaissance paintings; the "modern pictures" were "not much." The Bargello was a "fine Gothic building"; the court and stairs were "simply stunning," and the rooms were "beautiful" with "such fine proportions and vaulting." It was "a most successful and pleasing museum on the whole," with good collections of bronzes, tapestries, gems, sculptures and "good architectural fragments." At the Uffizi he listed the contents of individual rooms. The Pitti Palace "contains about 500 pictures practically all masterpieces. [There are] very few works of inferior merit." Raphael's *Madonna della Sedia* was "the sweetest picture I have ever seen" almost quoting Baedeker's recommendation, "The finished beauty of the figures and the unspeakable tenderness of the maternal embrace are touching and impressive." The Boboli Gardens adjoining the Pitti Palace, had "hill and vale and lake [with] many fine vases, fountains, [and] statues." The Ponte Vecchio was a "quaint picturesque bridge lined with shops which have belonged to jewelers since the fourteenth century." The Ponte Santa Trinita, was the "finest bridge." San Marco's frescoes by Fra Angelico, were "very fine."

He left Florence August 30th and stopped briefly in Pistoia and in Bologna, a "fine town" with "dandy arcaded streets and many fine buildings." It was the "best modern architecture in Italy" because the "new buildings harmonize with the old ones."

He was in Venice for the first week in September. He emphasized the oldest parts, "Byzantine Venice," the Piazza of San Marco and the Basilica, "a Byzantine church with Gothic embellishments." It had "hundreds of square feet of mosaics inside and out [which are] very fine in color," doors "from Constantinople," and an altar front that was a "very fine early work." The Palace of the Doges had a "fourteenth-century front" and was "beautifully decorated by Tintoretto and Paolo Veronese." The Libreria Vecchia by Jacopo Sansovino with his "Palladian principles" was "one of the finest Renaissance buildings in Europe." He echoed Baedeker: "Perhaps the finest secular edifice in Italy." St. Mark's Campanile collapsed in 1902, and although reconstruction began almost immediately, four years later, the masonry was still just "fifteen feet above ground." They were "making very slow progress."

As in Florence, painters interested him as much as, perhaps more than, architects, and he was less interested in architecture than Baedeker.. In the Accademia di Belle Arti. Titian's *Assumption* was a "great Picture, [and] the finest thing in the Gallery."

Tintoretto had "many large and beautiful things." At the Church of San Zaccaria, an important example of the transition from Gothic to Renaissance, Doyle liked the "many fine frescoes." He said nothing about the Church of Santa Maria Formosa; it was the art inside: a "very fine Madona by Sassoferato" and Palma Vecchio's *Santa Barbara,* which was, he said, "one of the fine pictures of Italy." The nearby equestrian statue of Bartolomeo Colleoni, a Venetian general of the fifteenth century, was the "best I have ever seen. The horse seems just about to move." On his last day he swam at the Lido, an "interesting excursion" at a "large bathing establishment on the Adriatic." The water was "too warm" and too shallow. He had "to walk half way to Trieste to get deep enough water to swim."

On September 8, he started west for Milan, stopping at Padua, at Vicenza, where Andrea Palladio had lived and worked, and at Verona. Milan, with few antiquities, got a little more than a day. It was in 1906 as it is today more important for commerce and industry, a manufacturing center of silk, woolen, and cotton goods and "art furniture." The cathedral was "very fine" with "a great view of [the] surrounding country from [the] top." In the Church of the Santa Maria delle Grazie, Leonardo da Vinci's *Last Supper* was "in bad shape." Baedeker said it was "in the last stages of decay."

On September 12, he started north for Paris and left Italy the next day. Doyle spent 190 days in Europe altogether, 135 in the south and only 55 for Switzerland, Germany, France, Belgium, and England. In 1906 he did not explain his itinerary. Fifteen years later he told his two draftsmen, Charles Greene and Donald Stewart, to emphasize the south: "I am decidedly of the opinion that Spain, Southern Italy and Greece first, returning to Naples and working slowly North is the way to get the most out of the trip."[26] He explained Greece's importance to Stewart: "There is not much new that is good that is not in some way based on something old that is good. And in these days when so many are running after false gods, there is a need for scholars trained in the classical traditions."[27]

When Stewart reported on his own trip, he thanked Doyle for the recommendation: "I feel extremely fortunate in having followed your advice to start with Greece. Developments have followed in their logical order, and it has been extremely interesting to trace the influence and relation of the earlier periods upon each succeeding one." In Florence, for example, he had the advantage of a grounding in Greece: "To me the early Renaissance artists (Brunelleschi, Donatello etc.) come nearer the spirit and perfection of Greek art than any succeeding generation."[28]

Doyle had an uncritical wonder of Greek and Roman art and architecture: they possessed a perfection for him later ages could only approximate.

He nearly ignored Germany, stopping only briefly in Strasburg, which Germany had absorbed in 1871, after the Franco-Prussian War. He said nothing about the rising colossus of the German Empire. He saw only things old.

> *[Strasburg is a] mighty picturesque old Germany city. [It is] very prosperous and busy looking. [There is a] corking fine cathedral of brownstone and fine old homes with beautiful carving and many very picturesque houses and buildings. [I] only spent a few hours here and would like to have stayed a few days. [There are] so many things of interest.*

The afternoon of September 14, he reached Nancy,[29] which Doyle thought "too modern." He liked Rheims much better. The cathedral, "early Gothic" and "very fine" with its "deeply recessed entrance," has "fine" rose window, many "fine" statues, two "fine" towers, and "beautiful" stained glass.

He spent three weeks in Paris. The "best thing" was how it was "laid out to many beautiful vistas and new things [are] built with [the] idea of preserving the beauty of the city and adding to it," with "fine open spaces and boulevards and fine wide streets," like the Place de la Bastille and the Place de la Concorde. The Bois de Boulogne was "a great park full of people in gladdest array on [a] fine P.M. And the Place des Vosges was a "fine old square [with] all old houses." Sainte-Chapelle was "very gorgeous." Notre Dame was a "great cathedral." Cluny Museum was "very interesting [with] fine ceilings and fireplaces, beautiful carved furniture [and] many good fragments of fine architecture." The Luxembourg Palace and Gardens were "very good."

In Paris, more than in any other city, he judged as he observed. The Opera (1874) was "magnificent but rather disappointing [and] over decorated particularly in [the] interior." The Hotel de Ville (rebuilt 1876-84) had "some good interior details [but] the exterior was not very happy." The Madeleine (1806) was "not bad but rather cold and lifeless." It was "very big" and the "interior [is] pretty good." He liked the Louvre but preferred the oldest parts; "Francis I's court is good." The exterior of the Bibliotheque de Sainte-Genevieve (1838-50), which may have inspired Whidden &

Lewis' Portland Library,[30] was "very fine;" but the "interior [is] not much." The Comptoir National d"Escompte (rebuilt 1883) Doyle said was "good modern French." The Ecole de Medecine in the Boulevard Saint Germain on the Left Bank, done a few years earlier in a "severely plain style" (Baedeker), Doyle thought "good." The Ecole des Beaux Arts, which was important to many contemporary American architects, he went to for the exhibitions. He said it had a "good collection of antiquities and casts [and] good copies of famous pictures." As in the earlier part of his journey, he was as likely to admire a painting or statue as a building. In the Louvre, he commented on the antiquities and casts from Egypt, Asia Minor, Greece, and Rome, the collection of Renaissance sculpture, and paintings of early French and Italian masters and whole collections like "the modern French gallery" and "great collections of gems, jewels, and small objects of art." Of the picture galleries in general he concluded, "Much … is mediocre and uninteresting but [there are] many masterpieces of all schools." In his time modern art, especially French, was exhibited in the Luxembourg Palace. His favorites were Saint-Gaudens, Meunier, Rodin, and Whistler.

He visited Chantilly nearby for the chateau and the racecourse, St. Denis for the ancient monastic church, Saint-Cloud for a park and fountain, Sevres for a "porcelain manufactory," and Versailles. He had several days on the Loire for Orleans and Blois, "a very interesting city," He could have spent "a month here drawing things." He liked the chateaux at Chambord, Amboise, and especially Chenonceaux. He returned to Paris by way of Chateaudun for the "castle," and some "fine old houses [with] carved wood Renaissance details."

He left Paris October 8 for Chartres. The cathedral was "a corker, one of the very finest I have seen. The taller of the two towers … the principal tower rebuilt [in] 1507 [is] very ornate but [it] is very graceful and beautiful." The west and oldest façade was "simple and fine." The interior was "stunning" and the "details all so good [with] fine stained glass, especially "the west Rose window." The Church of St. Pierre was "very good in imitation of the cathedral." There were "a number of dandy old fourteenth and fifteenth century houses;" especially a "half timber house near [the] fish market," with a "carved wood circular bay for stairs."

The next day, he started north, stopping briefly in Dreux for the nineteenth-century Chapel Royal, the memorial to the Orleans royal family. It was "very rich" with "too much decoration." Rouen was much better, "a fine town full of interesting old things." It was the "most interesting city except Paris that I have seen in France, all things considered." There was a "fine sixteenth-century building opposite [the] cathedral"; some "richly carved Renaissance houses"; other "very interesting timber houses"; and a "very interesting clock tower." The city museum, a "modern building nicely situated in the park" had a "very fine collection." Despite "too much decoration" the cathedral was "very good" with a "good" modern pulpit, some "fine" side portals, and a "fine" rose window. The Palais de Justice was a "beautiful late Gothic building" but "most of the over decorated interiors [was] modern." Best of all, "the finest thing in Rouen, was the Church of St. Ouen." Baedeker called it "one of the most beautiful Gothic churches in existence." Doyle thought it "much finer than the cathedral."

On his last day in France, Amiens was "somewhat disappointing after Rouen" although the cathedral was "a wonder," with many similarities to Notre Dame in Paris. Its interior was "very lofty and fine" with "very good details" in the best period of Gothic" although there were "no fine leaded glass windows as at Rouen and Chartres." There were "interesting monuments in [the] cathedral and fine iron grilles and gates to all side chapels and to [the] choir," where the choir stalls were "beautifully carved" and were "among the finest I have seen." There was "not much else" of interest. The new fountain and monuments were "mediocre." He missed "the fine old carved timber houses of other French cities." He concludes: "Town [is] too modern." It is interesting to note how often, as he described what he saw in northern Europe, he criticized excessive decoration in modern work. He preferred the simplicity of earlier times. Throughout his career he stressed simplicity and eschewed ornament, especially when it seemed superimposed by a designer. He liked the restrained work of craftsmen: molders, masons, carpenters, and carvers.

He had less than three days in Belgium to see Brussels, Malines, Antwerp, Ghent, and Bruges. Baedeker suggested a week and a half for these cities. He had an hour in Ghent; he said it was "a short time." He saw the cathedral and the Hotel de Ville which was "very picturesque." It was a "very interesting looking town."

On the evening of October 13, he crossed the Channel to England and Dover. In Canterbury, the next day, he found the cathedral "very interesting" with a "peculiar plan" from "various periods" especially the "old Norman nave" and "the central tower." The city was "very quaint and interesting with many picturesque views [and a] fine place to make watercolors."

October 15 he arrived in London, the center of the British Empire, at Victoria Station, where his diary takes up. He seems to have started walking northeast toward Trafalgar Square passing first [the Roman Catholic] Westminster Cathedral, then under construction, which "will be stunning when completed. [It is the] best modern church I have seen."

He had sixteen days in London but took few notes. The first day he bought a guide book that is in the Doyle Library at Reed.[31] He carefully studied this book, underlining attractions and drawing lines in the margin next to descriptions, yet he wrote almost nothing in his diary. Westminster Abbey was "pretty fine Gothic." St. Margaret's was a "fine late Gothic Chapel." Day trips out of London got a little more, especially Greenwich, with "some good buildings by Jones and Wren." But Windsor was just: "twenty-five miles from London, [the] grandest Royal Residence in England, fourteenth century, [and] Windsor Park." Nothing was said about Hampton Court: the name headed a blank page.

Twenty years later, on his second trip to Europe, he liked England better, and he thought about his disappointment in 1906. In 1926 he saw more of the countryside because he toured by car; in 1906 he traveled by train: "When I was here before, I saw very little of the English country outside a few of the larger towns and well known places. This time we have taken more time to it and have seen some good houses inside as well as out. There is some great stuff here in Tudor, Queen Anne and Georgian suitable for our climate in Portland and the bulliest English tile roofs you ever saw."[32] He liked the villages and cottages, "the simple roadside houses and gardens and the small places of northern England and Scotland [are] extremely simple and restrained. No moldings."[33] He did not like some contemporary architecture:

> *The architects here in England, London particularly, dislike large, restful, unworried spaces and unbroken lines. Most of the buildings are fussy and ornamental—unlike the people. The modern buildings I am referring to of course. With their heritage of Tudor, Queen Anne and Georgian buildings, one expects them to do better, but the modern influence seems to be French and German. … Plenty of Good things in London tho, but they are mostly over 100 years old. St. James Palace for instance. It is a gem.*[34]

On both trips he loved Oxford.

In 1906 he had three days to explore the colleges. He was impressed: "Very beautifully situated city with charming old college buildings. Everything [is] in good taste and substantial looking." He responded warmly to the spires, vaults, cloisters and gardens. He listed each of the colleges, three of which he gave two stars: Christ Church, New College, and Magdalen. In addition he gave two stars to the University Galleries, Christ Church Cathedral, and the Divinity School with "magnificent full groined ceilings and good paneling." Almost every entry was favorable except Oriel, "not much architecturally" and Keble, "Victorian, rotten architecture."

When he left Oxford, October 3, he went to Warwick, an "ancient town. Some old houses and two old gates remain, but the main thing of interest here is Warwick Castle." The next day, he found Chester a "fine, quaint, old town." He walked around the "ancient walls, very interesting, about two miles" and through the arcaded streets for "many interesting examples of half timber houses."

On his last day he stopped at Port Sunlight, a factory town that William Lever, an industrialist and an amateur social philosopher, had designed for the employees of his Lever Brothers Soap Company. The houses, shops, schools, and churches were nineteenth-century reproductions of traditional village craftsmanship. Doyle approved. It was, he wrote, "finely laid out" and "very interesting" with everything "English style."

He sailed from Liverpool, November 6, 1906.

There are many accounts of A. E. Doyle's life in nomination forms for the National Register of Historic Places and in biographical dictionaries of architects. In all of them he is said to have attended Columbia University; some even say he graduated from Columbia. In fact he was neither a registered student nor a graduate. I discussed this matter with the Columbia University Archives and with the University Registrar; there is no record of him at Columbia, although at the time the university recorded all registered students even if they were not candidates for a degree.[35] I think the explanation for the mistake is that these accounts have built on each other. At some time in the past, someone misunderstood the practice of permitting office-trained draftsmen to attend classes as "special students." A better term today might be auditors. "Special students" were unrecognized by the university administration. There were no "official records accepted by the registrar."[36]

At Columbia in 1901-1903, when Doyle was in New York, there were many "special students," draftsmen from architects' offices who attended lectures and audited courses but were not enrolled in the program because they did not have the qualifications to enroll or did not have the money to do so or did not choose to become full time students. The administration of the university disapproved of special students, who paid no tuition, and preferred enrolled students preparing for graduation. But William R. Ware, the director of the Architecture School at Columbia until 1903, contravened university policy and allowed draftsmen without degrees or college graduates with degrees in other subjects to attend courses. He believed that these office men "kept the regular students more in touch with the realities of practice and demonstrated a high proficiency in drawing." His disagreement with the university helped force his early retirement in 1903, Doyle's last year in New York.[37]

Doyle never said he attended or graduated from Columbia; he admitted he was an office man. In 1913 when he applied to design the Portland Post Office, he described his training: "The writer was with Whidden & Lewis in this city for over ten years and while in their employ worked on the competitive plans for the San Francisco Custom House. He has had four years experience in New York offices, three years with Henry Bacon, then a year abroad."[38]

In 1919 Charles Cheney did an article for *Architect and Engineer* on Doyle and asked for information about his training and career. Doyle told him essentially what he had said for the post office competition: "Grew up in office of Whidden & Lewis, Portland. Was with them 12 years, afterward spending 3 years in New York and a year abroad."[39] He repeated essentially the same thing on several other occasions.

The idea that he attended Columbia University gradually crept into his biography. In this earliest account of Doyle's life Cheney said nothing about Columbia because Doyle had said nothing to him about it, noting only: "He [Doyle] had three years in New York City."[40] In 1922 Charles Carey embellished the story when he published a brief biography of Doyle with those of other Oregon politicians, merchants, and professionals. Charles Carey was a friend; he and Doyle served together on the Art Museum Board, and both were members of the Arlington Club. Doyle probably said something to Carey about being a "special student" because Carey wrote that Doyle "pursued special courses in design at

Columbia University of New York City and in ateliers while working in the office of Henry Bacon."[41]

At the time of Doyle's death in 1928 his office changed the emphasis in an official obituary: "He went east to Columbia University to take special courses in design, while working in the office of Henry Bacon."[42] The Portland papers quoted the office's obituary with subtle changes of emphasis. *The Oregonian* said: "He went east to Columbia University to take special courses in design while working in the office of Henry Bacon."[43] *The Journal* went farther; it said, he "went to Columbia University to complete his work."[44] After that the story had a life of its own. By 1956 he was an enrolled student; the *Biographical Dictionary of American Architects* said he "went to New York to enter Columbia University's School of Architecture" and "graduated" from it.[45] In the *Macmillan Encyclopedia of Architects* (1982), "Doyle went to New York where he pursued design studies at Columbia University and worked in the office of Henry Bacon."[46] And the story of A. E. Doyle's university training has been repeated in the nomination forms for the Historical Register and in the most recent and authoritative biography.[47]

There is a similar history to the idea that he attended the American School in Athens. When he wrote Cheney in 1919, he said nothing about the school; yet Cheney wrote that Doyle had "a year in Europe, including some precious months at the American School in Athens."[48] Very possibly at some point he said to Charles Cheney that he had been at the American School. In 1922 Charles Carey amplified the statement: "Desirous of still further perfecting his professional knowledge he spent several months as a student in the American School of Archaeology at Athens, Greece and a year in foreign travel,"[49] and the obituary provided by Doyle's office repeated this. A number of recent biographies mention a scholarship; for example, "With a scholarship to the American School of Archeology in Athens Doyle left for study and travel in Europe."[50] He was at the school; he said he met his travel companion, Martin, there, but he neither enrolled in it, nor was he supported by it. I asked the school. There is no record of him.[51]

University training became increasingly important in architecture as in other professions in the twentieth century. On the German model, universities everywhere were developing graduate programs and schools, which gave professions "an institutional basis on which to standardize knowledge" and "a most powerful legitimization for their claims to cognitive and technical superiority."[52] By the 1920s there was a presumption that architects were university educated. As the idea gained popularity so did the assumption that Portland's most successful architect was a university product. I do not think Doyle misrepresented his training, though he was not averse to embellishing, "padding his dossier" as people would say today. His two years in New York he sometimes called three or even four years, and his six months and five days in Europe he said was one year. And very possibly at some point he said to Cheney that he had been at the American School, but he did not study there for months. He arrived in Athens May 26, 1906, and he left July 6, for a total of forty-one days. For seventeen of those days he traveled to Argos, Delphi, Eleusis, and Troy. Therefore he was only in Athens twenty-four days.

Throughout the nineteenth and even into the twentieth century, especially in places as provincial as Portland, the line separating architects from the other building trades was easily crossed because there was no licensing of architects, and, until late in the nineteenth century in the East and into the twentieth century in the West, there were no architectural programs at universities. In Doyle's time in Portland and elsewhere, all "who so chose could call themselves architects and could engage in professional activities." Young men (and sometimes women) learned architecture by "working and learning in the offices of those already in practice." Periods of apprenticeship varied, and draftsmen worked as junior employees or as pupils until they felt they could make it on their own.[53]

Probably few people knew Doyle as well as or liked him better than Thomas Lamb Eliot. They worked together on Reed College, on the Central Library, on a store and office building for Eliot in Hood River, and on a redesign of Eliot's Neahkahnie summer cottage. In the spring of 1928 after their friendship ended at Doyle's death, Eliot looked back on his contribution to Reed College in a short piece for the spring 1928 Reed College alumni magazine: "Mr. Doyle came to his position with Reed College after employment in a prominent firm of architects in Portland. He had spent several years with a distinguished New York office, followed by travel in Europe, and had taken up independent work in 1907 with rapidly growing success."[54] Eliot was a Harvard man. He was a founder of Reed College, as his father had been of Washington University in St. Louis, yet he did not expect an accomplished architect to be a university man.

The University of Oregon was founded in 1872, but for two decades its curriculum was strictly classical. There were two courses of study, Classics and Science, yet the emphasis even in science, which required Latin, was on classical and literary knowledge. The stated aim was "to cultivate the mind in a general way," to train "public speakers and writers, lawyers, statesmen, clergymen, and intellectual workers." In 1894 new, practical courses were introduced in civil and electrical engineering, in commerce, and in pedagogy for students preparing for careers in teaching. A journalism course was added in 1909. The university started a law school in Portland where it remained until 1913 when Eugene added a law school and the Portland school separated from the university to become the independent Northwestern School of Law. Gradually professional schools were established. Education started at Eugene in 1909; there was a normal school at Monmouth from 1856. Architecture began in 1914, and journalism in 1916.[55]

Among Portland's elite, there was some resistance to these developments. College was important to the children of the pioneer merchants. Even the women of Portland's better families at the turn of the century attended college, sometimes in the East. Liberal studies were a refinement. Only gradually would the prejudice dissipate that assumed a separation between education and professional training. Harvey Scott, the editor of *The Oregonian,* thought that college was for the elite, who should study the classics as he had done at Linfield. Professions, he insisted, should not be taught at universities: "School-made teachers," he wrote, "are often just such practical failures as school-made editors." This was not just a provincial prejudice. W. R. Ware founded the architecture schools, successively at MIT and Columbia, yet he had a high regard for office training. He had a similar view about study in Europe and participated in the founding of the American Academy in Rome. He was even chairman of the managing committee for a while. He resigned in a dispute over the supervision of the students who, he thought, should discover "their own examples of fine architecture, rather than studying only those dictated by the Academy."[56]

A. E. Doyle was office trained and self taught. In Europe he was uninterested in professionalism and the work of contemporary architects. If he noticed recent buildings at all it was usually to address their deficiencies, especially their over-decoration, in terms of early precedents. The architects he mentioned were long-gone advocates of classical principles like Andreas Palladio and Christopher Wren. In his diary he repeatedly mentions the accomplishments in wood, brick, and stone of nameless craftsmen long gone. He sought out old cottages and houses often in preference to buildings deemed to have architectural merit.

On his return to Portland, he had excellent preparation for his career. He had worked and studied architecture in New York, America's most important city, and he had traveled in Europe, where he learned about the sources of western civilization. He traveled as wealthy Americans of his generation did with copies of little red Baedekers in hand to see Europe's art and architecture, to experience its culture and sophistication, to admire artistic as well as natural beauty, and to trace the history of cities chronologically from Athens to London. But Europe was much more than museums and antiquities. It was an ancient perfection against which provincial Portland could measure and model itself. Portland was building; it was becoming a city. It needed architects who knew about cities, who had seen them and who had worked on them.

CHAPTER 3

Starting

Shortly after his return, Albert Doyle and Lucie Godley were married in Chehalis, Washington, on December 19, 1906. The town's weekly newspaper devoted more space and words to it than to most weddings that year. Doyle's brothers Edward and Arthur were ushers. Their sister Daisy was maid of honor. The best man was Harry Wentz. A reception followed at the home of Dr. and Mrs. G. W. Kennicott, whose house remodel Doyle planned among his first jobs. Dr. Kennicott's interest in the wedding may account for newspaper's notice of it; he was the town's leading physician and the proprietor of the county's only hospital.[1]

Mr. and Mrs. A. E. Doyle's house at 2136 NW 8th Avenue was in West Irvington, then a rapidly expanding suburb. Streetcars were creating the newer neighborhoods. Other areas of the city had horses and carriages, but not "newly developed Irvington." No one there had "the facilities for housing them." And automobiles were still in the future.[2] Just one mile from the Steel Bridge, the neighborhood had "the best service carline in the city." An electric line on Union Avenue (now Martin Luther King Boulevard) was two long blocks from the Doyles' house. Streetcars ran every

A. E. Doyle bought this house at 2136 NE 8th Avenue in 1904; in the first few years after his marriage, he remodeled it extensively to its appearance here as a stylish, if diminutive, Arts and Crafts. (Newhouse)

"three to five minutes," and "it takes only twelve minutes" to SW 3rd Avenue where Doyle could alight to walk to his office.[3] In his first two years, he was in the Commonwealth Building at SW 6th and Ankeny. Then from 1909 he was in the Worcester Building, built in 1889, a six-story, Romanesque office block between Oak and Pine on the east side of SW 3rd at what would now be 220, a well-recognized address of the building trades. Neither the Commonwealth nor the Worcester survives.

From the streetcar to their house was an easy walk of perhaps four hundred yards past early twentieth-century workers' cottages. It was not a fashionable address for a professional and his family, but in a tidy, first-ring suburb with paved streets and sidewalks; farther east, Irvington had grand homes. The Doyles' house was originally a working-man's cottage. He bought it in 1904 from Charles S. Dakyns, the janitor in the Concord Building, where Whidden & Lewis had their office.[4]

When the Sanborn Company first surveyed the area in 1901, little had yet happened on NE 8th Avenue. Between Tillamook and Thompson there were nineteen lots, but just one house. The next year, in 1902, Dakyns built his house. The neighborhood filled out quickly; by 1908 there were only two vacant lots. In the 1910 Census there was only one. The Doyles' house was two stories with a stucco exterior. Today it is sided with composition shakes. Yet there lurks a charm, which is surely to be attributed to Doyle, who altered it and gave the house the Arts and Crafts designation which it has in a recent survey of Irvington.[5] A gabled porch with exposed beams faces the street. At the back a gabled extension gives a second-story room and an open latticed porch below.

A. E. Doyle holds Jean, his third and youngest daughter, who is probably almost three years old. It is the summer of 1913, and they are on the front porch of the NE 8th Avenue house. He is thirty-six, young, but very successful. (Newhouse)

One of Doyle's first jobs was this house for Dr. Herbert Nichols. According to a Nichols family legend, Dr. Nichols cared for Mrs. Doyle and delivered Kathleen in exchange for Doyle's work on this house, which is still at 1925 SW Vista. (Author's photograph)

Doyle's plans survive for some renovations in 1908 and 1909 for a sleeping porch, which has become the second-story extension at the back, and for craftsman detailing in the dining room: a sideboard, wainscoting, and window and door trim.[6]

According to the 1910 Census, their neighbors included a grocer, a druggist, two real estate agents, a molder in an iron foundry, a railroad clerk, a baseball player, two salesmen, one in a cigar store and one in a hardware store, a book publisher, who worked out of his home, a concrete pipe contractor, and a laborer. More than one family lived in three of the houses. The house to the Doyles' south, for example, had seven occupants: a family of four, a married couple, and a divorcee. No wife in the neighborhood was employed outside the house. The Doyles were more prosperous than their neighbors; they neither shared their house with another family as did eight neighbors nor did they have boarders as did five. By the time of this Census, they had two daughters, Kathleen and Helen, aged two years and one year respectively. In addition, they had a maid servant, Ada May Burres, a young woman of twenty-three. Only one other family on the block had a maid.[7]

Albert and Lucie Doyle assumed responsibility for their parents. Doyle helped his family and hers with monthly allowances.[8] His mother's house belonged to him, and his sister and brothers continued to live there with their mother. The Godleys followed the Doyles to Portland. Henry was a tinner, and Sarah kept a notions shop. They moved often but they always lived within a few blocks of the Doyles. Henry died in 1916 and Sarah in 1927;

though the Godleys themselves were insignificant, there were newspaper obituaries because they were both pioneers who as children had crossed the Plains in covered wagons.[9]

A. E. Doyle's practice began modestly. Two of his early commissions were in Chehalis; neither was important. He remodeled Dr. G. W. Kennicott's house, where his wedding reception had been held. It was and is an unimpressive, stolid country doctor's home. And Doyle built anew for the Westminster Presbyterian Church where he had married. It remains much as he intended it: a shingled low English-style country church, 48 by 58 feet with an organ loft. Curved buttresses set off the entrance. A Mission-style belfry is 35 feet high and the auditorium of the church is 48 by 30 feet.[10] He regretted taking this job, explaining: "The church people got donations and made substitutions in the specifications, had a poor cheap contractor on the job who did not understand drawings very well. The result was that what little I got out of the job was eaten up in the making of trips to straighten out the tangles and at a time when I was very busy here."[11]

There was better work close to home. By 1911, he had designed eleven Portland houses. None was particularly large, like some of the mansions Whidden & Lewis did in Northwest Portland or on King's Hill. His clients were upper-middle class, prosperous people. Two were doctors; the others were successful businessmen.[12] There was also an awareness of current architectural trends. Most of the houses were Colonial and eight had Craftsman or Arts and Crafts elements.[13]

He also did a large Shingle-style summer house for an early and important client, Edward De Hart. It was a large two-and-a-half-story, T-shaped, shingled frame structure. The entrance through a vestibule led to a large hallway leading upstairs and to a living room and through it to a dining room, both with wooden floors, beamed ceilings, and large basalt fireplaces. An ample pantry and kitchen were beyond the dining room. Upstairs were four bedrooms; three had fireplaces and baths. In the attic were rooms for servants. This was an important early job; the house was for the retirement of a prominent businessman. Edward J. De Hart was nearly seventy when he gave this job to Doyle shortly after June 22, 1907, when he bought an acreage northwest of Hood River he called Lakecliff. De Hart had moved to Portland in 1876 and he started a firm which grew into Portland's largest hardware company, Honeyman, De Hart & Company (later, after De Hart's retirement, Honeyman Hardware). Edward De Hart was prominent in Portland. He was a long-time vestryman at Trinity Cathedral and a member of the Arlington Club. His large shingled Queen Anne was at the southwest corner of NW 20th and Glisan, where a streetcar-era apartment house, the Biltmore Apartments, is today.[14]

Prominence for Doyle came from one really important job. Within the first few months, probably by February 1907, Meier & Frank hired him for a new ten-story building at the corner of SW 6th and Alder, an annex to the five-story brick store on 5th between Morrison and Alder, which Whidden & Lewis had done in 1898.[15] An announcement was made in March 1908: "The style of architecture has not been fully decided upon, but will not follow that of the building now occupied except that the floors will probably be on the same level."[16] Doyle became the designer of the most important commercial institution of the city and one of the large department stores in the West. Through his career he worked often for the firm and for the Frank and Meier families; he had twenty jobs with the Meier & Frank Company or with the families. In later years, he did a monument for Sigmund Frank, a house in Portland Heights for Abe Meier, and a summer house at Menucha on the Columbia River for Julius Meier. Neither house survives.

If we knew why Sigmund Frank turned to Doyle, who was young and inexperienced, rather than to Whidden & Lewis,

This is a view looking north on SW 5th in about 1900. The 1898 Meier & Frank Building by Whidden & Lewis is ahead. (OHS 11931)

Sigmund Frank decided to build a white terra-cotta-clad department store like some in New York and Chicago. This is Doyle's rendering of the store as he intended it in 1909, from SW 5th and Alder. (Portland Architectural Club, Yearbook, 1909, no pagination)

who had designed the earlier Meier & Frank building, we would probably understand better why he was immediately successful. In 1983 Pietro Belluschi was intrigued by the question. As he approached the end of his career, he paused to answer it, to explain why his former employer got the contract. He admired Doyle, who was, he said, "a very convincing person and he got the job on his own. He was lucky." Sigmund Frank had a reputation for disregarding status and recognizing worth. "He always listened to any suggestion from the cashboy to the head of a department." He walked daily and regularly through the store and talked and listened to "the department managers and the least important clerks."[17]

In 1927, in his last months of life, Doyle recalled Sigmund Frank as a good friend: "I started to work pretty young and … one of my first friends in business was Sigmund Frank. He was a fine friend for many years. He was a truly great man and had a fine influence. I was very, very fond of him."[18] Friendship was important to Doyle, as he wrote in one of his many letters of instruction to his daughter, Kathleen. While visiting New York in 1923, he had a temporary membership in the Player's Club because he was recommended by

Henry Bacon, who, he wrote, "is just loved and worshipped here, so any friends of his are accepted without question. He is a real friend of mine and has been for more than 20 years." And there is a guiding principle to be drawn from the incident: "Well, Kathleen dear, next to being somebody yourself it's great to have friends who are famous."[19] Doyle was friends with the heirs of Portland's leading families. William S. Ladd died in 1892; his son William M. had a life-long, close relationship with Doyle. Henry Failing died in 1898; he left three daughters. Doyle knew two of them. And Henry W. Corbett died in 1903; Doyle worked closely with the three Corbett boys, as he called them, the three grandsons of H. W. Corbett: Henry Ladd Corbett, Charles Elliott, and Wesley. They were nearly his age.

Simon Benson knew Doyle from the Lewis and Clark Exposition and the construction of the Forestry Building for which Benson had supplied the timber. He was born in Norway and an immigrated at sixteen to Wisconsin, where he learned English, married, and had a store. When the store burned, he moved to St. Helens, Oregon, to find work in logging. He bought 160 acres of timber, which he sold when his wife became ill. In 1890 he began over. He mechanized by adapting steam power and inventing an ocean-going log raft to deliver timber by sea to California. Eventually he owned 45,000 acres of land, which he sold with his company in 1909 for $4,000,000, nearly as much as H. W. Corbett's estate of $5,000,000. Benson retired to Portland as a philanthropist and developer. In 1911 he had Doyle design a hotel soon after called The Benson. He also tasked Doyle to design the Benson Bubblers, because Benson advocated temperance, recognizing the harm of alcohol for timber workers, all men, barracked together for the work week and released for days off in taverns and brothels.[20]

Thomas Lamb Eliot, according to George McMath, was Doyle's patron.[21] He was likely Portland's most prominent citizen. In his early years in Portland after 1867 when he became the pastor of Portland First Unitarian Church, there was some resistance to Unitarianism among the conservative and traditional Yankee churches of Portland and some suspicion of heresy. Through Eliot's long service, the prejudice dissipated. Other ministers of Portland's Protestant churches came and went, but Eliot stayed. He retired in 1893 because of poor eyesight and to concentrate on causes for the city and the state which had long interested him: education, mental illness, the penal system, women's suffrage, temperance, the Humane Society, the Library and the Art Museum.[22] Eliot

The Eliot Building was Doyle's first job. It is still at the corner of Oak and 2nd Street (116 Oak Street) in Hood River, Oregon. Today the building is much as Doyle designed it. (Author's photograph)

Thomas Lamb Eliot (1841-1936), A. E. Doyle's close friend and patron. (RC)

wanted an art school in Portland, and he saw the Sketch Club as the forerunner.[23] He was independently wealthy, in a small way, a land speculator and developer with interests in Portland and Hood River. The Crocker sisters, Anna Belle and Florence, were questioned about the founders of the Art Museum, probably in the 1940s; they remembered Eliot as the "giant of the board, a great man." They added that "in addition to all his virtues however, it seems that he was a skilled financier, a very shrewd man in all money matters."[24]

His home was a three-story, frame, 1882 Second Empire with a mansard roof, in a fashionable neighborhood on the South Park Blocks at what would be 1025 SW Park Ave.; it is a parking lot today. He had a country house near Hood River where the family spent two months in spring and autumn, and in time he also had a cottage at Neahkahnie for the summer. He was forty-nine when he retired, and he traveled to Japan and Alaska. In 1906 he sold a large and valuable tract of river-front property opposite St. Johns. On the proceeds he and his family toured Europe, leaving in April 1906, the same month as Doyle. They sailed for England and he for the Mediterranean. They traveled south and he, north. They met by chance, August 23, 1906, in Florence. They talked about Eliot's plans for a two-story building in Hood River with a hardware store below and offices above. A Hood River architect, Paul Milton Hall-Lewis, had done drawings. Doyle made some suggestions, and the next day Eliot gave Doyle his first job. Doyle's last weekend in Florence was given to a drawing that he dated August 27. Two days later Eliot sent "Doyle's design" to Portland.[25]

Eliot was chairman of the Reed Board of Regents, which January 5, 1911, selected Doyle as architect for the campus and the first two college buildings. This was the most important job in Portland in the early twentieth century. Eliot was also the vice-president of the Library Association, which selected Doyle nine months later to design the Central Library. He may also have been responsible for two other library jobs. In the first few months of 1907, Doyle designed a temporary eastside neighborhood branch, a small craftsman cottage with weatherboard exterior, a hip-on-gable dormer roof, and two banks of casement windows. The one-story frame structure at SE 11th and Alder comprised one large room with one end for adults and the other for children.[26] In 1911 when he was selected for the Central Library he was already working on the permanent East Portland Branch Library.

Winslow B. Ayer was president of the Library Association in 1911. Since he had selected the cast collection that became the core of the museum and the models for the Sketch Club, he too must have known Doyle as a youth. Ayer made his fortune as Benson had in timber. In 1904 when he had Whidden & Lewis do a Colonial house for him (still at 811 NW 19th), Doyle, just back from New York, doubtless worked on it. Ayer gave Doyle a series of jobs including a house and outbuildings for a cattle ranch near Carlton, Oregon.[27]

⇜

The position of Whidden & Lewis in Portland was commanding, yet Doyle replaced them. "To this day, the decline of Whidden & Lewis's architectural influence has not been adequately explained."[28] In 1907, both Whidden and Lewis were about fifty. They maintained their office until Whidden died in 1929 although they had no significant job after 1915. Until Doyle went out on his own, they had worked for each of the major families of Portland" they had had four contracts for the Corbetts, three for the Failings, and five for the Ladds. Yet only two of these contracts (for the H. W. Corbett estate) were in effect after Doyle returned to Portland, and they were begun before and completed in 1907. In his first year Doyle had two Ladd estate contracts, three for the H. W. Corbett estate, and two for the H. Failing estate.[29] One of the Failings' jobs in Doyle's first year was for a fifteen-story office block. While it was not built, Doyle designed it and there was considerable interest. Thereafter he got much of the work for the three families, while Whidden & Lewis got none—he did twenty-eight jobs for the Corbetts, three for the Ladds, and seven for the Failings.. Whidden & Lewis were far less busy in their last seven years,[30] and it was in 1907-1912 that Portland grew most rapidly. It is probably significant that three of the twenty-one jobs they undertook in these years were for one person, the successful grain merchant, Theodore Wilcox: the Wilcox Building (still at 400 SW 6th Ave.), the Stevens Building (still at 812 SW Washington), and the Imperial Hotel (now the Hotel Lucia at 400 SW Broadway).

What makes the question difficult is that Doyle's work is similar to that of Whidden & Lewis. In the downtown buildings, the continuity between them has often been stressed: "Just as Whidden & Lewis had picked up where their parent firm, McKim, Mead & White, had left off on the Portland Hotel, so Doyle, too, picked up where his mentors, Whidden & Lewis, had left off on the Meier & Frank department store."[31] His work and theirs can be confused: "Doyle's early glazed terra-cotta buildings differ little from those designed by Whidden & Lewis."[32] His Central Library seems to acknowledge their Portland Library. The facades of both are dominated by a rank of large arched windows on the second floor. And both have three arched doors centered on the first floor.[33] Most of their work is compatible with his, like their Renaissance City Hall, the Stevens and Wilcox buildings, and the Imperial Hotel.

To provincial Portland Whidden & Lewis represented Eastern, even Parisian sophistication, which may not have always been an asset. They were preeminent over, even aloof from, other architects, who formed an early professional organization, the Portland Architectural Club, which William Whidden never joined. (Ion Lewis did join, late.) Despite Whidden's unwillingness to join, he was asked to serve as patron of the Beaux Arts atelier, because he was Portland's only Ecole-trained architect. When some architects recalled the atelier, they remembered his refusal, perhaps too the disdain in his terse response: he "did not care to serve."[34] E. B. MacNaughton had a searing encounter. Like Whidden and Lewis, MacNaughton was a graduate of MIT and an Easterner. Shortly after graduation in 1902, he came west, stopping first in Seattle, where he quickly ran out of money. He pawned his watch and went on to Portland to look for a job. He called at the office of Whidden & Lewis in the Concord Building but no luck: "A sliding window was opened, and he was told to get out."[35]

"Whidden was difficult,"[36] often distant and unapproachable and very different from Doyle, who was warm, open, and sociable. Doyle knew Whidden could be unpleasant. He regretted the façade Whidden presented and the distance in their relationship. When Doyle was dying, Whidden often came to the hospital. Doyle described the visits: "He seemed to be in much better spirits than I have known him to be for some time and was very pleasant, and I enjoyed him tremendously in his apparently changed attitude. He seems to be sweetening as he is growing older. I don't know that he has treated me differently than many of his friends, but perhaps I have felt it more."[37]

It is characteristic of Doyle's optimism and goodwill that he did not suspect what surely must have been the case, that illness and frailty softened Whidden, who came to comfort Doyle. Suffering and impending death tempered an usually querulous demeanor.

Personalities aside, there was novelty and style in Doyle's designs that gave an air of fashion and sophistication. While Whidden & Lewis eschewed Queen Anne, their proportions often seem influenced by it.[38] Doyle was part of a new generation of architects. Most of his earliest house plans showed Craftsman or Arts and Crafts influences. He sometimes included wood carving or stained glass, and he exposed rafters and supports. He liked the square upper columns resting on piers or on porch balustrades. In Europe, timber work, tiling, and carving fascinated him even on architecturally insignificant old buildings.

At the end of the nineteenth century in England, William Morris and John Ruskin advocated the role of the craftsman and the production of beautiful and useful objects. In the United

States, Gustav Stickley popularized the cause in his magazine, *The Craftsman*.[39] Stickley's ideas were popular in California and the bungalow spread widely through the work of Charles and Henry Greene and Bernard Maybeck. The formation of Portland's Arts and Crafts society is another example of how styles and ideas in Portland were brought here from the East and how much Portland could be influenced by the experiences of Portlanders who traveled and lived there. Julia Hoffman formed a Society of the Arts and Crafts when she returned in 1906 to Portland from Boston, where she belonged to the Boston Society of the Arts and Crafts. She had gone East after she was widowed so her children could attend school and university. Her son trained as an architect and later established the still important Hoffman Construction Company. Portland's Society of the Arts and Crafts, which included artists, craftsmen, and art lovers, was popular. In 1908 it had 85 members; two years later there were 135, and a program of instruction in painting, photography, sculpture, and weaving. I do not know that A. E. Doyle was ever a member. Some of his friends were. Ellis Lawrence and Harry Wentz lectured at the society's sessions. Charles Carey, Ellis Lawrence, and Morris Whitehouse were on the board, as were some of Doyle's early clients: Miss Helen Harmon, Mrs. Charles E. Curry, and Mrs. Gordon Voorhies. He was sympathetic with the organization's purpose to further "a knowledge of crafts that can be turned to a source of income" and to provide "an outlet for self-expression," because crafts are "a means to create beauty in the practical objects of everyday life." The society has developed and changed in the last century. Its successor is the Oregon College of Arts and Crafts with a campus at 8245 SW Barnes Road.[40]

In his downtown buildings, there was also a break with Whidden & Lewis. When he opened his office, they were completing the Corbett Building on the southeast corner of SW 5th and Morrison (now gone). It was a ten-story, steel-framed skyscraper with little exterior ornamentation. Like the 1898 Meier & Frank building, cater-corner from it (also gone), "windows occupy most of the façade filling the space between the brick faced column." Atop both buildings were "boldly projecting" slabs.[41] The steel structures of the two buildings seemed evident on the exterior. Doyle brought fashion, a New York influence, to the neighborhood in Classical or Neo-Classical forms expressed in white-glazed terra-cotta. The Meier & Frank annex was the first, but it was soon followed by his Selling Building on the southwest corner of SW 6th and Alder, Lipman Wolfe on the west side of SW 5th between Alder and Washington. and the Northwest Bank Building on the north side of Morrison between SW 6th and Broadway. This "white city" evoked classical temples and Renaissance palaces in the tripartite division of the new skyscrapers: a base, a shaft, and a capital. Base and capital were decorated with columns, pilasters, and arched windows. Spandrels were filled with ornaments drawn from the European past like acanthus leaves, lamb's tongue, bead and reel, and egg and dart. The taste for classical and Renaissance motifs had erupted in 1893 at the Columbian Exposition in Chicago, in the first of the white cities, largely designed by New York architects.

Doyle began his Portland practice having had significant experience in New York in the office of one of the country's important classicists, Henry Bacon. The Doyle family has among their prized heirlooms Bacon's wedding gift to Albert and Lucie, a silver loving cup, engraved with the names of the members of Bacon's firm who had known Doyle in New York. Doyle carefully maintained this relationship with Bacon. He wrote frequent friendly and personal messages, and he made a point of visiting Bacon. New York style was very important to Sigmund Frank, who gave Doyle his first significant job. Frank wanted his store to look like New York. He "made a close study" of the department stores in New York City "in order to map out the plans for a new home for the store in Portland."[42] The Library Board, when they decided to build anew, turned instinctively to New York. They began by engaging Carerre & Hastings, who were then completing the New York Public Library. Within a few months, the board decided to sever the relationship with this firm and Doyle got the job. For Meier & Frank and for the library, Doyle traveled east to New York to see what was being done as he planned for his work in Portland. Doyle's credentials as a New York-trained architect were nearly unique. William Whidden had come to Portland from New York but in 1888, five years before the Columbian Exposition and its influence.[43]

David Chambers Lewis might have challenged Doyle. He too had had New York training, but ill health cut short a promising career. Lewis was ten years older than Doyle and a Princeton graduate of 1890. He briefly worked for Whidden & Lewis, overlapping there with Doyle before returning East to Columbia for graduate work in architecture. Back in Portland, he opened an office late in the 1890s with an enviable list of clients, many of them relatives. He did a number of houses and downtown buildings that had "an affinity with Chicago office buildings."[44] He was well connected. His father, Cicero H. Lewis, had come to Portland in 1851 to establish a wholesale grocery business and to invest in real estate and is often mentioned as one of Portland's successful pioneer merchants in company with Corbett, Failing, and Ladd. He married Clementine Couch, the daughter of Captain John H. Couch, whose donation land claim is now much of northwest Portland. The family home was an 1882 mansion at NW 19th and Glisan, where Couch Park now is.[45] David Lewis' most significant accomplishment is probably Trinity Episcopal Cathedral, where he was a parishioner and his father, uncles, and cousins were vestrymen. When he became ill, he moved to California, where he died in 1918.

In 1909 Doyle was elected to the Arlington Club, Portland's most exclusive men's club for members of Portland's oldest and wealthiest families; only the most successful professionals could aspire to membership.[46] In 1913 he and Mrs. Doyle were listed in the Portland Blue Book, a register bound between blue covers of Portland's social, business, and professional elite, with their club memberships, their addresses, and the hours each week when they were "at home."[47] His signature in these years had gravity. As a youth he had always signed his name in his books, Albert E. Doyle, but from 1909 frequently and from 1911 always, he signed A. E. Doyle. To friends and family he was "Bert." To men who knew him well, even to other Portland architects, he was Doyle. To most of the people with whom he worked, all of the members of his office and almost all of his clients, he was Mr. Doyle. But to the public at the time and always, in the years since, he has been A. E. Doyle.

He was part of an increasingly prestigious profession. Architects were asserting that they were professionals, like doctors and lawyers. Portland architects were self-styled artists and arbiters of taste. In 1906, when Doyle was in Europe, some of the younger architects formed the Portland Architectural Club "for the purpose of bringing together the members of the architectural profession in social and educational relationship." In five years the membership grew from twenty to eighty. The club started annual exhibits of architecture, "instigated legislation beneficial to the profession," sponsored "public lectures and entertainments," and established "a higher sense of professional ethics."[48] The club worked for standards of art and architecture in Portland and Oregon and for the City Beautiful Program. It sponsored lectures on "travel, history, and technical subjects." It pressed for revisions in the building code and for legislation to license architects and to select "architects by competition for all state work amounting to over $5,000."[49] The members met on the top floor of the Sweeney Building (now the Bishop's House at 223 SW Stark). There was a drafting room for the atelier, a library, and a social room with two large fireplaces.[50] It "organized lecture courses, set competition programs, administered juries, and provided a library and a gallery of prints and casts." It tried to reproduce something of what was done in Paris in an atelier for architecture students. Doyle helped shape the educational program. He served on the club's first education and scholarship committees. Students were set specific, often archeological, problems. In 1912, for example, students were asked to design a courtyard appropriate to a house in Pompeii in the first century BC. Their work was sent to San Francisco to be judged. In 1912 several Portland architects talked to the students about the benefits of the atelier. Doyle said it would improve students' freehand drawing; draftsmen are often too mechanical and limited. Others told the students they would gain "a more extended knowledge of architectural words and phrases," receive "inspiration by friendly criticism," and attain "a more exalted view of professional duty" and a "greater regard for professional ethics."[51]

The Portland Architectural Club was an important first step in the development of a profession in Portland. It brought architects, draftsmen, and others interested in architecture together to display their work, to talk about their collective problems, to perform in amateur dramatics, and even to sing at a piano in the social room. It was a democratic organization. The 1910 *Yearbook* listed fifty-nine members without distinguishing between architects, draftsmen, engineers, and superintendents. City directories gave job titles; about half were architects.

In 1911 Oregon architects organized their own chapter of the American Institute of Architects, which was "the proper body to act upon public and professional questions." (Nationally, the AIA dated back to 1857.) Henceforth the club was "confined to social and educational work."[52] It ceased altogether in 1915, the year after the founding of the School of Architecture and the Fine Arts at the University of Oregon (later renamed the School of Architecture and Allied Arts). Like engineers, academics, doctors, and lawyers, architects increasingly limited "admission to and reputation within a community of peers." Throughout America there was an increasing insistence on professional credentials and professional organizations to maintain them. America's rapid growth of cities and communication made "unknown, perhaps unknowable people" interdependent."[53] Portland was no exception. It had grown to be a city and was united with the larger American society. Here as elsewhere "emergent professionals wanted to distinguish themselves from the swirl of amateurs, popularizers and charlatans."[54] The AIA worked to improve the standing of the profession on many of the issues heretofore the concern of the Club, like juried competitions, standardized fees, and licensing of architects. The advantage of the AIA was national standing and a Washington headquarters. Doyle was a founding member of the Oregon chapter of the AIA. As he was a practicing architect there was no question about his admission. Nor was there any question about his state license in 1919 when Oregon began licensing architects.

State licensing began in Illinois in 1897 and spread gradually. In Oregon in 1919 as elsewhere, the legislature prohibited anyone from calling himself an architect or pretending to practice the profession without a license. A five-member board of architects examined prospective architects in "mechanics as applied to building; superintendence, materials and construction, history of architecture in relation to architectural design, planning and design; practical knowledge of sanitary and electrical installation, heating and ventilating." Many were exempted from examination: "any person registered in another stated with equal qualifications" or anyone who had "practiced the profession for five years in another state," or anyone in Oregon who had practiced for one year "prior to the passage of the act."[55] There were differences of opinion about licensing. Some felt, "There are more grounds for licensing an architect than there is for licensing a physician." Others bridled at state control. Licensing restricts newcomers and does nothing about poor buildings of designers who do not call themselves architects. Examinations and diplomas do not guarantee good architecture. "A graduate of L'Ecole des Beaux Arts, or of Massachusetts Tech" or "Yale, Pennsylvania or Harvard" can be incompetent. The public can "pick the able from the inefficient, and no certificate from the state can be more effectual than public opinion."[56]

But that was the losing side of an argument. In Portland as elsewhere a loosely defined vocation was becoming a profession. As early as 1900, members of the American Institute of Architects wanted to require university training. The pressure mounted thereafter, the AIA Committee on Education made annual reports on the progress, and in 1912, an Association of Collegiate Schools of Architecture formed to set the standards for professional training. In 1911 the Oregon Agricultural College (now Oregon State University) offered some courses in architecture; until that time the nearest architecture program was at Berkeley and the next nearest was in Illinois. Finally in 1914 the University of Oregon began a degree-granting architecture program.

When Doyle opened his office, there were university-trained architects starting out in business in Portland at about the same time. Morris Whitehouse was from a prominent Portland family. His father was the manager of the Portland Gas and Coke Co. He attended the Bishop Scott Academy and graduated when he was eighteen in 1896. He went immediately to MIT but returned to Portland soon after. He went back in 1903 and completed his degree from MIT in 1906, when he received a traveling fellowship for work at the American Academy in Rome.[57] He returned in December of 1907 from his studies in Massachusetts and eighteen months of travel in Europe.

Ellis Lawrence was even more impressive. He had money and the background of an affluent Malden, Massachusetts, family, and had a privileged childhood and youth with the best schools, MIT, and European travel. Upon returning to the States, Lawrence worked briefly in Portland, Maine, before deciding in 1906 to move to San Francisco. On his way he visited Portland, where he learned of the San Francisco earthquake. He settled in Portland, and joined with former MIT classmate, E. B. MacNaughton, and Herbert Raymond in a firm for which Lawrence was the principal designer.[58]

Doyle, Whitehouse, and Lawrence were almost the same age, though Doyle was a couple of years older. They began their practices in quick succession. Lawrence was first in 1906, then Doyle in 1907, and Whitehouse in 1908. But here the similarities ended. Lawrence and Whitehouse assumed lives of affluence and prominence. Whitehouse comfortably returned to Portland society. The month after he returned from Massachusetts and Europe, the (Portland) *Spectator* named him one of the city's most eligible bachelors. He formed a partnership with a fellow MIT graduate, an engineer, and a member of the prominent hardware family, Bruce Honeyman, whose sister Whitehouse eventually married. In 1907 both Doyle and Lawrence moved to Irvington. But while the Doyle's home was modest, the Lawrences, with their inherited money, settled a half mile east in a fashionable neighborhood. Their large house, which Lawrence designed as Portland's first Arts and Crafts house, is still at 2201-2211 NE 21st Avenue. While the Doyles had to wait until 1913 to be listed in the Blue Book, the Lawrences appeared in 1908, when they moved to Irvington. Lawrence and Doyle had a cordial relationship. Doyle, who was chairman of the Westminster Presbyterian Church building committee, was probably responsible for Lawrence getting the job of designing the new church in 1912.[59]

The two men were both active in professional organizations. Lawrence usually chaired or presided while Doyle served on committees. Lawrence was president of the Portland Architectural Club, the Portland Chapter of the American Institute of Architects, and the Architectural League of the Pacific Coast. In 1908, just two years after he had settled in Portland, the Dean of MIT visited Portland and called a meeting to start a technology club for alumni. Thirty attended the first meeting and elected Lawrence president. Lawrence recognized Portland's limitations and devoted much of his life to improving them. He confided to a friend that Oregonians were "typical western Americans, knowing and caring little about aesthetics at this stage of their community life." Most Portland architects, he thought, were inadequately trained, and cared "little or nothing for architectural principles." In 1908, when he had been just two years in Portland, he advocated better education of architects; otherwise, he warned, "Shoddy and selfish designers will dominate." In 1910 he wanted a local chapter of the AIA to raise professional standards in the West. In 1913 he again voiced suspicions about some local architects who needed to escape "the mire and stench of commercialism."[60]

Shortly after he arrived in Portland, Lawrence taught a class of carpenters about architecture at the YMCA. A few years later he recalled the carpenters fondly if somewhat patronizingly: "It was inspiring work, the work of these fellows who came in there with their big hands, awkward fellows, with hearts and souls in their work." He became disillusioned with the program at the end of the year when the director of the YMCA told the students they were architects. Lawrence realized then, "It was wasted energy," which would result in "the usual type of domestic architecture perpetuated all over town." On his work as patron of the Portland Architectural Club's atelier, he was more satisfied but not enthusiastic because he wanted architects to be university trained without Beaux Arts influences.[61]

Lawrence supported criticism of the Beaux Arts system as early as 1913 at a Portland meeting of the Architectural League of the Pacific Coast. He had invited a young professor of architecture from Berkeley to speak, and Warren Perry began by praising the Ecole des Beaux Arts in Paris. It is "the most efficient and the same time the most elastic system in practice. ... It is a mighty institution." Yet, he went on, it comes from "very different conditions, a different people, and a different culture than ours." He thought the American Society of Beaux Arts Architects was also "excellent," but that it "benefits most the region immediately around New York" and has not worked well in the West. The West Coast, he thought, needed its own system, schools of architecture designed by architects in each of the western cities, because teaching cannot be "conducted at arms' length or, what is worse, at continent's breadth." A teacher cannot "pretend to teach anything" to someone he does not know, or who does not "know or trust" him. He must "hob-nob" with a student for days or even weeks "over any subject but architecture before he gains the student's trust." Perry said, "Give of yourself to your student; unbosom yourself before them, and they will not be slow to do the same before you. That is the thing that animates the dry bones of teaching into a living thing of flesh and blood."[62]

In the discussion that followed there was a good deal of approval. A Vancouver architect said he felt inadequate serving as the patron of the local atelier because he had not "studied the proper length of time in Paris." He agreed with Perry; conditions on the Coast "are different from those in the East." An architect from Seattle spoke supportively of how much better prepared such students would be than he had been; he had pursued a general course in the arts in college before he went to Paris.

John Bakewell from San Francisco raised the temperature of the discussion. He declared: "I do not believe in teaching architects." Architecture, he said, was a subject for general education, but teaching architecture is not the way to train architects. "If I were a young man starting out in the study of architecture, I would not go to college ... , I do not think very many architects would." Prospective architects should "work in offices and at the same time educate themselves." It is a great mistake "when boys go to college [and] they think that when they graduate they are going to be architects." Bakewell emphasized his disagreement with Professor Perry: "The Beaux Arts work is the successful principle because it is adapted to the draftsmen in offices and [is] not trying to teach men architecture in schools and colleges." He saw education as the responsibility of the student, not the teacher. He spoke of office men learning where they could. He could have been describing Doyle's education from textbooks, from his masters Whidden, Lewis, and Bacon, and from a Beaux-Arts Society atelier.

Then A. E. Doyle spoke. If he agreed with Bakewell that Professor Perry confused teaching and learning, he did not say so. He confined himself to endorsing the Beaux-Arts system which was, he said, "fundamentally right." He thought education would not be "effective" if done independently of the Beaux Arts Society. He affirmed that the program was "primarily for the draftsman and gives him a kind of work, and a kind of education that he cannot get in the office." It "is helpful for his entire career because it helps him to think quickly, teaches him to think for himself." The system is right because it "develops character and teaches a man to think."

While the future belonged to university-trained architects, at the time of this debate most students of architecture were "office men," at least in the West, where the only degree-granting architectural program was at Berkeley. In 1913, 193 students on the West Coast competed for Beaux Arts Society awards. Of these only eleven were from Berkeley. Some were members of the ateliers of the various architectural clubs of the cities, but others were simply office men submitting on their own. There was little interest in the Oregon Agricultural College's architecture program. Circulars advertising it went in 1911 to every architect in Oregon and most in Washington to alert "draftsmen to the fact that there was a course in architecture at the Agricultural College." The college received only one reply. In 1913 the professor of the program was discouraged; after two years he had seen little student interest. He said, "I have pretty nearly given ... up now."[63]

⋞

In 1917, ten years after A. E. Doyle began work, *Collier's Weekly* visited Portland and declared "its spirit" enduringly aristocratic and "concretely expressed" in the homes of the Corbetts, the

Failings, and the Ladds. Every city has such places. Chicago has Michigan Avenue; Philadelphia, Independence Square, and for New York, the Woolworth Building. So Portland had these houses, "Shaded by big trees ... patterned by neat walks ... with gardens of prim old fashioned flowers ... affluent, superior, immobile, aristocratic. ... They were in the beginning are now and ever shall be to all intents and purposes world without end." Their dominance was unquestioned and secure. Portland's principal families settled all matters of importance to the city like "municipal harbor bonds, a mayor's election, ... the length of bathing costumes ... new doctrines, new art. ... Only for a few revolutionists and impossible persons ... [do] untried or unsettled problems exist at all."[64] *Collier's*, of course, was poking fun at priggish Portland, but satire is no less true for being funny.

A. E. Doyle, Anna Belle Crocker, and Harry Wentz became the leaders of the Portland art community at the beginning of the twentieth century by the grace of Portland's families. Doyle's client list included many of the important names of Portland: Corbett, Ladd, Failing, Mead, Selling, Meier, Frank, Eliot, Ainsworth, Ayer, and Benson. He was a close friend of Frederick and Robert Strong, who were from an early family and who between them managed three of Portland's most important estates: those of Henry W. Corbett, William S. Ladd, and Stephen Mead.

Anna Belle Crocker was the curator of the Portland Art Museum because her employer, William M. Ladd, also the president of the Portland Art Association, believed in her. She described how her appointment arrived unexpectedly when she was studying in New

left: Anna Belle Crocker (1868-1961) was a close friend of A. E. Doyle and Harry Wentz. (OHS 001433)
right: Harry Wentz (1875-1964) was A. E. Doyle's best friend, his best man and pall bearer. (PAM)

York at the Art Students' League. She "was awakened in the early morning of a dark winter day to stumble down three flights up of a student boarding house to sign for a telegram." When Ladd explained this unexpected act of noblesse oblige or aristocratic caprice, he half joked: "Why not make some use of the art you are always studying." She knew his self deprecating declaration of philistinism masked a real concern about her. Mr. Ladd was, she wrote, "always interested in the ambitions of his clerks."[65]

Harry Wentz became Portland's most important art teacher because Crocker, as curator of the Portland Art Museum and as director of the Art School, appointed him an instructor in the Art School. He had studied in New York at the Art Students' League and at Columbia's Teachers' College and he too had traveled in Europe. Yet at the turn of the century back in Portland, there was little opportunity for an artist. He settled for teaching manual training at the East Side High School (later Washington High School) until Crocker turned her good fortune to his and gave him a job at the Museum School.[66]

CHAPTER 4

In Partnership: Doyle & Patterson (& Beach)

At some point in 1907 A. E. Doyle and William Patterson became partners.[1] The first record for Patterson in Oregon is 1901, when he was first listed in the City Directory as an architect. He worked for Whidden & Lewis in 1904 and 1905 when Doyle was also there, back from two years in New York before his European tour. Patterson was married but nothing else is known about his family. He made no pretenses about being a designer. He did not join the Portland Architectural Club or the AIA, and he was never licensed in Oregon as an architect.[2] Except for the Wells Fargo Building and his partnership with Doyle, his career and life were little noticed.

Yet, the two men were well matched. Doyle was a designer; Patterson was an engineer and a superintendent. William Patterson was a natural complement for Doyle since he had just completed the Wells Fargo Building, Portland's first skyscraper, which had been designed by the nationally known architect, Benjamin Wistar Morris III, a Portland native living in New York. Therefore,

In 1909 Doyle & Patterson moved their office to this nineteenth-century office block, the Worcester Building. (PCA A2004-002.667)

Patterson had been the superintendent on Portland's most important building when he and Doyle formed their partnership. Together they represented the latest in commercial architecture. Doyle was the only architect in Portland with significant New York experience, except for William Whidden, who had worked for McKim, Mead, & White before coming to Portland nearly twenty years earlier and before the skyscraper craze in New York. A friend Doyle had made in New York came out to work for Doyle & Patterson and to add to the firm's New York connection. Lewis E. Macomber was "an architectural renderer of exceptional skill," whose renderings of Doyle & Patterson's buildings, especially at Reed College, added to the firm's claim to elegance and flair. Dick Ritz recalled how Macomber's "skill was legendary in the [Pietro] Belluschi office more than thirty years after" he left Portland and returned to New York.[3]

Tall buildings were made possible by the developments of the steel skeleton and the elevator[4] and were necessitated by the centripetal force of the streetcar system, which assembled the city's growing population for work and commerce on a few downtown blocks. In 1907 in central Portland thirty-seven buildings were under construction, including one ten-story building, one eight-story building, two of seven stories, one each of six and five stories and twenty of two, three, or four stories.[5] Steel-frame buildings were of special importance to commerce because at the street level, on the sidewalk, there could be large display windows, impossible in walls wholly of masonry, which allowed only small and recessed windows

Two years later, *The Oregonian* reported, "More strictly first-class office buildings have been erected in Portland during the past three years than during the entire previous history of the city. Where builders had hitherto been putting up four, five or six-story buildings, they have more recently had plans for eight, ten, and twelve story blocks." New tall buildings "demonstrated clearer than anything else the change in Portland's growth from a city of ordinary class to that of the highest grade." The newspapers published pictures of canyon-like streets. "Portland has passed through the cheap and unsubstantial era of wood and brick." Wood dominated construction because Portland was near inexpensive timber and "remote from the heart of the steel and cement manufacturing centers."[6]

1907 began propitiously and ended in recession. On Monday, October 21, 1907, the Knickerbocker Bank in New York had insufficient funds to meet demands. On Tuesday there was a run on New York banks. On Wednesday and Thursday the government and some private financiers intervened and made deposits in New York banks to avert panic. As events unfolded, Portland worried, but *The Oregonian* did its part to retain calm by reporting with a false optimism first that bank failures would not come west and then, prematurely, that the crisis was over. Portland was affected; the problem had been in the making for much of the year as stock prices on Wall Street sagged and financial capital dwindled. On Friday, October 25, six small New York banks closed even though the clearing houses had issued certificates to cover deposits and the stock market had stabilized. By Sunday Chicago and Pittsburgh announced there would be clearing-house certificates. Still *The Sunday Oregonian* insisted Portland was unaffected, and the problem could be confined to the East. On Tuesday, October 29, as banks closed throughout the country, Governor Chamberlain of Oregon issued a proclamation ordering a five-day bank "holiday" with clearing-house certificates and bank checks in lieu of cash. What currency there was went for payrolls to keep some money in circulation. With credit short, the year's unusually bountiful harvest could not ship and property could not sell. Through August real estate sales each month had exceeded the total for the corresponding month in the preceding year. But in September sales fell off slightly. October was down by half in comparison to October of 1906 while November and December were about a quarter of the sales in the corresponding months of the preceding year. The total for the year was just short of the preceding year, $23,247, 544 in 1907 versus $24,306,844 in 1906.[7]

But the bank crisis of 1907 was only a temporary inconvenience, and Portland's economy rebounded in 1908. For most of the seven years of Doyle and Patterson's partnership, they prospered and became the city's pre-eminent architectural firm. After less than two years, at the end of 1909, *The Daily Journal of Commerce* marked their accomplishments: "This firm is winning its way by the character of its work and merits the success it has attained."[8] A. E. Doyle and William Patterson had begun their practice in a broad period of exceptional prosperity. The city grew rapidly and changed quickly until 1914, the year before they dissolved their partnership. This decade after the Lewis and Clark Exposition was a remarkable period, perhaps Portland's "Golden Age,"[9] very different from the 1890s, when there was a depression. In July 1893 a crisis permanently closed seven Portland banks; the others struggled. Credit was tight; jobs were scarce; and Coxey's Army made a brief visit in Portland on the way to Washington. The depression is evident in the building permits, which were 898 in 1891 and 1078 in 1892. They fell to 522 in 1893 and to 271 in 1894. Until the end of the century they remained low; in successive years through 1900 they were respectively 345, 193, 224, 154, 357, and 387. The building industry did not recover until 1902. While there were 445 building permits in 1901, there were 1260 in 1902 and 1611 in 1903. By 1907, there were 3890, in 1910, 6520 and in 1912, 10,902. Expenditures were even more astonishing. The total in 1900 was less than one million; in 1910 it was over twenty million. In the ten years after 1902 capital in Portland banks grew from $3,675,000 to $12,150,000. Deposits nearly tripled from $27,169,000 to $71,853,000, and bank clearings quadrupled from $155,000,000 to $600,000,000.[10]

Portland's population much more than doubled in the first decade of the twentieth century; the Census in 1900 gave it as 90,426, and in 1910 as 222,957. Following the depression of the 1890s, the growth trajectory returned to the earlier nineteenth-century pattern, when the population had more than doubled each decade.[11] The first decade of the twentieth century brought an "unusual influx" of single men attracted by the "building operations undertaken" and "new manufacturing industries established." They came alone to find work; they would later send for their families, who "are to follow when a house has been established."[12]

These were boom times. There was enormous wealth in land like Laurelhurst, which was developed in 1911 and 1912 from a farm, in the Ladd Estate. William S. Ladd had bought the 462 acres in 1874 for five dollars an acre or $2310. In 1909, his heirs sold it to the Laurelhurst Company for two million dollars or $4329 an acre.[13] The value of Portland real estate everywhere within the city increased rapidly. E. B. MacNaughton, one of Ellis Lawrence's partners, saw the possibilities and in time changed his career from architecture to development and banking. In 1903, after MIT, he arrived in Portland young, poor, and ambitious. He worked as a draughtsman for Edgar M. Lazarus, one of Portland's established architects, before going into partnership with Lawrence and Herbert E. Raymond. He saved his money, and by the time of the 1907 bank crisis, he had one thousand dollars in a bank that offered him seven lots in east Portland to cancel his claim. There were five lots, not seven, but he accepted the deal and found a contractor who was as desperate as he and eager for work. MacNaughton drew plans for a five-room house, which the contractor built and MacNaughton sold. The two worked together on the four remaining lots. According to MacNaughton, "Portland was a riot as far as real estate speculation was concerned." In areas of east Portland 800 percent profits were possible. MacNaughton heard about a lot in downtown Portland between Salmon and Main for twenty thousand dollars. He didn't have even five thousand dollars, but he had an account at U. S. National Bank. He screwed up his courage, approached the cashier, and asked for five thousand dollars in exchange for a note. He got the loan and the lot, and within two weeks he had sold the lot for twenty-five thousand dollars. Then he took his five thousand dollars and bought another lot in the center of the city, which he sold for an apartment house that he helped to design.[14]

Portland was the port, the market, and the transportation hub of an increasingly commercialized, extractive, and agricultural economy. The railroads followed river valleys. The first transcontinental line to the Pacific Northwest came down the Columbia to Portland in 1883, six years before rails reached Puget Sound across the mountains to Seattle and Tacoma. Portland relished how its web tightened on the region. There was a breathless excitement in 1909 when two railroads raced southward from the Columbia River into Eastern Oregon, vying to open a "territory approximately the area" and with "all the resources" of the state of Ohio with "untouched mines of precious metals, a virgin tract of pine" and "water power four times the aggregate of Niagara." There was boundless optimism in the newspapers.[15] A new line connected Portland to Tillamook and harvested the timber in between. Another from Eugene to Coos Bay brought to Portland's market the southern coast, which formerly had depended on steamers from San Francisco. Between 1900 and 1910 the number of freight cars handled in Portland nearly doubled and the number of rail passengers more than tripled. The Willamette River between Portland and Eugene was deepened and widened as was the Columbia between Portland and the Pacific. Locks opened at the Celilo Falls in 1914, and river-boat cargoes now reached Portland from Eastern Oregon and Washington without portage. The really important change to Oregon's economy, everyone thought, would be the Panama Canal. Through the Straits of Magellan, Portland was nearly fourteen thousand miles from both Liverpool and New York. With the canal, the distances became eight and six thousand miles respectively.[16] The canal opened briefly in 1914, but disruptions in trade by World War I delayed the expected improvements in transport.

Three distinct communities—Portland, East Portland and Albina—were consolidated politically in 1891.[17] Streetcars drew them together. The first streetcars, in 1872, were just on the west side, but the growth of the system was rapid. By 1900 there were one hundred forty streetcars a day across the Burnside Bridge; in 1909 there were a thousand. Between 1900 and 1904 ridership on the system doubled, and it doubled again between 1904 and 1909.[18] There were constant improvements. In 1898 there were just 100 miles of track; by 1909 there were 230. In the same period streetcars increased in size and comfort; in 1898 streetcars seated sixteen to twenty people; in 1909 some could seat seventy-five. Increasing power gave them access to every part of Portland. The last horse-drawn streetcars were seen in 1894. In 1900, with motors of just 25 horsepower, they could not climb steep hills. By 1909 some had four motors of 37½ horsepower, and there were lines "into districts that could not be reached by streetcars in the olden days."[19] In 1917 the Portland Railway Light and Power Company boasted that for thirty years the fare had been a nickel, "which by most measures had lost half its value." In 1886 this fare could take a rider only 2.71 miles. In 1917, "you can ride a distance of 18.7 miles for the same five-cent fare, or practically seven times as far as you could 30 years ago, thanks to our long suburban line and universal transfers."[20] The tracks on the east side from the Columbia River to Oregon City converged on central Portland along SW 3rd and 5th. The lines from the hills and Northwest Portland ran on Morrison and Washington. The streetcars reoriented the city from the riverbank where it had formed in the nineteenth century, and they concentrated the Portland commerce and professions on a few blocks west of the river.[21]

Turn-of-the-twentieth-century prosperity was rooted in economic change. In the nineteenth century, Oregon's important exports had been wheat and flour.[22] Lumber and logging were the growth industry at the beginning of the twentieth century. Oregon had "one-sixth of the standing timber of the United States," but in the early years Oregon's timber was "burned and removed" to permit farming. There was little market for lumber except locally. But at the end of the nineteenth century, forests grew scarce in Minnesota, Michigan, Wisconsin, and the South. By 1909 Portland was "the largest lumber producing city of the world."[23]

The Lewis and Clark Exposition in the summer of 1905 spurred growth in the city. By one estimate, "sponsors, participants, and visitors" spent $10,000,000, and this sum "multiplied and remultiplied its impact on demand for services and facilities."[24] The exposition also had subtle effects. It made Portland reconsider the facilities and institutions of the city. There were only two first-class hotels, the Portland and the Oregon, one department store, Meier & Frank, but no skyscrapers, and these had been appearing in other cities. Cultural and educational facilities were rudimentary. There was one high school and a Catholic college with a divinity school, Columbia University (now the University of Portland). The Portland Art Museum opened a new, small facility a few months before the fair; it had no original painting or sculpture in its collection. The Portland Library had recently become a free public library in the beautiful though cramped facility at 6th and Stark; there were no branch libraries. And the streetcars were inadequate for the crowds of visitors; a makeshift arrangement ran frequent streetcars from Morrison to the fair grounds in Northwest Portland. Trade fairs, like the Lewis and Clark Exposition, "unlocked the floodgates to what became a steady flow of goods and fantasies about goods." In 1876 the Philadelphia Centennial Exposition "was like lifting a veil"; it revealed "the size, the variety, and the beauty of the world."[25] In Portland in 1905 the Lewis and Clark Exposition commemorated an historical event, but "the theme was the potential of commerce" in the Pacific. "The motif was the pleasures and possibilities of twentieth century technology—airships and automobiles, incubators, and electricity."[26]

In 1857 when Aaron Meier arrived to open a dry goods store, Portland had forty such shops, all near the river, for a city population of perhaps twenty-five hundred. Meier too began on Front Street. By 1885, he had a large, two-story store on SW Taylor between 1st and 2nd and a partner, Emil Frank, whose brother, Sigmund, worked for them. Emil left to go out on his own. Sigmund stayed, married Annie Meier, Aaron's daughter, became a partner, and succeeded as manager when Aaron died in 1889. In 1898 Sigmund Frank had Whidden & Lewis do a five-story, half-block store at SW 5th and Morrison. For an expansion in 1909 he hired Doyle.[27]

Four large department stores were built in Portland in a three-year period between 1909 and 1912. Doyle designed three of them: the Meier & Frank annex, Lipman Wolfe, and the Holtz Department Store. For the fourth (Olds, Wortman, & King), Doyle & Patterson were the local architects. Patterson superintended construction, and Doyle planned the interior of the building by designing and arranging the display cases, counters, partitions, cabinets, and shelving in the various departments.[28]

Before about 1880 department stores did not exist. They appeared in the East when merchants learned about the presentation and advertising of goods. "What was new was the volume of showing off, the quantity of selling materials, and the intermingling and application of color, glass, and light on behalf of the movement of goods." Portland's merchants studied what was happening at Wanamaker's in Philadelphia, Marshall Field's, and Carson, Pirie, Scott in Chicago, Macy's in New York, and Filene's in Boston.[29] When Meier & Frank decided to expand in 1907, they repeatedly told the newspapers about studying East Coast models. Julius Meier explained: "We have a special architect in New York who is regarded as an expert on department store building in conference with Doyle and Patterson and every device that is known to modern building will be installed."

At first the annex was to match the yellow-brick, five-story, 1898 structure of Whidden & Lewis. As Doyle worked on the plans, Sigmund Frank went east. He was so impressed with the

Doyle's rendering for a new building for Lipman Wolfe. (McMath SB)

use of terra-cotta on new buildings that he changed his mind and instructed Doyle "to get up a design in terra-cotta for the facing of the new building." Doyle too went east to "visit the large cities for the purpose of observing the latest methods employed in the construction of department store buildings."[30]

Along one of the main north-south streetcar lines on SW 5th Avenue and between the two east-west lines on Morrison and Washington stood Lipman Wolfe (now the Hotel Monaco) and Meier & Frank (the original 5th Avenue five-story brick building by Whidden & Lewis was replaced with a Doyle design in 1915). Today they are at first glance a nearly matched set, although the Meier & Frank building is taller, whiter, and broader, with more detail in the ornamentation. Both are covered completely with white-glazed terra-cotta and both conform to the accepted pattern of late nineteenth- and early twentieth-century skyscrapers: there is clear demarcation between the base, attic, shaft, and cap. While the Meier & Frank building was cobbled together over a quarter of a century, Doyle's Lipman Wolfe building appeared entire for its opening in 1912. It was modern, sophisticated, indeed eastern and European. It brought to Portland an elegant institution of commerce and social life, principally for middle-class women, who were drawn by lavish displays of goods, restaurants, and lounges.

> *There is not a single part of the handsome structure that does not reflect an idea of usefulness or convenience. The keynote of the architecture is that the solid and substantial character of the building should do more than attract and please the eye … It should provide for the highest efficiency in the operation of such a large establishment.*

The nearly breathless newspaper prose described the opulence of the building bottom to top. In the subbasement were lockers for three thousand employees, who entered the building through a special entrance on Alder. The basement, or gallery basement, was a well-lit sales area with mahogany cabinets, counters, and shelves for books and linens. A "wide and artistic staircase of metal and marble" connected the basement and first floor. The first floor had a twenty-one-foot ceiling and there were six large elevators in the middle of the building. The third floor was "exceptionally handsome"; all the fixtures were of solid Circassian walnut to display ladies' coats and suits. In the northeast corner, there were "a series of French rooms to be used for the fitting of evening gowns."[31]

Aaron Holtz, who built Portland's fourth department store, which he named for himself, came to Portland from New York in 1902 as Meier & Frank's first advertising manager. He helped plan the Meier & Frank annex with Doyle and then went to work for Olds, Wortman, & King in time to assist Doyle with that new store's interior. The Holtz Department store (now the Mead Building, 421 SW 5th) was smaller than the other department stores. It had seven stories and occupied a quarter block. Five floors and the basement were used for sales. While there are terra-cotta accents for windows, doors, and cornice, the exterior is otherwise covered with beige brick. (Today the exterior has been simplified and streamlined, presumably to give it a more "modern" appearance.)

On May 25, 1912, a large crowd formed to await opening of the doors at 10:00. The technology was particularly impressive. Every sales counter had a telephone and a cash register rather than the

The Holtz Department Store was completed in 1912. It is now the Mead Building, on the northwest corner of SW 5th and Washington. (OHS 006285)

usual "common till," and the store had an "intensified arc light plan, conceded to be the best ever devised for department store illumination." Department stores were for more than selling; they were public institutions, with restaurants, rest rooms, and social areas. At the Holtz store there was a cafeteria in the basement called the Holtz Inn, a "women's lunch counter" on the third floor with "a restful and homelike atmosphere," and a sitting room on the sixth floor.[32]

These four department stores greatly increased the commercial space of Portland. Meier & Frank doubled the store's capacity with the addition of the annex. Lipman Wolfe nearly tripled its space when it moved from the quarter-block Dekum Building, where the store had occupied the first three floors. Olds, Wortman, & King increased its floor space four fold. And the Holtz building was a new store. By my rough calculation, in the matter of three years, between 1909 and 1912, total department store floor space increased over four fold.

Doyle also designed a commercial building in 1912 for the large retail and wholesale drug firm, the Woodard & Clark Co. The beige-brick, nine-story Woodlark Building at 813 SW Alder, named for the two principals of the firm, had a two-story ground floor with a mezzanine to sell drugs, cosmetics, and dry goods. Because the building has been renovated as an office building, the commercial organization is no longer evident. The mezzanine has become a full second floor. Whatever terra-cotta there was at the ground level is gone, and the original design is only evident on the upper stories, especially on the top floor windows, where there are terra-cotta arches.[33]

A. E. Doyle was introduced to important members of the Portland Jewish community when he worked on Portland's department stores. The Lipmans, Wolfes, Meiers, and Franks were first- and second-generation German Americans and members of the Temple Beth Israel, which after 1889 had a synagogue of Moorish and Byzantine motifs and two onion-domed towers at SW 12th and Main. It burned in the 1920s and was replaced with the present temple at NW 20th and Glisan. In 1878 Jewish men formed a club, the Concordia, because the Arlington was reserved for men from Portland's dominant Yankee population. Despite the divisions these nineteenth-century Jewish families with their German

Lewis Macomber's rendering of the Woodlark Building, which is still at 813 SW Alder. (OHS 56844)

and urban background were quickly integrated into Portland's business community. Portland Jews included a number of wealthy merchants; most of the rest "had attained middle-class status and few were poor."

Ben Selling was another of the wealthy Jewish merchants who employed Doyle & Patterson.[34] In 1910, Doyle designed a twelve-story office building for Selling, C. S. Moore, and Moses Blum across SW 6th from the Meier & Frank annex. He divided the Selling Building (now the Oregon National Building, 610 SW Alder)

The Selling Building (now the Oregon National Building, at 610 SW Alder) was done in 1910. This photograph was taken shortly after it was completed. The Marquam Building, which collapsed in 1912, is next door to the left. This photograph shows how dramatic A. E. Doyle's buildings were on SW 6th Avenue, which was then a well-developed street with large nineteenth-century office blocks. The striking and bright Renaissance features of Doyle's Selling Building contrast with the somber late nineteenth-century Romanesque masonry on the Oregonian Building, on the immediate right, and the Marquam Building. (OHS 106145).

vertically into three parts, a base, staff, and capital. Today, polished granite added in the 1930s to the lowest two floors replaces Doyle's cream-colored terra-cotta framing around large windows of seven shops along SW 6th and Alder. The staff was cream-colored brick with white mortar joints and cream-glazed terra-cotta trim.[35] It is now painted white. Only the top two floors remain as they were in Doyle's time, with an arcade of arched windows framed in cream-colored terra-cotta. The entrance to the office building is still on Alder, though it is much altered. Originally there was an ornate copper and glass marquee. The entrance inside had wainscoting with an inlaid tile floor and an ornamental plaster ceiling. There were three elevators for the offices above. Each of the eleven upper floors was divided into eleven office rooms. The five top floors were for physicians and dentists. Seven-foot marble wainscoting lined the hallways, which had tile floors.[36]

As the Selling Building was going up in 1910, Ben Selling probably helped Doyle get another job, Neighborhood House, still at 3030 SW 2nd, which was intended to help Jewish immigrants settle and adapt to America and Portland. At the turn of the century, poor immigrants came to Portland (as elsewhere) to find work in lumber, timber, and the railroads and often settled in South Portland for the city's least-expensive housing. Presbyterians, Methodists, and Jews established settlement houses in keeping with a national movement of helping immigrants. Many of the new Jewish immigrants were from rural and primitive areas of the Russian and Austro-Hungarian empires. They were as unacquainted with urban society as they were with America, and they were sometimes dissatisfied and alienated with ideas about revolution, anarchism, socialism, communism, Jewish nationalism, and Zionism. Some were responsible for bringing to Portland the Socialist Labor Party in 1877 and the Socialist Party in 1902. Middle- and upper-class Jews of Portland were usually of German descent and were established members of Portland's business community. They saw such ideas "as radical and dangerous."[37]

Ben Selling had a long-standing interest in helping immigrants adapt to America. He and his family were largely responsible for establishing Neighborhood House. Most of the money for it came from the estate of Philip Selling, Ben's father; the rest was

Neighborhood House is still at 3030 SW 2nd. (Author's photograph)

raised in a fund drive headed by Ben Selling and Rabbi Jonah B. Wise. Selling bought the land at SW 2nd and Wood. His wife was the first teacher for the organization which developed into the Neighborhood House. In the 1890s, as immigration increased, she organized sewing classes, which met in homes and synagogues. In time other classes were added. In 1905 Edgar M. Lazarus designed a first building which was soon too small. There was just one English class in 1906, with eleven pupils and one teacher; by 1909 there were three hundred students and fourteen teachers. They had social events and athletics, which attracted some Christians, but the organization was emphatically Jewish, with instruction often in Yiddish, with Zionist groups, and with the observance of Jewish holidays. As the Presbyterian and Methodist settlement houses developed, Christians, even Catholics, preferred them.[38]

On December 12, 1910, Doyle's building was dedicated. It was (and is) appropriately red brick and Colonial, thus American and patriotic. It is a three-story building; a double stairway rises from the street level to the first of the two upper floors where there were offices and classrooms. Below on the first story, there was a raised basement with abundant windows, a gymnasium, and eventually a swimming pool.[39]

In 1905 during the Lewis and Clark Exposition, Portland's tourists' facilities were inadequate. There were just two first-class hotels, the Portland and the Oregon, which opened at SW Broadway and Stark in time for the fair. Most visitors stayed at a number of small, inexpensive hotels. Private homes took in paying guests, and some boarding houses were hastily constructed for visitors near the fair in Northwest Portland. Portland's tourism continued to increase. Travelers arriving and departing tripled between 1900 and 1910. In 1911 and 1912 there was a spurt of hotel construction to accommodate the growing numbers. Five major hotels were planned: an extension to the Portland, the Princeton (now the Whitmarsh Building, 623 SW Park), the Multnomah (now Embassy Suites, 319 SW Pine), the Imperial Hotel (now the Lucia at 400 SW Broadway), and an annex for the Oregon (almost immediately called the Benson, as it is today). Three of these went to Doyle & Patterson. Several smaller hotels, in which Doyle was not involved, were also bulit around this time: the Carlton at SW 14th and Washington, the Congress at SW 6th and Main, and the Mallory (now the Luxe, 729 SW 15th).

Doyle's twelve-story tower for the Portland Hotel would have doubled the size of the hotel. A new hotel manager dropped the idea. (OHS 56918)

For the Portland Hotel extension, Doyle designed a two-hundred-room tower on the SW 6th Avenue forecourt.[40] The Princeton was designed for the 50-by-100-foot lot at the corner of SW Broadway and Morrison. The first two floors and the basement were for a store, and on each of the upper ten floors there would be seventeen rooms and thirteen private baths. Hardwoods would be used liberally throughout.[41] But nothing came of the extension to the Portland; a new management scuttled the project. The boom had its excesses. Instead of the Princeton, Doyle did a smaller, seven-story hotel which opened as the Ritz. Today it is an apartment house.

The Benson Hotel, on the other hand, thrives much as Doyle designed it with the exterior and some of the public rooms little changed. The *Telegram* called it "the Pacific Coast's most beautiful hotel." It "rises from granite, to terra-cotta, to reddish brick and a green-tiled mansard roof." Just below the roof at the cornice line there is "a highly ornamental terra-cotta balcony" which is encircled by a bronze rail "giving a rich effect to the ornate terra-cotta." (The rail is gone, and there is no longer a balcony.) The interior is luxurious. The main dining room is beautifully planned, as are the private dining room, reception rooms, and state suites on the first few floors. Floors five through ten have the main hotel rooms, each with private bath with plumbing fixtures "of porcelain of the highest quality." Every room has a telephone as well as a "tele-autograph, whereby any one calling in the lobby can record his message in the room" as does "the best New York hotel." The eleventh-floor rooms have French doors opening on the balcony "which will be one of the city's best viewpoints." There is a central "vacuum cleaner system" and everywhere "all the modern appliances that are found in the best hotels of the world." The twelfth floor is for business travelers and has suites with baths, private bedrooms, and parlors or sample rooms for salesmen to display their products.[42] The Benson brought East Coast or at least Chicago standards to Portland. Doyle frankly admitted the prototype. It was, he wrote, "inside and out largely inspired by the Blackstone [Hotel in] Chicago."[43]

Simon Benson financed the project as an annex to the Oregon Hotel next door, but it quickly became the Benson. The official opening was March 5, 1913, the day of Woodrow Wilson's inauguration. When a telegram arrived that Wilson had taken the oath of office, the hotel's doors opened.

In 1911, when the plans for the Benson were taking shape, Doyle & Patterson accepted a third partner, James George Beach, a thirty-six-year-old structural engineer with a degree from the University of Illinois, and perhaps not coincidentally, Simon Benson's son-in-law. The firm was busy with the Central Library, Reed College, and the Holtz department store. In Doyle's opinion, Beach was a talented engineer. Years later when Beach was living in San Francisco and in need of a job, he applied to a friend of Doyle's and asked Doyle for a reference. Doyle wrote that Beach was "quick [and] accurate and [that Doyle had] never known [a] better all round engineer."[44] This is unusually favorable for Doyle, whose numerous letters of recommendation are seldom so uncompromisingly positive. Yet Beach and Doyle had disagreements, and Beach remained with the firm for only two years. He left for California in 1913.

Doyle broke with Beach because he came between Doyle and Simon Benson, changing the plans for the hotel and adding to the cost. Doyle wrote, "Mr. Beach made it very plain to me on a number of occasions that this was his job and that when it was necessary to do any talking to Mr. Benson, he would do the talking." It "caused the break with Beach for I felt that if I could not control the work that he brought to the office and put it through

The Benson Hotel at 309 SW Broadway was completed in 1913. (This was the cover for Pacific Coast Architect of March 1913, the month it opened.)

in the regular way I did not want the work." He was writing to Benson in 1916 hoping for another chance. Benson wanted to remodel the hotel and to build an annex cater-corner from it at Broadway and connected by a passage under the street. Doyle hoped past difficulties would not exclude him.

> *I am very anxious to make up to you in the future work what you may feel was lacking in the former job and I would put the very best that is in me and my organization at your service if given an opportunity. I will be glad to look after any changes in the present building, and do any preliminary work on a new proposition at office cost without charging a commission.*[45]

Benson was conciliatory but distant: "No doubt Mr. Beach was to blame for part of this also myself for not giving matters more of my personal attention however, I have forgotten all about it now and have no further ill feeling thanking you for offer of assistance."[46] Doyle did not get the job. Benson gave it to Houghtaling & Dougan. Ten years later Doyle made some preliminary plans for a substantial annex, but it was not built.[47]

In the nineteenth century, a number of colleges with church affiliations appeared in western Oregon, like Willamette in Salem (1842, Methodist), Pacific at Forest Grove (1842, Congregational), McMinville, later Linfield, at McMinnville (1849, Baptists), Albany, which moved to Portland in 1942 and was renamed Lewis and Clark (1867, Presbyterian), George Fox at Newberg (1891, Quaker). In Corvallis, Eugene, and Monmouth, were the state schools: respectively, Oregon Agricultural College (1868, now Oregon State University), University of Oregon (1876), and the Normal School (1856, now Western Oregon University). In 1891 Methodists established a university in Portland. It failed and the (Catholic) Archbishop of Portland acquired the site for Columbia University in 1901. It is the University of Portland today. Many thought that Oregon needed a nonsectarian, private college, and that Portland needed a university in keeping with its growth into a city.

Thomas Lamb Eliot, whose father had helped found Washington University in St. Louis and whose distant cousin, Charles W. Eliot, reformed Harvard, discussed with Simeon and Amanda Reed as early as 1887 the need for a college or university. The Reeds were congregants and choir members at the First Unitarian Church as well as close friends of Eliot. They prospered in Oregon from river boats and railroads and other investments, often in partnership with William S. Ladd. Even after the Reeds left Portland in 1891 for Pasadena, Eliot wrote and visited to tell them about Portland's needs. Simeon died in 1895 leaving everything to Amanda, who died in 1904 and bequeathed $1,500,000 for a vague purpose: "an educational instrument for elevating the people" of Portland. Relatives contested the will without success, delaying planning until 1908. The trustees thought first of vocational training but concluded that the public schools were filling that need. They decided for a college because Portland unlike other comparable cities had no college of "an undenominational character."[48]

The legacy was invested in Portland real estate and became $2,500,000 in time for the planning. That was modest in comparison to a few contemporary bequests to universities, like $20,000,000 given by the Stanfords or $30,000,000 by the Rockefellers for the University of Chicago. Yet it was large for a college. Until the Civil War the largest gift to any college had been $175,000. In 1900 one hundred thousand or so dollars could finance a building, and older campuses were collections of various buildings in different styles, from different periods, reflecting the wishes of different donors. The Reeds' legacy, while small compared to some, still provided the opportunity to design a whole campus; the Reed endowment permitted planning "on a grand scale."[49] The college buildings, Eliot wrote, will be "more permanent than any other in the city's life." They will reflect "strength and beauty, truth of purpose and attaining of perfection." For Portland the college would be "a chief source of what must be bringing the highest good to a great people."[50]

Reed College was probably the most important Portland job in the early twentieth century. Ellis Lawrence wanted it badly. He asked his former employer and friend in Maine to write a former colleague of Reed's newly appointed president, William Trufant Foster. The friend complied. He wrote that Lawrence was "a thoroughly capable architect who has had careful training and education, and is fully qualified to handle such a piece of work."[51]

But on January 5, 1911, Doyle & Patterson got the job. According to the official announcement, they were elected unanimously. However, the ballots survive as small scraps of hastily torn yellow paper scrawled with the names of the principal Portland architects. There were the three well-established senior architects, William Whidden, Ion Lewis, and Edgar Lazarus. Lazarus had been practicing in Portland since 1894, nearly as long as Whidden & Lewis; already a member of the AIA in 1911 when the Oregon chapter formed, he was elected the first president. There were also the three young men of the new generation: Lawrence, Whitehouse, and Doyle. Each of the ballots lists several names; presumably there was a selection by elimination, and only Doyle & Patterson appear on all ballots.[52]

When the newspapers announced the decision, Doyle was in "exhaustive conferences" with President Foster about the "development of grounds and buildings." Foster had collected some three hundred "ground plans, elevations, photographs and sketches of universities at home and abroad." They would proceed now to do "a block plan for a century of development" and detailed plans for the first buildings. Doyle would soon attend a convention of the American Institute of Architects in San Francisco when he would visit both Berkeley and Palo Alto. Upon his return, he and President Foster "will practically camp out" on the site of the campus to study it "from the standpoint of grouping, from a scenic standpoint and from every possible related viewpoint."[53]

They planned for a large university. Lewis Macomber did beautiful, detailed renderings of Gothic buildings in a sylvan setting with dreamy spires and shaded quadrangles: a would-be Oxford in Portland. But there is an important difference between Oxford and what Doyle planned. He designed orderly buildings according to Beaux-Arts principles without the untidy irregularities characteristic of real medieval quadrangles built over centuries. However, there was "a kind of compromise between medievalism and classicism" because around the edges of Doyle's plan the "formal order gave way to a meandering architectural irregularity."[54]

As the buildings were going up in early 1912, Doyle gave a public lecture about them and their antecedents, especially about St. John's, Oxford.[55] He may have explained then, as he did on other occasions, that the Sally Port in the dormitory was "almost

upper: Lewis Macomber's rendering of Doyle's idea for one quadrangle at Reed College. The dormitory block, much as it is today, is on the left. To the right is a planned but never built administration building. (Pacific Coast Architect, 2 (1912), p. 215)

lower: The Reed College Hall of Arts and Science in a photograph taken late in 1912 when the building was completed and some debris from construction remains. In front of it is the imprint of a specially built railroad track which supplied the workers. (RC)

[an] archaeological reproduction of Compton Wynyates," a Tudor manor house in England.[56] The outside entrance to the chapel "was adapted from the doorway of the Pilgrims' Inn at Glastonbury." The staircase was limestone and brick and rough plaster to give "the feeling of medievalism" and the staircase and entrance were "adapted from the cloister in Westminster Abbey Church." The ceiling of the chapel "was taken from the form of ceiling commonly used in the guild halls in England," and the chapel "was inspired by the great hall in Hampton Court Palace." At the back of the chapel, a small balcony was adapted from the Palace of the Doges in Venice.[57]

Nine years later, Beatrice Olson, a Reed undergraduate writing about the campus for the 1922 *Griffin*, the college annual, reported on conversations with Doyle and others about the buildings, which were not in one style. Even the Arts Building (later Eliot Hall) was "predominately the modified perpendicular style, characteristic of the active building period of the fifteenth and sixteenth centuries" but with exceptions. The chapel "dates back to the tenth century, and earlier, if we are to include the apse. … The open timber ceiling

Macomber's drawing of the entrance to the Reed College Arts Building, later Eliot Hall. (Pacific Coast Architect, 2 (1912), p. 217)

survives from the seventeenth century. … These early periods have been brought together and modified to suit modern needs." There are "fifty details of architectural decoration." Those lacking "the trained eye of an architect" will not find them immediately, but they will gain "inspiration and unexplainable joy in discovering them." She enumerates some on Eliot Hall: "the rectangles of fleurs-de-lis, the Richmond roses, in the paneling around the archway, and in the support for the pendant post on either side of the archway, the trefoils filling the spandrels, or triangular spaces left by the arch, two lions each with a paw on an open book, the overlapping leaf design on the corbels supporting the oriel." As to the dormitory, Doyle "unconsciously unbent and with a smile" made it "domestic." He "searched the old English manor houses for the folklore and the grotesques, and local tradition for the features of a home." There are "little-boy and animal grotesques, some studious happy some snappily wide-awake, others sleepy." They "comprise a good part of the decorations and symbolize the use of the building for recreation and sleep and preparation for work."[58] When Doyle talked about his work for Reed he spoke of adapting: "We tried to get the spirit of the old English Collegiate Gothic while adapting the style to present day conditions. There are many little interesting subtleties in the design and details that are not apparent at first, things that we hope delight the students in discovering such as the seals of over eighty of the leading universities."[59]

The dormitory building at Reed College, which was originally called "The Boys' Dormitory" because a "Girls' Dormitory" was to be on the other side of the canyon. It was recently completed in 1912 when this photograph was taken. (The American Architect, vol. 106, #2011 (July 8, 1914), no page)

For the college, these two buildings, the Arts Building and the dormitory, were important symbols of tradition. According to William T. Foster, Reed's president, they were "the equal of any in the country." For the money, Reed could have had "twenty buildings of the usual type," the sort of buildings "which would present a fair appearance for ten or twenty years."[60] They were designed in the Gothic style because the Reeds were religious people, although they opposed any sectarian affiliation. Therefore, it was appropriate that "the first building erected from the income of their endowment should embody a chapel architecturally suited for Christian worship." He did not think that "Pagan" styles (presumably Greek and Roman) were as appropriate. Four centuries after the building of St. John's at Oxford, there is in America "the first building of a new college."[61] President Foster liked the association with Oxford. On another occasion, he explained: "If one were to enter the garden of St. John's College, Oxford, one would find a building erected more than a half a century before the landing of Pilgrims at Plymouth [which was] ... the immediate inspiration for the main arts building of Reed College." Yet he readily admitted differences. Reed had reinforced-concrete with brick veneer and "far more glass area at the sacrifice for the expanse of walls," because "the requirements for lighting for class rooms and libraries and laboratories are better understood today."[62]

By 1902 the Library Association of Portland was a venerable institution with a large collection in the Whidden & Lewis building on Stark between SW Broadway and Park (now gone), which also housed the Portland Art Museum. There was also a small, decade-old, Portland Public Library with three thousand volumes. While both were "public" libraries in that they both admitted the public, neither was tax supported. The Library Association's membership was by subscription. The Portland Public Library was open to everyone, but its only subsidy was a room in City Hall. Portland needed a public library system supported by taxes. In Massachusetts, nearly every township had one by the turn of the century. California had sixteen as early as 1887, and Seattle began supporting a library in 1890.[63] Thomas Lamb Eliot was active in the Library Association and advocated a free, publicly supported library as a prerequisite for modern, urban civilization. He wrote:

"The modern Library is the triumph of democracy, a giver of good things for the whole life of the people. Here is the history of a world's achievements. The library bridges the past and present. It is the enshriner of ten thousand servants of the race, and of their service and message to their own age and to future ages."[64] Libraries, it was widely believed, were like universities; they gave people the opportunity for self education. They bolstered democracies by informing the citizenry.

The Portland Library Association often debated becoming a free, public institution. The much smaller and poorer Portland Public Library, because it was free, might have expanded, but in 1900 the matter was settled, as so many were, by nineteenth-century wealth. John Wilson, who owned the store that was purchased from him and renamed by the buyers for themselves, Olds & King, bequeathed over eight thousand books and manuscripts and $2500 to the Library Association with a stipulation: his collection would be available to the public without charge. The Library Association accepted the bequest, decided to open to the public, and sought support from Multnomah County. To catalog the Wilson collection, Mary Frances Isom, a recent graduate of the Pratt Institute in Brooklyn, New York, came to Portland in 1901. In 1902, the director, David P. Leach, resigned, and Isom replaced him. The library closed briefly, absorbed the Portland Public Library, and rearranged to accommodate many more patrons. Within a few months the subscription library of one thousand members became a publicly supported library with eight thousand registered borrowers.

The East Portland Branch Library (1110 SE Alder). (The American Architect, vol. 105, #1995 [March 18, 1914], no page)

The library building on Stark was too small. Reading rooms opened in neighborhoods with staffs of volunteers, and the Art Museum prepared to vacate the second floor, which it did in 1905. In 1907 there were three neighborhood branches in Sellwood, Albina, and the eastside central district. A. E. Doyle designed a small wood-frame, temporary, eastside branch among his first jobs. In 1911 the Carnegie Foundation gave funds to build permanent structures for the branches, and Doyle got the eastside job. Like other Carnegie libraries, his East Portland Branch Library (1110 SE Alder) was in a traditional, recognizable style, Renaissance Italian. It had one floor and a daylight basement. A generous stairway led to imposing main doors entering on the ground-floor public spaces. There were reading rooms for children and adults.[65] Doyle liked the exterior of "tapestry red brick with pinkish gray terra-cotta trim" and the roof of green Spanish tiles in "a variety of shades." He thought the interior had nothing of particular interest except the children's fireplace.[66] The building was remodeled first in 1956 to accommodate library offices and again in 1967 when it was sold. The nearly eighteen-foot ceiling now accommodates an added floor to make a two-story office building.

In its first decade the Portland Library, which was later called the Multnomah County Library, went from a membership of 8,107 to 66,000 and an annual circulation of 110,665 to 1,0365,894.[67] In 1911 the library board decided they needed a new building. Isom visited the nearly completed New York Public Library and engaged its architects, Carerre & Hastings. In the fall of 1911 the board sold its valuable site at 7th and Stark with the understanding that the library could remain for two years as a new building was prepared, terminated Carerre & Hastings, and gave the job to Doyle, Patterson, & Beach. Doyle and Isom traveled east to visit recently completed libraries as they planned a building in which, Doyle admitted, architecture was subordinated to library work. Reading rooms surrounded work rooms and eight levels of stacks for three hundred and fifty thousand volumes. Doyle credited Isom with the idea of "building around a stack room" that governed the "disposition and relation of the rooms according to her definite ideas of library administration." It made no "compromises for the sake of architecture" but gave "honest architectural expression to the practical requirements of the building." In their travels they had seen many new libraries, often beautiful buildings, which served library work poorly. Librarians complained about them. The Central Library was different. It was a librarian's library.

The Central Library was completed in 1913. (The American Architect, vol. 105, #1995 [March 18, 1914], no page)

Today it is arresting for its grandeur. The three arched entry doors atop broad steps beneath a rank of tall, arched windows on the second floor and a row of square windows for the third floor dominate a façade topped by a balustrade. The building is set back from the street and surrounded by benches, fences, and shrubs for distance and dignity. Inside, the central staircase rises from a capacious entry to the second floor and a domed landing off two matched reading rooms, 105 feet long and 30 feet high, lighted by the arched windows. Charles Cheney, whose evaluation of Doyle's early work appeared in 1919, admired the "clean-cut handling and simple design." He thought it showed Doyle's ability in "the classic style" which was very different from the Gothic of Reed College. Yet they are, he said, "more than equally successful." Doyle was good: "An able architect deals ably with any type of work he undertakes."[68] Doyle said he liked Georgian architecture and appreciated the opportunity "to work in this style," which is "most closely connected with the early history of the nation and is the most typically American architecture we have." It has "a certain refined dignity befitting a library building" providing "surroundings of quietude and refined good taste." Yet often when he talked about the library, he spoke not of its beauty but about economy and efficiency. It cost just twenty-one cents per cubic foot, far less than most libraries, especially "memorial libraries" like the New York Public which was "over a dollar per cubic foot."[69] When the Denver Public Library asked about it in 1915, he said nothing about aesthetics or even the architectural style: "The Portland building is a big plain building built for a little piece of money. It has a lot of big reading rooms; administration is economical, and it is a much used and popular building with the public. Miss Isom is very happy over it."[70]

Eight years later when asked about the plan, he was petulant: "Of course we think the stairs are located in the best place or we would not have put them there." Placing the stairs "near the center of (the) building enables us to use all outside, well lighted space and ... to plan a building without corridors." The large reading rooms around the central staircase needed no hallways and lowered costs. "Corridors are waste space and usually are very expensive in public buildings, requiring marble wainscot [and] floors." He was frugal throughout: "wainscots are not high" and the marble is "the least expensive available. All materials are honest materials, however, and permanent."[71]

⟡⟡⟡

The firm's work was nearly completed as was Portland's expansion. For much of the next decade, Portland's downtown would change little because, with a slowing economy, the central city had enough hotels, offices, and stores. When the Central Library was dedicated September 6, 1913, three office buildings which Doyle had designed were also about ready.

Opening in early October 1913, the Morgan Building, on the south side of Washington between Broadway and Park, was to provide the home office for the Morgan-Bushong Investment Company, whose president was W. L. Morgan. It is an eight-story, steel-frame building whose base and capital are covered with cream-colored terra-cotta while the shaft is red tapestry brick with white terra-cotta accents. Cream-colored terra-cotta and a large terra-cotta key stone outline the entrance and accent an elaborate cornice. A large restaurant on the ground floor faced Broadway. Two-story shops even today line the Washington side of the building. The seven upper stories were mostly for medical offices. The developer, the Morgan-Bushong Investment Company, had the southeast corner of the top floor.

The Northwestern National Bank Building (621 SW Morrison) opened January 1, 1914, on the southern half block at SW 6th Avenue, Broadway, Morrison, and Alder, on the site of the former Marquam Building, a towered, red-brick and stone, Richardsonian, office building, whose brick was of poor quality. Shortly after it was built in 1889, problems developed in the eight-story masonry

The Morgan Building is still at 720 SW Washington. (The American Architect, vol. 105, #2009 [June 24, 1914], no page)

The Northwestern National Bank Building (now the American Bank Building, at 621 SW Morrison) replaced the Marquam Building, which collapsed in 1912. This is a rendering by Lewis Macomber. (OHS 58586)

walls, which were three feet thick at street level. By 1912 it was also the subject of dispute when the original owner, for whom it was named, Philip A. Marquam, an early lawyer and later a county judge, declared bankruptcy. The First National Bank, which held a mortgage, foreclosed. E. B. MacNaughton, then in partnership with Ellis Lawrence and Herbert Raymond, was charged with shoring the building up and with opening windows on the street for shops. MacNaughton soon discovered the walls were giving way, apparently because Marquam, to save money, had poorly trained Chinese laborers with no experience manufacture the bricks on his land on Marquam Hill. MacNaughton reported the problem and was nonetheless told to proceed with the changes. The job was nearly finished when the northeast corner crumbled suddenly in the middle of the night. MacNaughton feared the end of his career; other architects in town in a good-natured gesture of sympathy wore black crepe arm bands. Doyle, Patterson, & Beach were given the task of clearing the site and building anew.[72]

By February 1, 1913, the site was ready. The steel frame went up in June and July, and was closed in by mid-September.[73] It was advertised for its central location:

> *Attorneys who take space in this building will be near the courthouse and city hall and will have neighbors who will furnish the best class of clients. Insurance and real estate men will be on one of the main thoroughfares of the retail section. Lumbermen and timbermen whose patrons come from out of town will be near all the leading hotels. The family man who has theater tickets to buy will be only a step from all the amusement houses.* [74]

The new building had fourteen numbered floors and a mezzanine in the ground-floor lobby of the bank. It was 191 feet high. A penthouse on top added another 15 feet for a total of 206 feet. It was the tallest building in Portland. From the fifteenth floor an ornamental iron staircase ascended to an observatory for "an excellent view of the entire surrounding country" of "the hills, the rivers and a considerable section of the valleys." It was not just a skyscraper; it was, in a term coined by the newspapers in talking about it, a "skypiercer." City boosters expected the observatory to be "one of the attractions for tourists."[75]

The developers of the building, its owners, and the principal tenants of the basement, first floor, and mezzanine were two conjoined banks, Portland Trust and Savings and the Northwestern National Bank. The classically themed outside of the building advertised the banks in it; the tripartite, vertical division had Corinthian pilasters at its base and at its capital. According to contemporary thinking, banks conveyed "stability, dignity, and security," when they looked like Greek and Roman temples.[76] Inside each of the thirteen upper stories were thirty-eight rooms and two lavatories of white marble. The building was fireproof throughout: steel frame, exterior walls of brick and concrete, interior walls of tile, floors of cement and window frames and outside doors of steel. Of particular interest was the "ample provision" for light; each room had "two big 40 watt lamps."[77]

It is curious how the newspapers praised both the Morgan and the Northwestern National Bank buildings and ignored the architects. For example, one review of the Morgan Building said: "This building is the particular product of Mr. Morgan's brain. It was he who first conceived it. He nursed the idea along and labored ardently to bring it into material form. While his associates helped him it was his guiding hand that directed the enterprises from its embryonic status to its present magnificent state of completion." Doyle & Patterson got a brief mention for drawing the plans: "The detailed architecture is the product of the office of Doyle and Patterson of Portland, although many original ideas of the owners are embodied in the plans."[78] As the building rose, the papers recounted the progress on a regular basis, yet said little about the architects. They were ignored, for example, in an article about the plans; the early ideas were reported at length, but nothing was said about Doyle. When the steel skeleton was taking shape, *The Oregonian* had a long article but did not mention Doyle, who had designed it, or Patterson, who supervised the construction. In May 1913, the *Morrison Street Bulletin*, which was a temporary publication about the developments on Morrison, devoted one issue of four pages to the Northwestern National Bank Building which it thought very good. Nothing was said about Doyle & Patterson.[79] A few months later *The Oregonian* published a long list of craftsmen and merchants who had worked on the Northwestern National Bank Building—the suppliers of the window shades, electric light fixtures, mortar, plumbing fixtures, woodwork, and grillwork. Even the firms who had done the hauling and painted the signs were named. Doyle & Patterson were not identified; the article mentions the architects but not by name: "the architects have taken advantage of all the late improvements in the field of electricity."[80]

The newspapers' neglect of Doyle & Patterson seems strange today. Their indifference provides a corrective to our evaluations based on hindsight. Doyle looms large today because of post-mortem evaluations of his life's work and because of an inclination today to accord architects more responsibility and more professional status than his contemporaries did. Doyle worked closely, amicably, and respectfully with his clients. He was naturally modest and self-effacing. Ellis Lawrence thought Doyle conceded too much to clients. He wrote, "I wouldn't pay the price for it all that he [Doyle] pays according to my standards."[81] Doyle willingly adapted his clients' ideas and admitted that he had done so; he was dismissive of architects who claimed autonomy and sole responsibility: "They [architects] build for people and have always built what people want, using their imagination, and suggesting, if they are worthy of their calling, something better than their client imagined."[82] Doyle could make his clients look good.

In the early summer of 1914 Doyle & Patterson completed the Pittock Block, which was unlike all their other office buildings by occupying, as the name suggests, a full two-hundred by two-hundred-foot block between Washington and Stark and SW 9th and SW 10th. It was named for Henry Pittock (1836-1919), the publisher of *The Oregonian* for more than sixty years, whose home had occupied half the block where the building rose, before there was a Pittock Mansion in the West Hills. Pittock retained the freehold on the block and signed a ninety-nine-year lease with the developer, who agreed to erect a building worth at least $650,000 and to name it Pittock.

The Pittock Block at 921 SW Washingtonin a rendering by Lewis Macomber. (OHS 93489)

The reinforced-concrete construction proceeded rapidly. The first floor was poured October 15, 1913. Forty days later, November 16, the roof was finished. The building was eight stories on Washington Street, but two stories on Stark, although the plan was to complete the entire block to eight stories in 1914. Doyle eventually added the six upper stories on the Stark Street side in 1923. The most significant feature of the building was its large basement that was 53 feet deep on the west side. The building's developer, Herbert Fleishhacker, a San Francisco capitalist, had broken the monopoly of the Portland Railway, Light and Power Company. His Northwestern Electric Company was the principal tenant; it occupied some of the above-ground office space and the entire basement where there was an electric sub-station and a distributing plant for Portland's westside.[83]

The Pittock Block was the last of Doyle's classically styled office buildings. There was a two-story base, a five-story shaft, and a one-story capital, but the ornamentation was subdued in comparison with his others. Terra-cotta pilasters and panels adorned the base, which was divided between the first two floors by a belt course. The second floor was separated from the third by two terra-cotta bands of scrolls, medallions, and panels. The shaft was buff-colored brick and the capital at the eighth floor had medallions and panels between the windows. There was a slight cornice at the top. A balustrade atop the second story between the two wings gave an edge to the south facing court.[84]

⇠

Doyle & Patterson's final job was to replace Whidden & Lewis's Meier & Frank with a larger building in keeping with Doyle's annex at a cost of $1,250,000 and $250,000 for fixtures. When Doyle did the annex, he had planned to replace the 1898 building, but this was delayed for years. Sigmund Frank died in 1910, and the sons of his former partner, Aaron Meier, succeeded him. Abe Meier became president and Julius Meier was the general manager. Not only were they replacing the legendary Frank, who had charismatically dominated the firm for more than a quarter of a century, there was a large problem with what to do with staff, stock, and customers. While the old building was demolished and the new one built, the store moved temporarily across 5th Avenue to the Failing Building (now the 620 Building at 620 SW 5th). The new building continued the exterior design of the annex, but it was

Doyle & Patterson's twelve-story Meier & Frank building on SW 5th between Morrison and Alder. Notice the annex is two stories shorter than the 1915 addition. (OHS 84109)

The H. E. Albee House at 3360 SE Ankeny was done in 1912 for the then-popular Portland mayor. (Author's photograph)

two stories higher. It was a large job and all the more important to the firm because construction was slow in Portland. When Abe Meier announced the project in the early spring 1914, he spoke of the recession: "There is a lull in building operations which has thrown a large number of deserving workmen out of employment, and the construction of the building will alleviate this condition to some extent."[85]

Nearly a year later, on Lincoln's birthday, February 12, 1915, Meier & Frank closed to celebrate the completion of the steel skeleton. After speeches about patriotism and economic development, a band struck up "The Star Spangled Banner." Silk flags were raised upon the steel skeleton, and store employees and construction workers wore small flags distributed by the company.[86] Through the summer the construction crew worked up the building. As each floor was completed, store clerks and stock filled the new spaces. In the last months the company had an ongoing "removal sale" from their temporary building across SW 5th Avenue.

Between 1910 and 1914, the firm concentrated on downtown. They worked on a few summer houses and two town houses for special clients. C. E. Wolverton was a lawyer by training and an Oregon Supreme Court justice when Theodore Roosevelt appointed him a federal judge. He was a Reed College trustee and a member of the Arlington Club. Doyle's Craftsman-style home for him is still at 1808 SW Laurel. Also in 1912 Doyle did a large Colonial mansion (still at 3360 SE Ankeny Street) for H. E. Albee, one of Portland's most liberal and successful mayors, who had arrived from Illinois in 1895 as an agent for Northwestern Mutual Life Insurance Co. and bought out a machinery business before entering politics in 1903.[87] His house is well preserved and stands today on eight lots on a slight rise at 3360 SE Ankeny. It was built in the new subdivision made from the W. S. Ladd Hazel Fern Farm in east Portland, which was and is called Laurelhurst. It looks out toward the south over Laurelhurst Park. When the house was built, Ash Street separated it from the park, but in 1927 the street was vacated, and the house now adjoins the park.[88]

Also on the east side in 1914 they did an assembly plant for the Ford Motor Company (still at 2505 SE 11th Avenue). It is a reinforced-concrete building with a brick veneer and large paned windows like other contemporary factory buildings. The building was constructed as part of the Ford Motor Company's program to decentralize automobile production. Parts were manufactured in the East and shipped to Portland for assembly. The building, unexceptional except for the detailing, has terra-cotta ornamentation on the exterior; a recessed entrance is framed by Doric columns.[89]

In these busy years between 1910 and 1915 Doyle did thirteen of his twenty-one downtown buildings. When he looked back on his work in this period, he dismissed most of it, like the department stores and office buildings, which Portland now prizes, as "practical stuff of a commercial nature, architecturally the less said ... the better." He took some pleasure in the Central Library, for its efficiency and economy. Reed was his pride. He wrote, "The Reed College work has perhaps been the most interesting work I have had."[90] In these five years the majority of his contribution to Portland was made when he was in partnership with William Patterson and briefly with George Beach. Their names will be forever joined with his in the history of Portland architecture. Yet theirs was at best an unequal partnership. Beach, to his cost, interfered with the normal practice by making decisions on the hotel that Doyle should have made. Reed has many letters on file from the firm of Doyle, Patterson, & Beach. All are signed by Doyle except one from Patterson.

Neither of these men was important personally to Doyle at the time or later. George Beach left the firm for California July 1, 1913. In 1926 he returned to Portland and to Doyle, with some hope he would be made a partner (I do not think Doyle encouraged this expectation). There was some friction then too; clients and some members of the firm had problems with him and complained. In a deathbed distribution of the assets of the firm, Doyle formed a partnership with some of his long-time staff, A. E. Doyle and Associate. He denied Beach an interest in it.

William Patterson left the firm in the summer of 1915. Doyle, when he gave thumbnail biographies of his life, said he had left in 1914, but I have found letters signed by Patterson and contracts in his name into 1915, which seems reasonable since that was when the Meier & Frank building was completed. The last definite date I have for his association with Doyle is a letter Patterson signed as a member of the firm, April 8, 1915.[91] In November that year Doyle, when asked about William Patterson, replied that he was no longer in the firm and that his office was in the Board of Trade Building.[92] On December 31, 1915, Doyle wrote Patterson to say that he would be late in making a payment, presumably as part of the dissolution of the firm.[93] In 1918 Doyle admitted he did not know where Patterson was and that he had not seen him for over a year.[94] Ten years later, on January 18, 1928, five days before Doyle died and after he had been seriously ill for years, Patterson wrote: "I have just learned of your illness and am very sorry to know of it. Should there be any way I can be of assistance kindly let me know. I hope that you will soon be on your feet again as lively as in the days of our association."[95]

Like other competent and confident people, Doyle seldom delegated, and he reluctantly shared recognition and responsibility. He worked best alone.

CHAPTER 5

Alone

After 1875 Portland's post office was in the Federal (now the Pioneer) Courthouse, which was enlarged in 1904. Over the next seven years postal receipts in Portland nearly tripled; a new post office was "urgently needed because of rapid growth of postal business."[1] In 1911 the Treasury Department bought the block bounded by NW Hoyt, Glisan, Park, and Broadway. The block fulfilled the U. S. Government's "latest policy in locating post offices as near as possible to transportation centers." It was "hardly more than a stone's throw" from the two principal train stations: Union Depot (still at NW 6th and Irving) and the Bank Depot (no longer) at NW 11th and Hoyt. In 1913 the U. S. Treasury Department announced a competition to choose an architect for the new post office. It was to be a substantial building, not the one- or two-story low-rise usual for a city of Portland's size.

A. E. Doyle applied on behalf of his firm, Doyle, Patterson & Beach, and he boasted of their size and accomplishments:

An undated photograph of A. E. Doyle, probably about 1915. Doyle normally avoided showing his profile. He may have been sensitive about the prominence of his nose; he joked self-deprecatingly about it. (SUPBP. Box 219, Peasley-Jourdan Photographers, 407 Morrison Street, Portland)

We have a force of twenty men, including engineers, and have had a good share of the work done here in the last few years. Last year we had six business buildings under way at the same time in the heart of the business district, aggregating in cost about two million five hundred thousand dollars. And in addition the Reed College buildings were built, and the new public library, covering a city block, was started. This library building is well along, the plastering being about completed, and the building will be finished in July. In the business section we have two buildings under way this year. The foundation work just completed on both of them. They are large buildings, and the combined cost will be about one million six hundred thousand dollars.[2]

But Portland's Golden Age was about to end. The planned U. S. post office in Portland would be one of only a few important jobs for years. Slowly Portland came to speak of stagnation, recession, even depression. Portland had experienced growth each year since 1907. There was some reason for optimism. The long-awaited Panama Canal opened August 15, 1914, and everyone knew it would shorten the distance and shipping time from Portland to East Coast and European markets. But World War I began the same month, and the Pacific fleet withdrew to the Atlantic to supply Europe. Freight costs in Oregon increased as much as 50 percent. There was a substantial drop in the demand for lumber.

Building had slowed before war broke out. In July 1914, the month before hostilities, A. E. Doyle described a recession in building. Some building materials, he said, were as much as 30 percent cheaper than they had been in 1911.[3] In November 1914, Ellis Lawrence wrote a piece on professional activity in Portland. He asked Doyle and other architects to list their work. Doyle's reply shows how much things had slowed down. He mentioned, of course, the Meier & Frank building, whose steel frame was beginning to rise along SW 5th between Morrison and Alder. His

The Reed gymnasium was built in 1913 west and north of the dormitory. It was razed in 1965. (RC)

other important work was finished: the Northwestern National Bank Building, the Morgan Building, the Pittock Block, the Benson Hotel, the Central Library, and Reed College. More recently, he said, he had designed four houses. The two most expensive, for Col. Henry Cabell and for Capt. Gordon Voorhies (by Doyle's estimates worth $75,000 and $45,000, respectively) were never built.[4] He completed the large Colonial (still) at the corner of SW Vista and Carter Lane (2010 SW Carter Lane) for A. Oberdorfer in 1916, but a house for J. G. Edwards was delayed until 1926. Otherwise, he had "some work scattered around like the Normal School Gymnasium at Monmouth, a passenger station for the Eugene Electric Railway (still at 27 E 5th Avenue, Eugene) and a one-story brick Carnegie Library at Goldendale, Washington (still at 131 W Burgen), but they, Doyle wrote, "are hardly worth mentioning."[5] The Eugene Station and the Goldendale Library are now on the National Register of Historic Places. The Eugene Station, which was the largest of these projects, was completed in the summer of 1913. In the same year, Doyle designed a gymnasium at Reed to resemble an Elizabethan theater. It was demolished in 1965.

The planned U. S. post office in Portland would be one of only a few important jobs for years. Doyle & Patterson (Beach had left for California in the summer of 1913) and fourteen other Portland firms applied to the Department of the Treasury for invitations to compete. There were seven invitations. Doyle & Patterson were included, as were the two other obvious Portland firms: Lawrence & Holford and Whitehouse & Fouilhoux. The Portland architects had been selected "after a careful study of such evidences of skill as were submitted." The other four had not asked to compete. The supervising architect and Secretary of the Treasury William G. MacAdoo added Bliss & Faville from San Francisco and three firms from New York: John Russell Pope, Clinton & Russell, and J. H. Freedlander.

There were problems with the post office competition. The contract was to be awarded by the Secretary of the Treasury without a jury of architects; and the architect chosen would receive a commission of 5 percent. In Portland questions about fees and juries had arisen at the earliest meetings of the Portland Architectural Club in 1906. In 1911 Oregon had its own chapter of the American Institute of Architects so that Portland architects gained powerful allies and a national voice for their claims—they were artists with special technical and scientific training; they could be judged rightly only by other such artists and scientists. The AIA was especially concerned about government jobs, because of their importance and size. They should be open to all professionals and awarded with the advice of professional architects who alone had the competence to judge architecture.[6] Architects should never compete on price. Marketplace rivalries are demeaning. Professionals receive reasonable fees; they do not haggle with clients and they should not consider jobs which pay less than 6 percent. But was this trade unionism?

That was a sensitive issue. In Portland, in April of 1912, at one of the early meetings of the fledgling local chapter of the AIA, Edgar M. Lazarus, one of Portland's senior architects and the first president of the Oregon AIA, answered critics of the newly formed chapter who thought the professional organization no better than a labor union. He took pains to explain the difference in a talk about professionalism and the qualities and standards that governed a professional organization. The AIA, he said, did not oppose competition. It favored "the advancement of art." Competition must be by "merit" not "in price." Prices charged by architects are "moderate and not excessive." Six percent is "only fair." Architects who charge less show "evidence either of professional ignorance or intention to swindle the client by accepting moneys other than the fees received from his employer."[7]

The distinction between a professional organization and a labor union was not always convincing. When some school teachers wanted to form a union under the American Federation of Labor, they claimed architects had done so. A. E. Doyle bridled at the suggestion. He wrote personally, not as a member of the AIA, which of course he was, to one of the teachers: "Ethical architects almost 100% strong throughout the nation" want no unions, which "have steadily lowered the standards of workmanship" instead of raising "the standards of the building industry." While employers "in no instance" have "been other than conciliatory," unions are always "belligerent, uncompromising and defiant."[8]

Yet Doyle and other architects collectively and through the AIA tried to influence the government to pay more and to jury the post office competition, even though they had understood the Treasury Department intended to do neither when they applied for invitations to compete. Doyle and Ellis Lawrence wrote to the other invited architects about meeting with Secretary MacAdoo to complain about the competition, and they wrote for support to the AIA and to the two senators from Oregon, Henry Lane and George

W. Chamberlain. Only one New York firm, Clinton & Russell, declined to join the protest. As to Secretary MacAdoo, he disdained to reply to the request for a meeting. He sent out telegrams to the protesters informing them that their invitations to compete were withdrawn. The Treasury Department then published a new list of competitors with only one firm retained from the original list—Clinton & Russell, who had refused to join in the dissent. Just one firm from Portland, Goodrich & Goodrich, respected architects but not in the class of the three originally invited Portland firms, was included.

Oregon's senators, Lane and Chamberlain, wrote to Secretary MacAdoo, who replied that the Oregon architects had "importuned the Treasury Department for invitations." When they were invited, they were told "the conditions of the program." Nevertheless, "each competitor sent unqualified written acceptance." Only after they had been invited did they object. Secretary MacAdoo felt that "the protestants' objections went to the fundamentals" of the department's regulations and of the conditions for such competitions. He decided that it was "useless to discuss the question with them, and I, therefore, withdrew in the interest of the Government, the invitations." He could not reconsider. There could not be a jury of professional architects because the legislation for the Portland post office did not allow for such a jury, and "the secretary of the Treasury is restrained by law from accepting gratuitous services." Moreover, the Treasury had an architect on staff as an "expert adviser." As to the 5 percent fee, it was adequate because the Treasury's architect would perform some of the functions which normally the contracting architect might undertake.[9] Secretary MacAdoo proceeded with the new competition.

Secretary MacAdoo, without a jury, selected the architect, Lewis P. Hobart of San Francisco, and paid him 5 percent. The post office, now called the Federal Building or the 511 Building, because it is at 511 NW Broadway and because the postal service moved across Hoyt Street in the 1960s, became an office building for the Department of Homeland Security, and is to be transferred to the Pacific Northwest College of Art, the successor of the Museum School, which Anna Belle Crocker and Harry Wentz helped to found.

The Oregon Chapter of the AIA was just two years old when this dispute ended. It was a fledgling organization and some were suspicious of the members' motives. Yet it could conclude the dispute with the U. S. Treasury Department with some satisfaction. Portland architects had worked together in advancing their professional standards. They had communicated with and gained the support of architects in New York and California. They had secured the voice of the national office of the AIA, which agreed with them without reservation. And they had been aided by Oregon's two senators. Unfortunately they did not convince the U. S. Treasury Department. Doyle probably summed up the feelings of others: "There was absolutely no justice in the action of the secretary. We do not question his right, but it is hard to imagine a man whom we had looked up to as being a big man do a thing as small as this."[10] Doyle had a point. Secretary MacAdoo's response had been petulant; he was concerned as much about his personal authority as about government policy or architecture. As if to confirm Doyle's suspicions and to defy the architects of Portland, the cornerstone of the building, placed at NW 8th and Glisan, has incised in bold capitals three names. On the first line in large stately capitals is William G. MacAdoo, Secretary of the Treasury. Below appear first in smaller letters: James A. Wetmore, Acting Supervising Architect, and then last in still smaller letters, Lewis P. Hobart, Architect.

On August 17, 1914, Mrs. Doyle was at Seaside with the children, the family maid, and a young nursemaid when Mr. Doyle, in Portland, completed preliminary drawings for a new house. Their home on NE 8th was neither appropriate nor suitable. He was then Portland's most important architect, and they had four children.[11] He sent his drawings with a letter, the only written correspondence between the two during their marriage that has survived. It is typed on Doyle & Patterson stationery, purports to be the cover letter to a client with plans enclosed, and is jocular and self-effacing.

> *I thought possibly you might like to look them (the plans) over with your daughters while at the beach, but if you are there merely for rest and recreation you may not feel like thinking about as serious a matter as building a house. If so, just put the sketches aside for consideration on your return to the city. Your husband may or may not be interested; I usually find that the husband does not care to be bothered with the details and gets peevish when the height of the Dining Room Dodo is discussed at length, or when you are*

upper: In 1914 Doyle planned this colonial house for his family. He never built it although he always wished he could. (SUPBP, Safe Drawer 2, "Mr. Doyle's Portland Heights House")

lower: This portrait of Mrs. Doyle and the four Doyle children is undated. It was probably done in 1915. Billy, about three, is on a chair. Mrs. Doyle is clutching Jean, who is about four. On Mrs. Doyle's left is Kathleen, who is about eight. Helen, about seven, is on her right next to Billy. (Newhouse) undecided as to whether the noodle post would be oak or mahogany. His principal interest being of a sordid nature—that of the total cost of the house, he usually makes an appropriation of about one-third the necessary amount to build a fitting home for one of his standing in the community, so if you can in some way induce Mr. Doyle to increase his appropriation, I will be able to improve on the sketches submitted and perhaps build a home more in keeping with your ideas.[12]

It is signed "O. U. Kiderarchitect." Beneath the signature there is a bearded and tousled-haired smiling face.

The house was to be distinguished, commodious, and Colonial.[13] The Doyles never built this house; and although he joked with Mrs. Doyle when he wrote her about it, he always wished they could have. In 1921 when a client asked about a Colonial house, Doyle sent several plans including some for this house, and he explained, "It is in the simplest Colonial Style, and I wish I could afford to build it."[14] Another personal project soon occupied him. Two weeks before he wrote his wife in Seaside, he had completed drawings for a beach cottage. On August 20, he revised the original plans, and in October he designed a single-car garage.[15] With a few minor changes, he built this house for his family.

The Doyle cottage is one of a group of four he did at Neahkahnie on the Oregon coast, eighty miles due west of Portland and eleven miles south of Cannon Beach. His first was for Mary Frances Isom in 1912, when Doyle was already working for her on the Central Library. In 1914-16 he designed three more cottages for himself and his two life-long friends, Anna Belle Crocker and Harry Wentz. These were not Doyle's first vacation houses. In his first year of practice he had done two cottages on the Long Beach Peninsula in Washington, one for Fred Page in Long Beach and the other in nearby Klipson Beach for Mae and Ann Shogren, who had a successful ladies' dressmaking business in Portland. He also designed a large Shingle-style country house for E. J. De Hart on the Columbia Gorge near Hood River. In 1909 he did another cottage for the Shogrens near Mosier in the Gorge.[16] Isom's cottage was built to the specifications for the Page house; Doyle crossed out "Page" and inserted "Miss Mary Frances Isom."

When Doyle first went to Neahkahnie in 1912, a few houses dotted the slope of Neahkahnie Mountain for the magnificent, uninterrupted ocean views. Such views were unavailable at Seaside, Gearhart, and on the Longview Peninsula in Washington, which were the earliest beach developments because they were

Neahkahnie was little developed when the Doyles first went there. This photograph was taken January 31, 1915, when work was about to begin on the Doyle cottage. The Neahkahnie Tavern is in the immediate foreground, and the Isom cottage is just north of it on the bluff above the beach. (Newhouse)

close to the steamers and trains from Portland. Neahkahnie had few trees. Before the Whites came, the Indians regularly burned the mountain to encourage elk grazing; later, the steep slope was suited to pasture. Sheep kept the hillside cropped and the mountain was stark, rugged, and windswept.[17] Today spruce have returned to reclaim the side of the mountain nearly to the shore.

Neahkahnie was remote in 1912, two miles from Nehalem, and four miles from Wheeler, a lumber town with a stop on the Tillamook to Portland railroad, which was completed in 1911. Until then a tugboat with a barge was the principal means of transport. The road south to Tillamook was primitive. North to Seaside there was the "Mail Road," a trail around Neahkahnie Mountain, fragile and perilous, 825 feet above the surf, and a foot and a half wide.[18]

Neahkahnie was developed by Samuel Gordon Reed, who began searching north of Tillamook for beach property in 1906. In 1911 Reed built a house at Neahkahnie and moved his family down from Portland. Mrs. Reed, who was pregnant, walked the eleven miles from Cannon Beach around Neahkahnie Mountain on the Mail Road.

In 1912 when Doyle came to Neahkahnie, trains ran regularly from Portland daily except Sunday at 7:20 in the morning. Even in 1926, the journey was primitive and uncomfortable. Stewart Holbrook regretted using the line twice:

> *The Tillamook Line was composed of ancient coaches, each heated, after a fashion, by a coal-burning stove, and lighted by kerosene*

> *lamps. The seats made no concession to the human spine. The cars were filthy. The so-called right of way was such that huge fir trees were often blown down across the tracks. The baggage car always carried sufficient saws, axes, peavies, and wedges to have equipped a small logging camp.*[19]

The train reached Wheeler about 1:20 in the afternoon.[20] For Neahkahnie, travelers took first a launch to Nehalem and then a motorized "jitney" the last two miles. In 1912 Reed built a large, rambling, shingled inn nearly on the beach for vacationers and

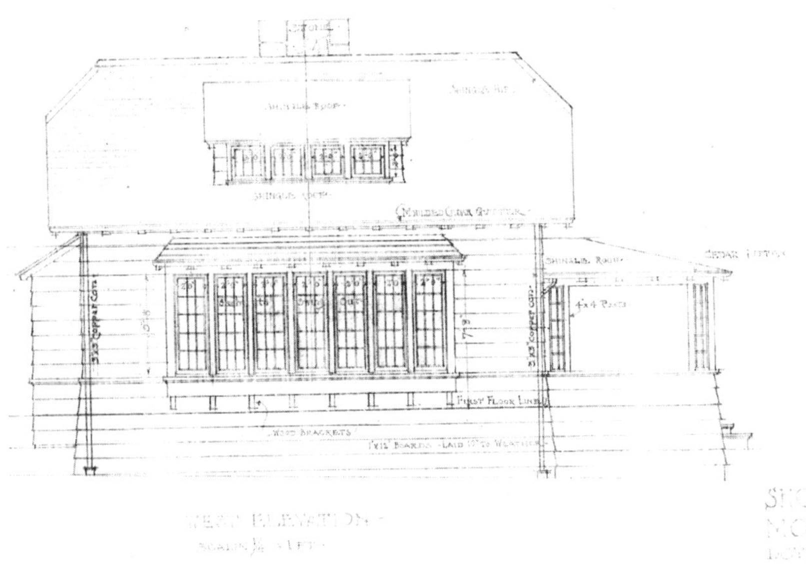

Doyle's plan for the Isom cottage in 1912. (SUPBP, Drawer #25)

The Isom cottage, now called Library Cottage, is today much as Doyle planned it. (Author's photograph)

prospective vacation-homebuilders. Ellis Lawrence designed the simple and rustic Neahkahnie Tavern (now gone). Floors were bare wood, and the walls had exposed studs. There were thirty guest rooms and a dining room, which served meat, dairy, and vegetables from Reed's farm near the inn. A development brochure claimed every modern convenience: "all the comforts of the city... electric lights, pure mountain water, [and] telephone." There were even plans for "golf links."[21]

The Isom cottage is "nearly conventional Arts and Crafts architecture." It is shingle clad with a jerkin-headed gable. A long shed-roofed dormer looks out to sea. The interior is simple and

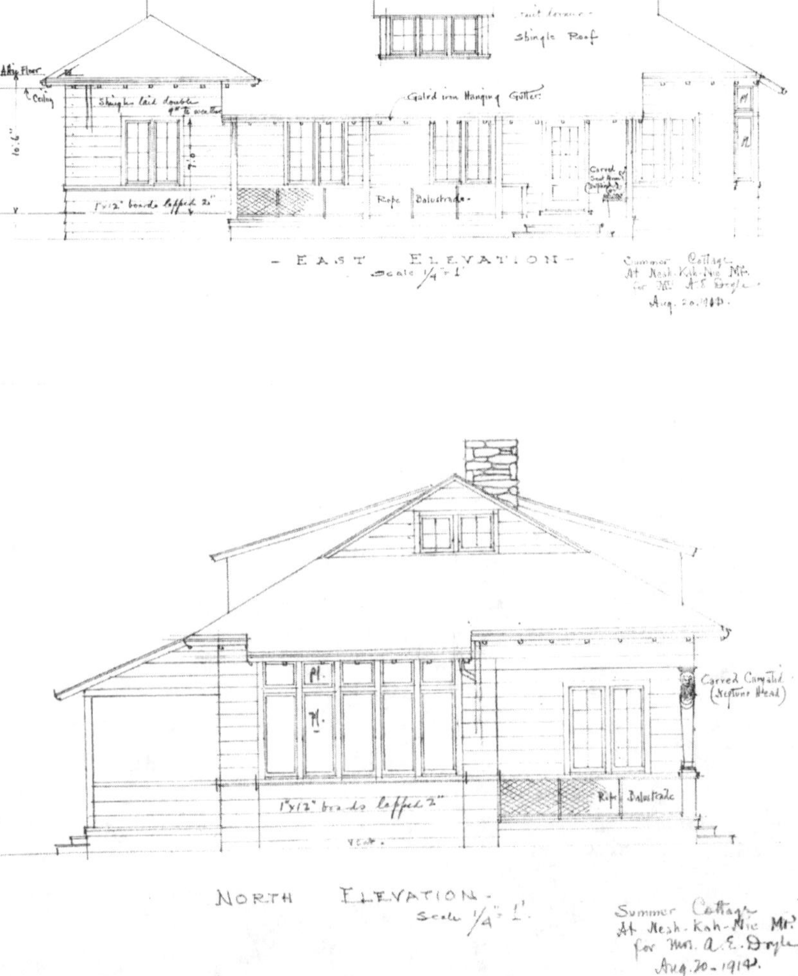

upper: Doyle's plans for his own Neahkahnie cottage. This is the view from the east. Notice that even in this early drawing the dormer, which was initially planned but is not there today, was to be omitted. This drawing is by Doyle; notations and title are in his hand. (SUPBP, Drawer #4, "Summer Cottage at Neah-Kah-Nie Mt. for Mrs. A. E. Doyle")
lower: Doyle's cottage from the north. (SUPBP, Drawer #4, "Summer Cottage at Neah-Kah-Nie Mt. for Mrs. A. E. Doyle")

informal. On the ground floor, there are four rooms put together as a "T." The head of the "T" is the living room/dining room with a "wide west-facing window bay originally fitted with many small panes." Behind in the shaft of the "T" are the kitchen, two bedrooms, a bathroom, and stairs to a bedroom and sleeping loft above.[22]

Doyle began planning his own cottage as he worked for Isom in 1912. That summer he bought a lot at the intersection of Neahkahnie Mountain Road and 2nd Street. (The streets, though platted, were not graded until much later.) In 1915 he bought the half lot immediately south of his so that he had a site approximately 50 feet east and west by 150 feet north and south. Neahkahnie regulars sometimes question Doyle's choice of lots when so many were available because the view west to the ocean was blocked then as it is now by the house that the Reeds had built in 1911 as their first home in Neahkahnie. But Doyle valued the mountain view, which is unimpeded because the site is on the edge of a canyon.

He called the house "Mt Zion." It is low to the ground with porches on the east and west. The roof has a slight gable and spreads out over the structure. Inside there is a rustic simplicity like that of Isom's cottage and an efficient and informal floor plan. A large living and dining room surrounds an open stone fireplace. Walls are one by twelve inch board and bat. Off the main room there are a small kitchen and a small hall leading to a bath and four bedrooms. Upstairs is a sleeping loft under the low roof. The exterior is not all shingled as Isom's is. At sill level and below, the

The Doyle cottage today at 37480 2nd St., Neahkahnie. (Author's photograph)

wall is one by twelve inch unplaned spruce boards slightly lapped. Above the sill and to the roof are shingles. As for Isom's house, he had a large bay window to capture the view. Here it faces north and Neahkahnie Mountain.

Doyle incorporated into his own cottage two wood carvings, a head of Neptune, which was a support for the porch (now enclosed) on the northwest corner of the cottage, and a dolphin arm rest on the bench on the eastside (the front) porch. They were by Alexander Phimister Proctor (1860-1950), a sculptor known in Oregon for *The Rough Rider* in Portland, *The Pioneer Mother* on the University of Oregon campus, *The Circuit Rider* on the State Capitol grounds in Salem, and the Portland Art Museum's first original sculpture, *Indian on Horseback*.[23]

In the next year Doyle completed cottages for Anna Belle Crocker and Harry Wentz. On these two cottages, the shingles on the exterior walls disappear. The overlapping wide unplaned spruce boards, which Doyle used to sill height on his own house, cover the exteriors. The roofs are shingled. The Crocker cottage is low with gabled front and wing in a "T"-shape. The living and dining area are at the head of the "T" with a fireplace on the east wall; two double-casement windows on the west look out to the ocean. On the north a five-windowed casement looks toward the mountain and to the south there is a double-casement window. East of the living room is a hall leading to a back bedroom and a staircase to the second floor. The kitchen and bath occupy the center of the building. An alcove on the south side of the kitchen opens on a south-facing porch.

The main entrance to the house is on the north. Today the cottage is much changed. Its entrance is now on the east because Neahkahnie Mountain Road when graded was about 12 feet below the level of the house. A large addition, a north-south wing on the east, was added after Doyle's death and after Crocker sold. It holds the entrance and a large library with an A-frame window toward the mountain.[24]

The Wentz cottage is well preserved because it has received iconic status. Its setting is more stunning than that of the other three cottages.[25] It rests precariously on a bluff above the ocean. In early days before the spruce grew up to obscure the view north, it appeared to nestle against the mountain. Harry Wentz was much involved in his house; one story has it that in 1914 he received eight hundred dollars for a Tiffany glaze he painted in the Pittock Mansion. His first idea was to use the windfall to return to Paris;

Anna Belle Crocker's in 1938. It is today much altered. (Author's family's photograph)

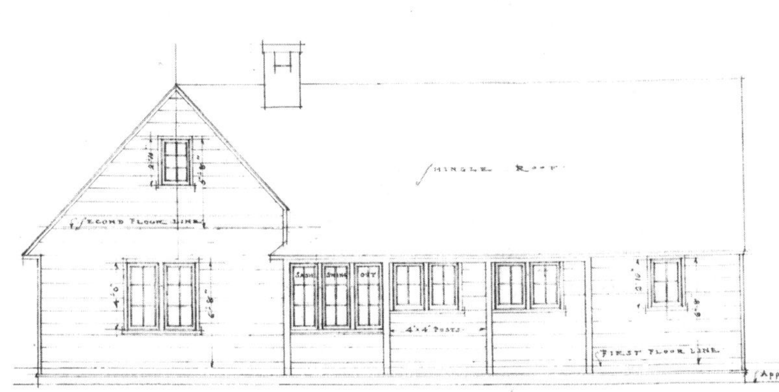

Doyle's plan for the Crocker cottage from the south. (SUPBP, Drawer #38, "Seaside Cottage for Miss A. B. Crocker")

The Harry Wentz cottage today, at 38070 Beulah Reed Road, Neahkahnie. (Author's photograph)

but he then decided to build at Neahkahnie. He worked closely with the local carpenter, Fred Humke, and kept careful records of the expenditures for labor and materials. The total cost was $1050.50.[26] While Doyle and his staff drew the plans for these cottages, he received no commission.

The Neahkahnie cottages have common elements, perhaps even a logical progression. The shingled exterior of Isom's cottage gives way first to a combination of shingles and weather boards for the Doyles' and then to all weather boards for the Crocker and Wentz cottages. The bay window in the Isom cottage faces west, not north as in the others. It originally had small panes. However, even in the Isom cottage there is a large casement window on the north toward the mountain. For the Doyle cottage there is a large unpaned bay window. The Crocker cottage has a larger north-facing casement window but no bay. The Wentz cottage seems to combine the two windows; it has a bay window but it has become a "studio window, here simplified and refined to almost Miesian quality."[27]

All of the cottages are informal and simple without dining rooms or large reception rooms. They were summer houses seldom used in the cold and wet months. Their internal arrangements were adapted to the family groups who vacationed in them. Isom was unmarried, but she had an adopted daughter. Her cottage had two downstairs bedrooms with spare rooms upstairs. The Doyles had four children, and they were accompanied by a maid. Their cottage had four bedrooms on the ground floor; there was a sleeping loft above. Anna Belle Crocker never married; she lived with her sister Florence and her mother. Her cottage had a downstairs bedroom with sleeping areas above. Harry Wentz was a lifelong bachelor; his cottage was the most informal of all. The floor plan is a 16 x 28-foot great room with a kitchen adjoining. There is a simple staircase to an attic bedroom.

These cottages are often cited as important for the development of the Northwest Regional style. They and others looked to "the indigenous rural architecture of Oregon: the barns, outbuildings, and utility structures that are found throughout the state."[28] George McMath questioned how much Doyle was influenced by vernacular, regional buildings: "For a man of Doyle's background and training a more historic source would certainly have suited him better."[29] Some have emphasized similarities with Greene & Greene, with Bernard Maybeck, with the Arts and Crafts Movement or with the Craftsman style. Some have even looked for borrowings from Japan which is, in my view, dubious; there was not one book in his library on Japanese architecture.

To my knowledge, Doyle never said or wrote anything about the architecture at Neahkahnie. He did say something about a house sometimes linked with the Neahkahnie cottages. Edward Ehrman's summer house on the Columbia River Highway about one mile east of Corbett, Oregon, on a three-acre site with views of the river, was completed a few years after the Neahkahnie cottages. It has been classified as English or English Cottage. It is much grander than the Neahkahnie cottages. It has a great hall for gathering and dining, numerous bedrooms, and a large kitchen and service wing. Despite the size, here as at Neahkahnie there is informality. It features shingle, stucco, and stonework and is built low to the ground with a prominent roof and dormers, several clipped. Doyle described it modestly: "It is an extremely simple exterior of stucco and shingle with shingle roof. A purist would perhaps call it an English house, but it follows the style of the Early English small house or cottage type."[30]

He had a fascination on his tour of Europe for indigenous houses constructed by skilled and unschooled craftsmen. He wrote more in his diary about simple cottages or small houses than about the works of recognized architects, especially when they had skillful woodwork, plasterwork, and carvings. And he admired a modern village, Port Sunlight, near Liverpool, where modern architects replicated the traditions of old English craftsmen.

In 1909, three years before Doyle began his work at Neahkahnie, he bought *Picturesque English Cottages and their Doorway Gardens* by P. H. Ditchfield (Philadelphia, 1904), about the beauty and simplicity of English cottages. It surveys the "endless" variety of English traditional building types, because they emanate from the countryside and the ingenuity of the people who have produced them. Village craftsmen use the "materials which Nature provided" and there is therefore "a vast difference in methods of construction and in the appearance of the cottage homes of England." Materials of construction should be what "Nature herself supplies in the neighborhood wherein the cottage is to be reared."

At Neahkahnie, Doyle worked with a local carpenter and with local materials. Cedar shingles are out of the foothills of the Coast Range inland from Neahkahnie. The weatherboards are spruce from the mills in Nehalem and Wheeler as were the fir boards on the interior walls and floors. The stones for the footings and the fireplaces, which were the focus of the informal gathering rooms, were from the beach. A local carpenter, Fred Humke, built the cottages. He lived along the Old Nehalem Road in a still striking small cottage with an interesting roof line and shingle pattern. Doyle counted on him to care for his own cottage, to watch for wood rats, to unlock it in time for the arrival of the family and guests coming down from Portland on the train, or to check on it after a break-in.

Doyle did preliminary drawings for two other Neahkahnie cottages; neither was built. He helped to remodel a cottage that T. L. Eliot bought in 1917 and which resembles the cottages Doyle designed at Neahkahnie. He did drawings of it, made suggestions for improvements in it,[31] and consulted with Humke about work on it. The Eliot cottage remained in the family until 1969; it is much as it was in the 1920s. The walls are shingled in a pattern of alternate narrow and wide overlaps. The windows are unpaned casements. Rafter ends support a wide overhang and add a slight ornament.

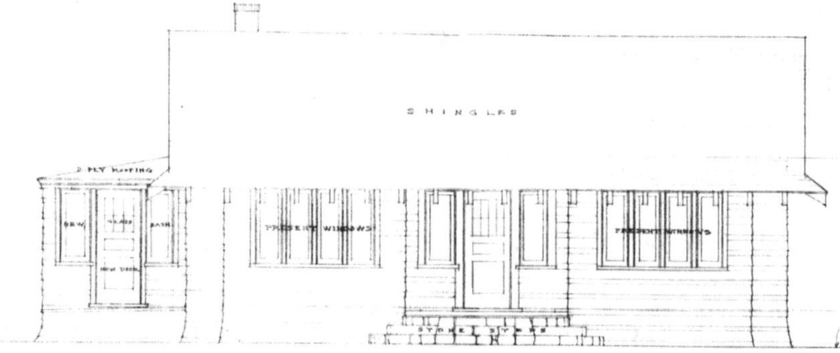

upper: When Mr. and Mrs. Eliot bought an unfinished cottage at Neahkahnie, Doyle did some drawings of it and made some suggestions about completing and improving it. This plan is in Doyle's hand. (SUPBP, Drawer 6, "T. L. Eliot Building at Hood River," misfiled)
lower: At the Doyles' cottage: Billy Doyle on the right is seated next to Jean Doyle. Two friends are to Jean's right. Notice Neahkahnie Mountain in the background; Doyle liked the view. (Newhouse)

Doyle also found jobs in the towns around Neahkahnie. He designed schools in Nehalem, Mohler, Wheeler, and Tillamook, and he did some preliminary plans for a small movie theater in Nehalem. Ellis Madden of Nehalem wrote him in the winter of 1916 after the Neahkahnie cottages were completed about "a good plan for a small one-story concrete motion picture show building without too much expense." Doyle admitted he had no "experience in movie theaters," and he had "nothing of the sort in my library." He did not even know where to find examples, but he would look. In the spring when he had some preliminary sketches, Madden was unable to complete the project and asked for the bill.[32] When Doyle became busier in Portland, he was less interested in jobs at the beach. Bay City wanted him to do a high school in July of 1919. He declined, although he agreed to meet with the superintendent while he was in Neahkahnie.

He never had more than a few days at a time at Neahkahnie. He was usually there in early July to help his family settle at the beach for July and August. They were accompanied by the family maid and, while the children were small, a young nursemaid, a teenager. At the end of August or the beginning of September, he went down to close up the cottage and return the family to Portland. Mrs. Doyle went by train; he drove with the children. Since the train was faster than the car, he wrote ahead to Fred Humke to have the house ready for her. There was convenience in having a car at Neahkahnie, to run down the beach to Manzanita at low tide; there was no Beach Road then to connect the two. He could also use a car to meet clients, though they would need to telephone him through a neighbor or the Neahkahnie Tavern because the Doyle house had no telephone. A messenger would come up the hill to fetch him. It was possible to drive to Neahkahnie as early as 1912; *The Oregonian* thought the road along the Miami River from just east of Garibaldi on Tillamook Bay to the Nehalem River was very good: "a hard bed of river gravel laid years ago (and) kept scrupulously in repair." But the trip from Portland through Newberg and Tillamook then north to Nehalem and to Neahkahnie was a hard day's drive, some of it primitive. The Grand Ronde Indian Reservation was often impassable with "nine miles of dust and corduroy in hot weather, nine miles of awful mud in wet." In 1919, when the road was much improved, a drive from Portland to Tillamook was still "six to eight hours depending on the driver." By the early twenties there were stretches of macadam and asphalt.[33]

Neahkahnie was a magical retreat; Doyle wrote of its beauties. In early spring when it "was carpeted with wild flowers," he thought it was like Monterey, "just about right."[34] He liked it better than the California coast where the weather was warmer, "if the sun would only shine, next best place is Monterey Bay."[35] On the freighter through the Panama Canal he saw brilliant sunsets in the tropics, "never anything to compare with them up north," except "we have had some good ones at Neahkahnie."[36]

⋘

Most of Doyle's men left to find work elsewhere. Lewis Macomber returned to New York to a position in a furniture company. Huston M. Reeves found work in Seaview, Washington. Jameson Parker enrolled in the University of Pennsylvania. The staff of twenty that Doyle had boasted of in 1913, when he applied for the post office competition, dwindled to three by November 8, 1915, when Doyle wrote Wilfred Higgins, who had gone east to find work: "We have nothing at all in the office but am holding on to Reese, Charlie and Merriam and hoping that things will be better."[37]

These three were long-time Doyle men. Harry Clyde Reese and Charles Greene had been with him since 1908 or 1909 and Charles Allen Merriam since 1911. There was another member of Doyle's staff, a young secretary, an Englishman of twenty-two. David Jack started with Doyle in 1915. He became central to the firm. Even in 1915 he was Doyle's personal assistant. When Doyle was away, he asked Jack about office business and through him directed work in the office. Doyle called him Dave, though his usual practice in addressing most men with whom he had a professional relationship was to call them by their surnames. Doyle would even ask Dave to check on his children. There is a noticeable improvement in the quality of the firm's files in this period. The records are fuller and more orderly.

Doyle struggled to keep the office going. He begged creditors like the Portland Auto Club, whose clubhouse he had done two years earlier. He made them a special deal, gave them a reduction "in the regular commission," agreed to payment in installments. Even so they did not pay. After a year he wrote: "I am appealing to you to see if you can not have the account settled."[38] The Northwestern National Bank paid nothing for eight months. He was understanding but firm: "I would appreciate a payment on account if not in full as soon as possible. In rendering a final statement I took into account the business condition and the condition of your building from a rental standpoint and did not charge any commission on a number of items for which a charge should be made."[39] He asked the owners of the Morgan Building for any part of the balance "you can spare." He explained: "I have a good deal in unpaid balances on the books and a note at the bank that I am very anxious to clean up so I will appreciate it very much if you can do something."[40] At the end of December 1915, he admitted to W. B. Patterson that he could not meet a payment of nine hundred dollars that was owed on the termination of the partnership. He could only pay four hundred dollars, he wrote: "I may have the balance sometime during January, but I cannot promise definitely."[41]

In the autumn of 1915, he completed the Reed president's house. It is a gracious house but it has not been a residence for half a century; presidents long ago preferred to live off campus. The house was designed for entertaining and a family. The ground floor had a large living room, a dining room, and a library. Upstairs were six bedrooms, three bathrooms, and two sleeping porches. The house was frame with a shingle exterior, "an English type of residence."[42]

William Truffant Foster, Reed's president, was away from Portland when it was done. He wrote to thank Doyle, who replied with more than his usual modesty: "I appreciate your expression of

The Reed College president's house was completed in 1915. (RC)

satisfaction very much. I do not feel, however, that I was of much help to Mrs. Foster in your absence, and there are many items of architectural detail about the house that I should like to have seen carried out better—$500 or $1000 more spent judiciously on good detail would have given the house better character." Doyle insisted that no blame should be assigned to the contractor who "gave you as much as anyone could for the money."[43] Reed was frugal like the rest of Portland in the years after the boom; its endowment was invested in depressed Portland real estate; there was no money for large collegiate Gothic buildings.

In 1916 the national economy improved; Oregon was not so well off because of problems in bringing lumber and grain to market. But building permits improved in value if not in numbers.[44] Doyle thought in the spring of 1916 that business was looking up. He now had seven men. In addition to Merriam, Reese, Greene, and Jack, Huston M. Reeves, who occasionally worked for Doyle, was back. Herbert Angell and Fred Moore both started with Doyle in this upturn.[45] Angell was about thirty-two and had some experience in other Portland offices. Fred Moore was, Doyle said, "a new boy."[46]

Two philanthropic projects would not have seemed important a few years before, but they helped to keep the office going. The White Shield Maternity Hospital for Wayward Girls was built with bequests from the will of Henry Wemme, president of Overlook Land Company and vice president and Manager of Willamette Tent and Awning Company, and a known, local personality. He had Oregon's first automobile and first airplane. He never married and died without heir, leaving the bulk of his sizeable estate to six Christian Science churches for a residence and hospital for young unmarried, pregnant women. While he was not Jewish, he

Doyle designed the Henry Wemme Home for Wayward Girls, now the White Shield Center, in 1916. Part of his building survives at 2640 NW Alexandra Street. (OHS 106090)

The Martha Washington (now Montgomery Hall, a dormitory of Portland State University, at the southeast corner of SW 10th and Montgomery); Doyle designed the first wing in 1916. A second wing was added by Ellis Lawrence. (Author's photograph)

was a German immigrant and close to some of Doyle's clients of German (and mostly Jewish) descent. The Wemme Home (some of it still survives at 2640 NW Alexandra Street) was at the end of a continuation of Thurman across a viaduct above Cornell Road near Forest Park, in a still-remote forested location, because the trustees hoped "to keep the institution away from prying eyes and, at the same time, to give it an atmosphere of the country with all the advantages of the city." It was a two-story colonial building "of large and ample dimensions." It was like an "old English manor with a warm homelike atmosphere." and none of "the harsh lines ... [which] seem to cling to public institutions."[47]

The Martha Washington Home was also a red-brick Georgian for an organization formed in 1887 to house "young women wage earners who are strangers in the city" in a residence in Northwest Portland at NW 14th and Flanders. As Northwest Portland became increasingly industrial, Doyle planned to build at SW 10th and Montgomery. According to the contemporary reviews of the building, bright and airy rooms looked out into a garden court or tree tops. Sunny porches on the first three floors opened to the garden. Furniture in the halls and lobby was wicker. The living room had comfortable chairs and couches. The dining room was a bright room with gay chintz hangings, soft-gray walls, and ivory woodwork. A social hall had hardwood floors for dancing, a piano, and a phonograph for the "girls" to "enjoy themselves." In the basement there were a laundry and a sewing room. In the youg women's rooms the furniture was white and "the girls were allowed to add individual touches and arrange their own personal belongings."[48]

Myron Hunt, a Los Angeles architect, heard good things about the Martha Washington and wrote to see the plans. Doyle replied:

> *The tribute to the Martha Washington Home is very much exaggerated I'm sure, for it is a very modest, frugal building in every respect. I am very glad to send the plan to you and hope they may be of some use, but you will no doubt be disappointed for the building is a very ordinary, cheap building. It has, however, served a useful purpose in providing bed and board for working girls at a low price.*[49]

Myron Hunt was impressed: "After studying the plan of your Martha Washington Home, I am sure it is not the building which is modest but you. This is a good building, well thought out and I want to congratulate you on it."[50] The Martha Washington was completed and dedicated early in 1917. It is now Montgomery Court, a Portland State University dormitory.

The Frank J. Cobbs house and garden in about 1918, shortly after completion. While the address is 2424 SW Montgomery Drive, this is the view from SW Vista above and behind the garden. (Cheney, "The Work of Albert E. Doyle," p. 50)

There were only two important jobs between 1915 and 1922: a house for Frank J. Cobbs and the U.S. National Bank. Both were started in 1916 and completed in 1917.

The Cobbs house is Doyle's largest and the "grandest Jacobethan house in Portland."[51] Because it is between SW Vista and Montgomery, its size and setting are easily viewed. The formal gardens contribute to the elegance of the mansion which was representative of a national movement. Many successful Americans expressed their wealth in brick and dressed-stone Jacobethan manor houses, which they associated with the English gentry. The Cobbs house had large oak-paneled reception rooms: a central hallway, grand living room, dining room and library; there were also modern conveniences like multiple attached garages.[52] Cobbs came from a wealthy Midwestern timber family who moved the family firm to Oregon early in the twentieth century, as did many Midwestern timber men. He also began a lumber yard in Salem which became Copelands, and he was a major stockholder and director of the U.S. National Bank.[53]

The U.S. National Bank is today one of the most striking of Doyle's central Portland buildings. He began on the quarter block at the northwest corner of SW 6th and Stark. The four-story Roman temple bank was extended west in 1922 to cover the entire half block on the north side of Stark between SW 6th and Broadway. The U.S. National Bank helped to define the financial center of the city and further emphasized the gradual realignment to the west away from the river. As the department stores a decade before had moved west of SW 5th along Morrison and Alder, Portland's banks were moving to SW 5th and 6th and settling along Stark. The First National Bank moved from SW 1st and Washington to the Corbett

The U. S. National Bank at SW 6th and Stark was completed in two parts. This photograph was taken probably in 1918, shortly after the first part, on SW 6th Avenue, was completed. (PCA A2004-002.568)

Block at SW 5th and Morrison in 1907. Ten years later it had its own new building at SW 5th and Stark. Earlier the Canadian Bank of Commerce, the Bank of California, Hartman & Thompson, and the Lumberman's National Bank had all settled on Stark Street and the Northwestern National Bank had moved to its Doyle-designed building on the corner of SW 6th and Morrison.

Doyle readily admitted the U.S. National Bank was a copy of a New York bank, the Knickerbocker Trust, which McKim, Mead, & White had done in 1904. The façades of the buildings are strikingly similar. There are free-standing Corinthian columns at the entrances. Corinthian order pilasters range along the side framing recessed, metal windows. The contrast of the pilasters and the windows in the shadow of them emphasizes the classical temple. The overriding impression is grandeur and power. Doyle avoided such grandiose descriptions. His characterization was simpler: "The U.S. National Bank here has been very well received by the public as well as by the patrons. It is a very practical banking room and at the same time good looking."[54]

He especially liked a review in the *Oregon Voter* that emphasized the warmth of the building, not its monumentality:

> *This new home seems to breathe living warmth. While its proportions are monumental and its architecture is classic, there is nothing of the tomb in its appearance or atmosphere. Neither exterior nor interior inspire awe or forbid close acquaintance. Perhaps the gentle harmony of the color scheme is responsible for this sense of warmth and welcome. The exterior is a delicate brown—not the brown of dead leaves, but rather that of ripened grain. A little lighter shade of the same brown pervades the interior, and in most delightful contrast thereto are the shades of dainty, subdued blue in the ceiling decorations. It would seem as though a more perfect exemplification of the harmony of contrast could not be conceived. The eye delights to rest upon every part of the interior. Details and general effects all invite satisfied contemplation.*[55]

Doyle was so pleased he wrote the editor. While there was "a mushy spot or two," he said, the newspaper expressed "the atmosphere of the place we tried so hard to get." He was delighted to know that someone he had never met could appreciate "just what we had striven so hard for."[56]

⋘

Ahead of the completion of these buildings, by the summer of 1916, work in the drafting room was falling off. Despite Doyle's confidence in the spring that business was looking up, his men were leaving. In early July Charles Greene was in New York, where he met up with a group of former Doyle men: Frank Logan, John Hatten, Jameson Parker, and Lewis Macomber. Frank Logan, who saw them all from time to time, observed that Doyle had an "ambitious representation" in New York.[57] Jameson Parker completed his work at the University of Pennsylvania in the spring of 1916 and wrote Doyle for advice about returning to Portland or finding work in the East. Although Doyle could offer him a job, he advised Parker to stay in New York: "The Eastern experience will be of more value to you than anything I have to offer."[58] Doyle helped; he wrote Henry Bacon and McKim, Mead, & White and recommended Parker as having "a lot of native ability and good taste and I would like to see him get a chance in a good office."[59]

By September Greene was going on to San Francisco where Doyle smoothed his way by writing Athol McBean, whose firm supplied much of Doyle's terra-cotta: "He is making a trip to the principal cities for the first time and has not been in San Francisco before. I thought perhaps one of your boys might show him some good roofs and some of the other things in San Francisco that are interesting."[60]

There was too little work to keep two engineers; Merriam had seniority. In May 1917, just a little more than a month after America's entry into the war, Doyle regretfully wrote a Spokane architect recommending Reese.

> *Mr. H. C. Reese who has been in my office continually for ten years is one of the most useful men I have known, he is not a designer but I have had him make the plans and details for almost all of my most important work. He is quick and accurate and his drawings look well. He has had a good all around experience and if you have a designer to work with him he ought to make the man you are looking for. I hate to let him go, but I haven't anything to do.* [61]

⋞⋞⋞

Among the Doyle papers, there is a list of jobs and commissions between June 1, 1915, and November 13, 1916, and a list of the payments made to him from the firm's income. It is the only such accounting of the firm I have found. In this period there were only two significant commissions: the Meier & Frank Co. for $20,280 and the U.S. National Bank for $6,538.88. There were also some good-sized payments from earlier jobs like the Pittock Block ($3,750) and the Northwestern National Bank ($1,917.52). But the White Shield home brought in only a thousand dollars and the Portland Women's Union just five hundred. There are several house plans with significant commissions: A. Oberdorfer for $1,605.53; W. B. Ayer, who was then building a country house and outbuildings near Carlton, Oregon, for $1,279.52; and F. J. Cobbs for $1000. But most of the payments were for less, like twenty-five dollars for an alteration in the Selling Building and the same from Reed. The total for this nearly eighteen-month period, from the end of the partnership with Patterson, was $47,977.93. From this Doyle took $15,172 or nearly a third, for an income on average of $211 a week or $10,972 for a year. He received payments on a weekly basis although in some months he took just one payment. Usually the payments were round figures of varying sizes: $250, $400, $500, and on two occasions $1000.[62] These were significant sums. For example, Frank Logan wrote from New York the week after this account was concluded because he wanted to return to Portland and have a job there when he arrived. He offered to work for Doyle for thirty dollars a week. Logan was an MIT graduate and an established architect. He had been Edgar Lazarus' partner for two years, an AIA member even before there was an Oregon chapter, and an officer in the Oregon chapter's first year. Doyle replied almost immediately. There was, he wrote, no one he would rather have in the office, but there was "little work," and without more soon "I can't keep the fellows in the office busy."[63]

When Doyle joined the Arlington Club in 1909, Whidden & Lewis were engaged in the construction of a new club building (811 SW Salmon), which is in use today. They were the obvious architects. They had designed the previous club house in 1892. They were members, indeed, the only architects who belonged until Doyle joined. And they were still Portland's most important architectural firm, although Doyle & Patterson were beginning to compete for that title. When the new building opened in 1910 it was "outstanding in architecture and appointments." There was "no small furor in Portland." It was "one of the finest buildings of its type in the nation."[64]

In the summer of 1916, when business slowed, Doyle began agitating for a renovation. What he did and who agreed with him was recorded in letters and reports that he bound loosely with renderings of renovated Arlington Club rooms.[65] In a number of these letters he explained his purpose as he did to the brother of his former New York employer. Francis Bacon manufactured fine furniture reproductions which Doyle wanted for the club. He began firmly: "I was not the architect of the building," but then he seems to have lost his way as he became a bit unsure about how to proceed. He wrote a sentence. Then he changed his mind and crossed it out. The original is still legible: "While on the Board of Directors I started a movement to use some of our surplus in fixing up our house, desiring to remain in the background." What he replaced this with sounds less conspiratorial. Next to the crossed-out section he penciled: "but I wished." The letter continues: "to have the work undertaken by the House Committee through the architects." As I read this passage and interpret Doyle's original admission, he saw himself as having hatched the plan, remaining always in the background, by turning the project over to a committee. He was in a delicate position in suggesting renovations. William Whidden and Ion Lewis were his mentors and long-time members (Ion Lewis was even a resident of the club). Doyle explained to Francis Bacon: "I do not wish to take an active part; but do want to see our club fixed up right."[66] He wanted a committee to "secure the cooperation" of Whidden & Lewis "as it would make it much easier for you and I (sic) to have them to do it."[67] Bacon understood; in reply he referred to "the delicate situation between you and Mr. Whidden."[68]

Doyle thought the interior of the building was pretty bad. He did not like the vestibule where he wanted "a decorative painting on each wall." There was an inappropriate wainscot of inferior marble. "I do not think it possible to do anything good with this marble."[69] Inside the vestibule in the windowless lobby, much was awry. It is "not too good Colonial painted white." There was need of a new fireplace and mantel; and "nothing can be done for the stairs."[70] Also in the lobby "the service is pretty much in evidence." They should conceal "the telephone switchboard, register desk and office." He proposed going through the club, room by room, to "get the architecture—walls, floors and ceilings right, and in right relation to the furnishings—in other words doing an entire room or lobby at one time." They should not work piecemeal "by buying an occasional chair or doing a little bit here and there." The whole building must be redone. "The ceilings in all rooms and lobbies are very plain," and "A rich ceiling counts for more than most people realize."[71]

He wanted color and brightness. In the upper lobby, the walls were "canvassed and painted" in "grayed buff." They needed "considerable color" in "rugs in blue, yellow, and gray."[72] New bright rugs "might make the walls glow and with a few pieces of the right kind of furniture this hall will be much more attractive." In the lobby there should be "somewhat stronger color as this lobby is entirely artificially lighted."[73] He wanted richness and dignity. The Arlington Club, "should be distinctive and not look like a hotel lobby—dignified and rich but not showy."[74]

Not much was accomplished in 1916. In 1921, after the war, Doyle wrote another report and made the case that the club was "the principal social organization of its kind in the Northwest" and "an exponent of the culture and refinement of taste of the people of this section." Visitors to the area and the club "form from its appearance something of an impression of the city and its inhabitants." The necessary improvements had been delayed by "a variety of circumstances" including the war "despite general agreement of the importance of it."[75]

In February of 1917, when Doyle was several months from completing the U.S. National Bank, *The Architect and Engineer* wrote to him about doing an article on his work. Doyle's only responsibility would be to provide drawings and photographs, especially of the U.S. National Bank. The editor explained, "We have some very favorable comments of it."[76] In reply Doyle was reserved. He had no "suitable photographs" because "the building business has been so poor I have had to do some hustling to pay necessary bills." As to featuring the bank, it would not be completed until July 1; so there could be no good photographs before then. He may have thought he was too negative. The letter ended with a pencilled explanation: "Of course, I would like to have some of my things published but I don't want to have it done unless it can be done well and that means getting some good photographs."[77]

It was two years before the article appeared. Charles H. Cheney, an architect and city planner based in San Francisco, who had consulted on planning with the City of Portland while Doyle was on the Planning Commission, provided a brief write-up to accompany the photographs Doyle eventually supplied. In fact, Doyle wrote much of the article by way of a letter he sent to Cheney explaining the photographs.[78] For example, on Reed College, Doyle wrote: "The Reed College work has perhaps been the most interesting work I have had. We tried to get the spirit of the old English Collegiate Gothic while adapting the style to present day conditions." Cheney repeated phrases and Doyle's evaluation: "The Reed College work has perhaps been the most interesting Mr. Doyle has done. He has contrived exceedingly well to get the spirit of the old English Collegiate Gothic while adapting his style to present-day conditions."

On Meier & Frank, Doyle wrote: "A twelve-story building covering most of a block 200′ x 200′ white terra-cotta; nothing to it except bulk. It is a big dry goods box punched full of holes for light and it looks like it." Cheney quotes Doyle to make the article's only negative comment: "The Meier & Frank Department Store is a 12-story building of white terra cotta covering three-quarters of a block. As Mr. Doyle says, 'It is a big dry goods box punched full of holes for light and it looks like it.'" And finally, Lipman Wolfe is, Doyle said, "better in design both inside and out" while Cheney said, "It is more attractive and better in design both inside and out."[79]

As the article was nearing completion, the editor asked Doyle to help with some of the costs of publication either by underwriting it or by naming Portland suppliers who might advertise in the issue. Doyle was not cooperative; he would not subsidize the article and rejected outright the idea of submitting a list of possible advertisers.

When he received the proofs, he thanked Cheney. He had no corrections except that William Whidden's name was misspelled. He wrote: "I am of course very much pleased with the nice things you had to say and want to thank you very heartily for your interest in seeing the thing through in such good shape."[80]

A few years later, when Seattle was considering zoning changes, Doyle wrote the Seattle Planning Commission and recommended Cheney, whom, he said, he knew from Portland planning. He said nothing about Cheney's article.

⇜

The United States declared war on Germany on April 6, 1917. Two and a half weeks later the editor of the *Western Architect* asked Doyle how the war would affect Portland construction. He was optimistic as usual. It would enhance "the very general healthy condition of business in all lines which has existed for some time," by expanding factories and adding housing.[81] In fact, 1917 was the worst year for construction in Portland during Doyle's career, with about one-sixth of the permits there had been in 1910. The war brought new industry. Portland had some experience with building wooden ships, especially as Oregon business and agricultural interests had become increasingly responsible for transport into and out of Portland with the withdrawal of the Pacific fleet to the Atlantic to supply the belligerents. But the important and dramatic change was in steel ships. Construction began very suddenly and mushroomed into a major industry in a few months. There had been no steel shipbuilding before the war. In 1914 the Willamette Iron and Steel Works without prior experience repaired a steel ship that had been damaged by fire in the Portland harbor. The Northwest Steel Company began shipbuilding in May of 1916 when it received an order for eight steel ships from Norway. By December of 1917 there were about seven thousand men employed on wooden ships, about the same number on steel ships, and another twenty-five hundred more indirectly employed making parts for steel and wooden ships. Combined, these numbers were "the largest for any single industry the city has ever known."[82] A year later, at the end of the war, thirty-four thousand men worked in shipbuilding in Portland and thirty thousand worked in other manufacturing, while before the war there had been no more than eighteen thousand men employed in all manufactures in the city.[83]

Plants for war work and houses for workers boosted construction. Yet most of this was inexpensive housing for shipyard workers; there was no fireproof construction.[84] Doyle did several buildings for the Northwest Steel Company. He tried unsuccessfully to bring his firm into the war effort. In 1917 he applied for a contract to build a grain elevator on the docks. He was so confident that he wrote Reese about it and invited him back, but he did not get the contract and Reese stayed put. By January 1918 he was trying to get into steel ship construction: "Many businesses have been practically wiped out by the war and I have been thinking for sometime that I must turn to something that is part of the war game—and I naturally turn to the building of boats as the most suitable thing, for it is a structural problem primarily and one requiring speed."[85]

Eventually Merriam went off to the war and Doyle called Reese back, but there was a "ban on non war construction."[86] In June 1918, he had on staff only Reese, Angell, and Jack, and there was "hardly enough work to keep them busy." They were surviving on "a bit of housing" and "some bank alterations and other small alteration work."[87]

Doyle did his part for the war. He volunteered for the Federal Food Administration, which was working to conserve food and to send what could be spared to Europe. The administrator of the program in Oregon was W. B. Ayer, his long-time patron. Doyle was coordinator of a large section of eastside Portland. He also worked on the savings bond (the Liberty Loan) drive. Almost a month to the day after the Armistice, he was cleaning up his desk to start anew, and he answered a letter that had awaited him. He explained why he was late replying: "I was in the midst of war activities, at a time when I was spending practically no time in my office."[88]

CHAPTER 6

After the War

With peace, A. E. Doyle thought, prospects looked "very good" for government projects, "small town banks and schools, [and] bank alterations and additions," and "many of the war profiteers [are] considering the erection of homes." He was hoping for work at last. "I am expecting to have several good houses next year."[1] By the end of December 1918, Doyle needed help. He wrote Charles Greene, who was stationed at the medical detachment at the Vancouver Barracks: "I have considerable work that needs to be done soon, and I would rather not put on any new men if there is a prospect of your returning soon."[2] Charles returned and by the spring Merriam and Dave Jack were both back from the army engineers. Merriam had served in the East while Jack had been in France.

Many thought Portland could retain its new industries, but shipyards and factories closed. Construction during and immediately after the war was for factories, public garages, and moderately priced housing for shipyard workers. Despite Doyle's optimism, there was little work for architects. For houses under ten thousand dollars, builders had "a great number of stock plans," and an owner "does not find it expedient to spend much money upon architectural service." Moreover, the economy was overheated and prices were high. In Portland building costs, both materials and labor, doubled in the war years and "peaked in August 1920," when they were two and a half times what they had been in 1915. After the summer of 1920 costs fell. By the end of 1921 they were 20 percent lower. There was reason then for optimism especially for the "types of buildings which call for architectural planning."[3]

In spring and summer 1919, Doyle received two honors, two public acknowledgements. In March a jury invited by the Oregon chapter of the AIA announced the "ten most notable examples of architecture ... within ten miles of city hall." Four of the ten were Doyle's: Reed, the Central Library, the F. J. Cobbs house, and the U.S. National Bank. Lawrence & Holford had two on the list; Wade

Pipes, F. A. Narramore, and Whitehouse & Fouilhoux each had one. The Portland Hotel was included and credited to McKim, Mead & White, who designed it, not to Whidden & Lewis, who did it. In the summer, the long-awaited article by Charles H. Cheney finally appeared after wartime delays. It was forty-seven pages of written and photographic appreciation of Doyle's work.[4] Still there were several years of adjustment.

In July 1919 when he took the family to Neahkahnie for the summer, he visited Mohler and Bay City about new schools. A month later Doyle admitted things were slow. Reese was working on an Elks Club building in Pendleton. The rest of the staff was "busy on details of houses." Doyle was "trying to make drawings for some schools, and [doing] a little superintending."[5] In November he wrote a job seeker: "Things are picking up fast and I am getting quite busy again." But he did not have enough work to offer a job.[6] He was looking for work as far away as Louisville, Kentucky. He wrote a bank president there about the success of the U.S. National but, he admitted, "The only practical arrangement [for him to do a Louisville bank] would be in respect to design and consultation, working with you and your local architect."[7]

In early August, he wrote the Mayor of Portland, George L. Baker, about hiring architects because builders, even when skilled, know "nothing about proportions" and give "little thought to the general design." A city's architecture, he expounded, "is an educational factor and a valuable asset to the city." An architect has many attributes of value in planning buildings:

> *He must be an educated man and citizen, to come in advantageous contact with many classes of clients, to understand the thoughts and interest of others and give intelligent advice. In addition to being trained in the science of planning and in the art of designing, he must be familiar with endless details of materials, methods of work and special appliances, to be able to specify what is needed and to see that it is properly furnished. He must also be a reliable business man. But the architect's special privilege is to make design a very important part to the end that, each building shall definitely express its purpose and appeal to both educated and uneducated people, a common possession in which they take pleasure and civic pride.*[8]

Doyle wanted to do a planned new Meier & Frank warehouse. In Cheney's article there is a drawing for it, which Cheney praised; perhaps Doyle thought by including it among other examples of his work he might win the contract. He wrote to advance his claim:

"[I am] hoping that when the time comes you will let me help you design a building suitable to the needs of the Meier & Frank Company." He explained the advantages of his firm.

> *Merriam had corking experience during the war on concrete construction on a large scale, being the engineer in charge of construction of enormous warehouses and shell loading plants at Tullytown, Pennsylvania. He has designed and superintended the reinforced concrete work on the Pittock Block, Ford Building, Reed College and Public Library. ... He has had a wide experience, is entirely reliable, and I do not believe has an equal in the Northwest as a concrete structural engineer.*

His staff were "a class of fellows that not an office in the Northwest can equal," who have "learned how to do team work." They would give Meier & Frank better service than any other firm in the Northwest: "I know your problems better than anyone else does and will have more patience in helping you to solve them."[9] He did not get the job. The building, now converted to condominiums, The Avenue, at NW 14th and Irving, so resembles his drawing that it has sometimes been attributed to him. But it was by Sutton & Whitney, a Portland firm, with whom he often competed.

In July 1920, building costs peaked. Doyle admitted he was not busy, but he expected improvement. Six weeks later, Doyle tallied their work: "a few houses, a couple of good bank jobs and college buildings that will provide a meal ticket for a few of us this year."[10] Seattle had not participated in Portland's boom in 1910-1912 but had not suffered a building recession in the early stage of the war. In 1914, when Doyle was planning for the half-block extension of the Meier & Frank store on SW 5th Avenue, he approached Frederick & Nelson, the Seattle department store, about a new building.

> *We can save you a great deal of money in planning your building and design a building to properly house your merchandise, on account of the experience we have had in this class of buildings. We can give you service that no architect or firm of architects on the Pacific Coast is in position to give, as we have an organization that has had experience in all the branches of department store work.*[11]

In the winter of 1916, he was thinking about opening a Seattle office; he wrote, "Seattle has a bright immediate future," yet he was unwilling "to do much gambling." He would wait until he had a "profitable job" in the Portland office "to use the profit in maintaining an office in Seattle until it can be made self-supporting."[12] Three years passed; in early spring 1919, he was looking for department store and bank jobs, and C. A. Merriam went to Seattle to head an office that was called Doyle & Merriam. By May he had a department store for J. S. Graham at 119 Pine in Seattle that is now on the National Register and has been renamed the A. E. Doyle Building. A year later he was selected to do the Seattle National Bank Building.

In 1920, Doyle's other long-time engineer, H. C. Reese, went to Pendleton to open an office. Doyle & Reese was unsuccessful. Aside from a lodge for the Elks, there was little business. Doyle early saw it was hopeless. After several months he wrote Reese, "It's about time we stirred something up, don't you think?"[13] Three weeks later, Reese cabled Doyle asking for plans for small churches. Doyle avoided church work. He did only two, the Westminster Presbyterian, in Chehalis, which had been a problem for him, and in 1913 another Presbyterian church in Raymond, Washington. He sent sketches of them, a pamphlet "Parish Churches of England," and fourteen plates "from our files."[14]

Reese and Merriam were engineers. In Doyle's small office, and especially when the office staff was thin, they, like Doyle, did whatever was needed. When they established satellite offices, Doyle closely supervised design. Because the Seattle office was for a while busier than either Portland or Pendleton, Charles Greene went to help, but Doyle supervised even him from Portland. He explained that Greene need not prepare full-sized drawings for the terra-cotta modelers because "A good modeler will do a better job from scale drawings than he will from full size, so don't waste time on full size terra cotta drawings."[15] The Seattle office did not have a library. Doyle told Merriam: "I appreciate that you are crippled for books." In the fall of 1919 the Seattle office had three Washington banks: "the National Bank of Commerce in Seattle, the Washington National at Ellensburg and Yakima National at Yakima."[16] Doyle wanted more elaborate windows on one. He wrote Merriam, "Have Charlie try for a little more terra cotta below window sills on side elevation, perhaps an enriched sill with panel below or something."[17] Merriam felt inadequate. He asked Doyle to bring examples of their old jobs, especially the Women's Union, the U.S. Bank, and the Central Library. He wrote, "It is positively amazing to find how little we know about detailing, and it is of vital importance to a job."[18]

⋘

The Doyles' home from 1920 is still at 2111 NE 23rd. (Author's photograph)

The Doyles gave up on their planned big West Hills Colonial; they could not afford it. Their house on NE 8th was small for their family of six and a live-in maid. The four children were approaching adolescence; Kathleen, the oldest, was twelve in 1919; the other three ranged in age down to seven. The family got a larger house by trading with Nelly and Lilly Fox, whose house on the northwest corner of NE Tillamook and 23rd became the Doyles' home for over thirty years.[19] The Fox house was considerably larger, on a double corner lot, set back from the street in a neighborhood of substantial and prosperous homes. In addition to the NE 8th Avenue house, the Doyles gave the Fox sisters eleven thousand dollars.[20]

A. E. Doyle and Nelly Fox knew each other. She had worked for the Public Library since 1903 when she was secretary to Mary Frances Isom. In 1908 she took over the supervision of the three branches of the main library, and she was in that position when Doyle planned the permanent East Side Branch Library in 1911. She was also an early member of the Arts and Crafts Society. Lilly was the assistant in the Rose City Park Branch Library.

Doyle remodeled the house extensively, making some structural changes, adding bathrooms, and modernizing the kitchen and wiring. Though the house was built in the 1890s, it appears today as more appropriate to the 1920s because Doyle added an entryway on the east side so that instead of a front-gabled presentation with the entry on Tillamook, in the Queen Anne fashion, the new front door is on 23rd on the side-gable. The address changed from 755

Tillamook to 437 E 23rd N. The modern address of the house is 2111 NE 23rd. Inside there was much redecorating with 968 hours of painting.[21] Some plans in Doyle's hand survive. He put the children on the third floor where there was a new bathroom and new cupboards and wardrobe. Kathleen and Billy had single rooms; Jean and Helen shared. On the second floor were a large master bedroom, a guest room, an extra room, and a new bath. On the ground floor, the new vestibule was placed within a porch facing 23rd. It opened onto a large redesigned living room. There were also a large dining room and a remodeled and enlarged kitchen. Outside a single-car garage was added fronting on the street.[22]

The Foxes vacated the house in early February and moved to the NE 8th house and the Doyles temporarily moved to 2516 NE Tillamook, to a house then unoccupied and uncomfortable. Doyle reproached the landlady for the condition:

> *The plumbing had been frozen during the cold spell several months ago and had not been put in shape, for every fixture in the house was out of commission, and most of the piping was split and blown out. We had plumbers working for several days to put just the kitchen sink and back toilet in shape, and the plumbers are now working in the bathroom.*[23]

Their newly remodeled house was not ready for them for three months, until the end of April 1920.

Charles K. Greene was twenty when he started in Doyle's office in 1909 after two years with Whidden & Lewis. In the lean early-war years, Doyle kept Greene on.[24] When Merriam went to Seattle, Greene went along to take charge of the drafting room. While Doyle from Portland or on frequent visits to Seattle supervised the commercial jobs, Greene was given reponsibility for residential work. Doyle told one Seattle client: "Charles Greene in this firm is doing some house work and doing it well."[25] Greene's income increased with his responsibilities. In 1919 his annual income was $1600; in 1920 it nearly doubled to $2783.[26]

But Greene needed more training. Except for some American travel and some time in New York, he had been in Portland. He spent much of 1921 and 1922 in Europe. Doyle helped plan the trip and advised about preparations. He offered his itinerary from 1906, but he could not find it. "If I can't find it, I can cook one up from my notebooks. I'll jot down any pointers as I think of them and be prepared to talk the thing over more fully the next time I am in Seattle. The thing for you to do now is to get your passport."[27] Two days later he found the itinerary. But he advised against being too fixed in making plans. "I don't think that you need to lay out a hard and fast itinerary as to dates. Some places repay a much longer stay than others, and they you will recognize when they appeal to you."[28] Doyle also helped finance the trip with fifty dollars a month that he called salary. Greene recognized his responsibilities. He reported frequently in long, detailed letters, which, when they reached Portland, were typed by the secretary and distributed to the staff.[29]

He set out in May 1921, with a stop in New York, where he had lived briefly six years before. He wanted to see recent developments, but the city disappointed him. He wrote home, "I can't seem to have the same childhood enthusiasm over this place that I had on my former visits."[30] There was no more question for Greene, than for Doyle, of classes or a degree. Greene needed Europe, and he was eager to sail. He wrote: "The trip is going to do me a world of good. [I] hardly realize yet that my life long dream is to be realized."[31]

Greene's letters were florid and wordy travelogues. He punctuated with gasps his account of the voyage from New York to Naples on an inexpensive and crowded French freighter: "I only hope I will be able to completely forget it in the beauties that are in store for me. Never have I seen such filth and rotten food." He was left much to himself. His fellow travelers were French and Italian "peasants." One died at sea. Greene at first suspected the food; he was relieved to learn it was tuberculosis.

He landed in Naples on June 18, 1921. He followed Doyle's itinerary. On Capri, villas covering the hillside were "white against the deep green of the olive groves," and flowers "fall in great masses over the old garden walls." Pompeii disappointed him: "almost everything of value has been removed to the museums" and his guide showed him "the most obscene of paintings and … the depravity of the people of Pompeii." As Doyle had fifteen years before, he hurried to Athens. He loved the museums, especially the statuary: "To see the manner that the drapery is carved and painted is really unbelievable." He traveled out from Athens visiting the major ancient sites. When he left Greece, he went first to Venice, then to Bologna and Florence. He traveled alone.

He was unmarried, unattached, and without family except for a brother in Portland; their parents were dead. He was lonely, and he wrote about his isolation to Merriam, whom he had known for eleven years and with whom he had worked closely the previous two years in Seattle: "I often wish you were with me so we could enjoy together all these wonders. At times one becomes very much depressed being so much alone and seeing such gay throngs all around." Florence, he wrote in a later letter, "must be beyond a doubt the most beautiful city in the world. I only wish you could enjoy some of the walks with me." He described his room; there is a "huge window … with its little balcony and potted bamboo tree … [and] a marble floor with a few blocks missing, a very good bed and a funny little stove and a few cracked dishes where at noon I have my bread, cheese and beer and at night one hot dish with lots of wonderful fruits and melons and wine." He concluded the letter with an apology: "You must pardon me but you are the only one I can rave to in this manner, and it just seems as if I unload on some one, for I am so filled with the charm of it all." Merriam was apparently not embarrassed by the intimacy of these letters; he had the secretary type and distribute them.

Unlike Doyle, who had carefully worked out his travel with Baedekers, Greene was unsystematic. In Rome he "did not pretend to do anything but wander around trying to get my bearing." He got "pleasure out of wandering suddenly upon some old familiar friend standing there before you in all its glory trying hard to remain isolated from its present surrounding and to retain the dignity and splendor of the days of old." When he did try to plan his time, he was turned away at the American Academy when he asked to see the library "so as to make sure I would not miss anything that I should see," and to work in the studio. "Imagine my surprise," he complained, "when I was refused," and "treated like a small boy." He was even denied admission to villas open only by permission of the Academy because, he was told, they were only for "those traveling on scholarships." He was bitter: "I probably said more than I should have." Greene had encountered a professional bias. Academic credentials had become important. Fifteen years before Doyle, like Greene without college or university credentials, had been permitted into the American School of Classical Studies in Athens and the American Academy in Rome.

⇠⇠⇠

In September 1922, just before Greene returned from Europe, Doyle was short staffed and wrote Rudolph Weaver, the Professor of Architecture at Washington State University in Pullman, Washington, for recommendations. Weaver replied with a name that would be important to the Doyle office over the next few years and to Portland architecture for two generations. Donald J. Stewart had worked for Weaver for three years; he was planning to keep him in his office because "he is a very promising man" who "will become a good designer. He also promises to have ability in water color rendering and everything that he touches has elements of beauty in it." Weaver was "glad to let him go in order to get him into an office where he will receive as much encouragement and opportunity as I know he would in yours."[32] Stewart was twenty-seven years old, a veteran, and unmarried. He had originally planned on a career as an illustrator, but, he wrote, "Due to the need of financial aid at home and two years of army service, I determined to study architecture as a surer means of earning. Since I have learned something of the profession I am not sorry of the

Doyle planned a twenty-one story office tower for the U. S. National Bank. It was not built because it would have diminished the bank's lobby. (OHS 62501)

choice I made and am intensely interested especially in design, rendering and lettering." He explained that, while a student, he had worked summers in Weaver's office, where he did "some rendering, full sizing, detailing and a little clay modeling." He hoped eventually to study at Columbia and to travel in Europe. He expected to find his career as a renderer.[33]

Doyle was working on an extension to the Pittock Block to raise the two stories on Stark to eight stories, the height of the Washington Street side. The additional 120,000 square feet made the Pittock Block Portland's largest office building at the time. He had several other important projects. The Corbett estate wanted a fifteen-story office block. The U.S. National Bank had grown into Portland's most important bank by acquiring several smaller Portland banks, most recently the venerable Portland house, Ladd & Tilton. It wanted to double the lobby on the ground floor and to build a twenty-one floor tower above it, to make it Portland's tallest. Reed was growing again with needs for a library and housing for students and faculty.

These were major projects, but they were scaled back. Portland was on the move but with less enthusiasm than two decades before. The Corbetts decided on ten stories rather than fifteen; the Pacific Building was the result. The U.S. National Bank demolished the Elks Building on the corner of SW Stark and Broadway to double Doyle's original temple bank and the lobby but decided against a tower because "the steel bracing necessary for a tower of that character would have used up much of the space otherwise available for lobby purposes."[34] Reed showed restraint. Not only was the library delayed, but the new buildings were wood frame with shingle or stucco not the reinforced-concrete, brick-faced, college Gothic of Doyle's original plan. Reed's endowment was in Portland real estate; its value had shrunk in the recession that began in 1914. Doyle's campus plan of 1911 and 1912 had expressed the optimism in the boom years when Portland expected to vie with San Francisco. By 1920 Portland had been overtaken by Seattle and Los Angeles. It was becoming the fourth city of the West Coast, and falling increasingly farther behind. Reed reflected Portland's reduced optimism. Doyle's additions in the early 1920s were charming enhancements to the original English spirit of the campus, without the grandeur. The faculty houses were simple English, shingled cottages. They have long since been turned to other uses like offices and language instruction. Anna Mann was a seventeenth-century country house with a bright, large living

Doyle's faculty houses are still at the east end of the Reed campus. These shingle-clad, English cottages provide offices and language houses. (RC)

The Reed Commons is today the Student Union. Its shingled exterior has been replaced with brick. It has also lost its rolled eaves which simulated thatch. (RC)

The Anna Mann Cottage was a Reed College women's dormitory. (RC)

The Butler Bank is at the corner of 3rd and Oak in Hood River, Oregon (301 Oak Avenue). (Author's photograph)

room, dining room, and enclosed porch. The Commons, now the Student Union, was an English great hall with exposed, rough-hewn trusses and with minstrel galleries at either end.

Doyle feared mediocrity. His work load was "the usual run of smaller buildings and residences" but he expected "a pretty busy office."[35] He had contracts for designing a number of banks for prosperous small Oregon and Washington towns like Hood River, Pendleton, Tillamook, Oregon City, and La Grande, of which the Butler Bank in Hood River was probably the most significant. Completed in 1924, it was small, a 40-by 94-foot one-story with mezzanine reinforced-concrete structure with a flat roof and sandstone facing. Construction costs were seventy-five thousand dollars, (one hundred thousand including expenditures on the furnishing and the lot), not a large job, but it was Doyle's only, and one of Oregon's few, buildings in the Egyptian style. Various motifs thought to represent ancient Egypt became popular especially for "mortuaries, movie houses, lodge halls, apartments, and commercial buildings" after 1922 and the discovery of Tutankhamen's tomb.[36]

For the rest of his life, Doyle would plan for the Reed library, a free-standing masonry building to complement the original dormitory and arts buildings. It was an important addition to the campus, which until then had used as its library the western end of the first floor of the Arts Building (now Eliot Hall). There was a need for a much larger collection than the present holdings of about fifteen thousand volumes and two hundred periodicals. Planning for the library was far enough along in January 1922 for an announcement in *The Oregonian*. The new building would have alcoves for classroom use as well as shelving for "duplicate copies of collateral readings which displace text books in the Reed curriculum." Doyle explained the plans to a librarian at the Los Angeles Public Library whom he wrote, among others, for advice about "what is needed in library, seminars, study rooms, quiet alcoves, in addition to two reading rooms and reference libraries." There was little nearby to guide him. "I don't like the University of California or University of Washington libraries. I don't think they help us much to solve our problem, and they are much larger schools than Reed will ever be, although we hope Reed will become famous for its research library."[37]

But the Reed Library was not built until after Doyle's death. It was designed by Pietro Belluschi and was scaled back from what Doyle was considering because of financial constraints in the early 1930s.

In December 1922, Doyle finally sounded confident: "My office is taking on something of the old time busy appearance of a few years ago, and next year will be a fine year, with a much better class of work than we have been getting."[38] By April 1923, when a Los Angeles architect wrote him about finding a couple of good draftsmen, Doyle bragged: "If I knew of a good draftsman or two I would nail [th]em myself. Things are pretty busy here now."[39]

A month later, there was an ominous development. He was planning a trip to Seattle to consult with C. A. Merriam, when he canceled suddenly because he had a tonsillectomy. He complained he was "rather miserable the past week, cross as a bear with a sore foot." As was his practice, he repressed his complaint with usual good humor: "Am decidedly on the mend, though, and expect to feel fine in a short time."[40] He would not know for some time how grave his future was. His throat may have provided the first signs of the disease which would kill him. Nephritis can begin with strep throat, and Doyle recalled when he was near death in 1927 that he had been sick for four years.

He increasingly delegated. Charles Greene, back from study in Europe, assumed more responsibility. Greene's income reflected his increased responsibilities. In 1920, his last full year of employment, he was paid $2,783. In 1923, his first full year after his European tour, his income jumped to $3,773. In 1924 it was $4,100 and in 1925 it was $5,900, which was more than double what Doyle had offered an experienced architect in his office. By 1926 Greene had been promoted from a draughtsman to an "architectural designer."[41]

⋄⋄⋄

The Bank of California had decided sometime during the war to move its branch office from the Chamber of Commerce Building at SW 3rd and Stark to SW 6th and Stark, directly across the street from the U.S. National Bank. Doyle first learned of the plan in 1918 when the Bank of California acquired the quarter block on the northeast corner of SW 6th and Stark and wrote the U.S. National Bank for information about building costs. The letter was referred to Doyle, who briefly answered their question and then explained his interest and his experience, but it was four years before planning began. The choice was between him and Sutton & Whitney. He was worried and determined: "I am very anxious to do the job as it is on Stark Street opposite the U.S. National," he wrote a San Francisco friend he thought might have some influence. "Sutton & Whitney's work has run mostly to garages and industrial work, and nobody does this class of work any better, but their ideas of a high class job and mine are a long way apart. [He describes a recent job by Sutton & Whitney] There is no evidence of an artist anywhere." He did not know how else to get his message across. "I can't tell the bank people all of this for I don't want to get business by knocking the other fellow and I like Sutton and Whitney personally, but they shouldn't do bank work. Whitney is a good engineer and likes to do big industrial plants, and he does them well."[42]

The Bank of California (330 SW 6th Avenue) was the first of Doyle's office buildings in the Renaissance Palace style. (OHS 53623)

Flowers festooned the lobby of the Bank of California on opening day, July 20, 1925. Doyle attended the dedication. (OHS 63173)

Doyle got the job; work began May 1924 and ended a year later. He cut short his vacation at the beach to attend the dedication, July 20, 1925. He fussed over the details: "I went into the bank to see that the janitor had cleaned the windows and floors so the room would look its best." He admitted, "These openings are always so embarrassing. The architect doesn't like to hear the kicks in the presence of the flowers and mobs of people."[43] *The Oregonian* said the bank is "a highly modern new building."[44] Doyle would not say it was modern. He admitted to Athol McBean, who provided the terra-cotta, that a modernist would not "get much of a kick out of it." But he was proud of it. He relaxed somewhat his usual modesty. He sent a photograph and wrote that it was "a good job of terra cotta. It is also a pretty good building—for a little one it has scale."[45]

"Modern" was used in two ways. Doyle was talking about architecture. *The Oregonian* meant the banking facility was up to date. There was a commodious lobby on the ground floor for the tellers' windows and the desks for officers. Above were a mezzanine and two floors for the offices of the bank. Vaults were in the basement.[46] The outside of the building was traditional, perhaps even historical. It was a subdued Florentine Renaissance Palace. Arched windows 24 feet high and 12 feet wide peered out at the street and bathed the interior in light. Tiles covered the hipped roof and terra-cotta the exterior walls. But much of it was only in appearance historical. The terra-cotta for the walls was cast

Doyle's English Cottage for Cora Wheeler is at 1841 SW Montgomery. (Author's photograph)

to resemble rusticated stone. Inside walls were covered with an "integrally colored plaster, formed to look like travertine marble." Only the floors and tellers' counters were of "genuine marble."[47] Doyle considered it one of his best buildings. It had simplicity, without "a frill"; art "should not be complex."[48]

In 1918 Mr. and Mrs. Coleman H. Wheeler bought a house from the Dekum family at the crest of the southwest hills with commanding views of Portland. They lived there and thought about what they would build in place of it until Coleman died in 1920. Like Doyle's clients Simon Benson and Frank J. Cobbs, Coleman Wheeler was a successful and self-made timber baron. He owned extensive forests in western Washington and Tillamook counties. Wheeler, Oregon, which housed the railway station near Neahkahnie, was a company town with the family name. After he died his wife, Cora Bryant Wheeler, who was from a lumbering family with interests in Clatskanie, Oregon, continued to direct the firm and to plan for the construction of their home. Doyle had completed plans sufficiently in early December 1922 to send her his estimates.[49] The house (still at 1961 SW Montgomery Drive) was completed in 1923. While it is said to be in English Cottage style, it has 7,427 square feet of living space. The English style is enhanced by an ersatz thatch roof, which was achieved by bending shingles on the eaves and ridges of the hipped roof. The sides are covered in a variety of materials—shingles, half-timbering, with some brick and stucco to give the appearance of aged masonry, stucco, and timber.

In these years, Doyle worked for a number of self-made millionaires who wanted large houses in traditional styles with spectacular views in beautifully landscaped gardens to approximate the villas and manor houses of European aristocrats and to give the impression of ancient craftsmanship and centuries of aging with modern materials. In 1915 he began planning a retirement house for J. G. Edwards; it was built a decade later on a commanding one-acre site in the Portland Heights (still at 2645 SW Alta Vista Place). Edwards was a Welsh immigrant who settled in Montana in 1872. He raised cattle and horses in Montana and Wyoming until 1898 when he bought a ranch near Madras, Oregon, where he bred sheep. Doyle admired Edwards; he told T. L. Eliot that he "is the most remarkable man I know." In Montana he was a rancher when there was "no law or government." While "he associated with the roughest type of men for many years, yet he has remained the highest type of cultured English gentleman who is received and enjoyed everywhere and has traveled everywhere."[50] The house is in Norman Farmhouse style, two and one-half stories high, with steeply pitched gables. Hollow tile walls "are covered with stucco distressed in a pattern simulating aged medieval walls." There are banks of multi-paned casement windows. The house is entered through a vestibule to a large central hall (20 by 30 feet) with a fireplace and staircase leading to the hall on the second floor nearly as large (20 by 26 feet). Around the hall downstairs there are a study, a guest bathroom and coatroom, a very large living room, and a dining room, behind which are a butler's pantry, a kitchen with a servants' dining alcove, and a servants' hall. On the second floor there are two bathrooms, two bedrooms, and a large sitting room on the southeast corner, "which commands views of Portland and mountains to the north." Servants' bedrooms are also on the second floor but in another section of the house reached by separate stairs from the service wing.[51]

Nearby at 2040 SW Laurel Street, he did an English Cottage for the retirement of Bert Ball, whose fortune was from wartime shipbuilding. He came from Pennsylvania to Portland as a young mechanical engineer to buy with others the Willamette Iron Works, which then provided steam-powered logging equipment. Under new management it constructed railroad locomotives until it built

The Bert Ball house at 2040 SW Laurel St. (Author's photograph)

ships for World War I. He retired in 1922 as president of what had become the Willamette Iron and Steel Works. The house, according to George McMath, is Doyle's best English Cottage. It is spacious with an exterior of rough cast stucco; the roof is shingled with rolled eaves. The garden is particularly attractive; it enfolds the house. On the ground floor there are a large central hall with a staircase and living room, dining room, and library. Beyond the dining room is the service wing with butler's pantry, kitchen, and breakfast room. On the second floor around a spacious hall are three bedrooms, two sitting rooms, and four bathrooms. There is a ballroom on the third floor.[52]

In 1925 Aaron Holtz returned to Portland after a decade of working in the East. He had been active in the development of the department stores in Portland when he had worked with Doyle on the Meier & Frank Annex, on the Olds, Wortman, & King building, and finally on his own, the Holtz Department Store (now the Mead Building), which he closed in 1914 after two years when the Portland economy began to sour. Holtz then went to Cleveland to become the merchandizing head of the May Department Stores. He was never happy there, and he returned for visits. In 1925 he came back to Portland as president of Lipman Wolfe & Co. after it had been purchased by National Department Stores.[53] Doyle designed a Jacobethan mansion for Holtz on King's Hill near the entrance to Washington Park (still at 2370 SW Park Place). The site is as impressive as the house, which is of stone, brick, and slate with bay windows and parapets.[54]

⋘

In March 1923, Doyle heard from Portland's most successful war profiteer. Joseph R. Bowles was traveling in Europe when he wrote from Florence about doing a house in "Italian and near Italian style." It was to be a major house with sleeping rooms and "combination dining and sitting room" for four servant girls because "they are entitled to consideration" and because "a better class of help can be held by such accommodations." Bowles wanted "four or five off-hand sketches" ready upon his return April 30, 1923. One sketch was to include "an inside court or patio design with removable glass covering."[55] This was no minor job. When finished, the Bowles' house was 4559 square feet and cost $250,000.[56] It was "a prize commission" and the finished and well-preserved house is "A. E. Doyle at his best and a great architectural jewel for the city of Portland."[57]

Joseph Bowles was born in Portland in 1869. After school he began as a shipping clerk working on the Willamette. He scrimped, studied, and eventually went to work for the Northwest Bridge Company. In 1914 he formed from it the Northwest Steel Company, which in 1916 began building steel ships, even before America entered the war. He was skillful in contracting with the U.S. government; "he obtained the most favorable steel contract ever granted to a war era ship builder." He continued with the company until 1923, when he retired and his interest turned to the house he had Doyle plan and build for him. Bowles was widely mistrusted. He was indicted "for bribing a government official and convicted of contempt of court" and was considered "a greedy, domineering and difficult person, with no sense of civic responsibility."[58]

The job was with the firm for more than four years until the end of 1927, principally because, according to those who worked on it, Bowles managed every detail. He was prickly. Doyle and J. R. Bowles were both members of the Arlington Club. When Bowles wrote Doyle from Florence about his house, he addressed Doyle as "Bert," as friends did. Yet as his staff became increasingly exasperated because Bowles intervened at every stage, Doyle admitted he had misgivings: "I am just as sorry as I can be about it all and I take all the blame, for I thought I could handle him."[59] Bowles hired plasterers to replace the ones hired by Doyle, who was furious: "I had a very beautiful lineup for his furnishing, but he would hardly look at it. If we work out something fine, he jumps on us for it. So it is pretty difficult to get anything any better than he can understand."[60] Bowles questioned Doyle's choice of Francis Bacon to supply furniture. Doyle wrote Bacon about the problem: "Mr. Bowles is a changeable cuss, and I have had quite a time with him about many things. Your scheme was so fine I don't see how he can help seeing it."[61] Bowles considered different colored tiles for the outdoor pool and delayed the tiler. He studied a sample of linoleum for the basement. Dave Jack scarcely repressed sarcasm when he described the result: "He [Bowles] has a piece of this linoleum now at the house experimenting with same before allowing them to lay it."[62] For the hardwood floors, the workmen complained, "Mr. Bowles practically passes on every stick."[63] To finish the floors, they tried several varnishes, "none of which have been entirely approved by Mr. Bowles as yet."[64] The problems and disagreements were widely known. Abe Meier bribed one of the watchmen with a box of cigars and toured the house with a group of friends. Bowles was furious. He conducted an "investigation" to find and fire the "guilty" watchman. The story got around "much to Mr. Bowles' annoyance."[65]

By 1924 the city was on the move to replace the Second Empire mansions of Portland's pioneer merchants, the Corbetts, the Failings, and the Ladds, where their widows and daughters continued to reside in the middle of the burgeoning business center of Portland. In 1924 the Failing house was razed from the block between SW 5th and 6th and Taylor and Salmon. The Ladd mansion went in 1926 for a hotel, which was never built; Belluschi's Oregonian Building occupies the site today.[66] The Ladd's Jacobethan-styled stables still stand on Broadway cater-corner from the Oregonian Building. Its original function survives in its name, the Carriage House, which has been reconfigured as a three-story assemblage of shops and offices. As I write, it has been removed while an underground garage is built. It is to return to its original position when a modern high rise is completed next to it.

The Corbett mansion endured longest. Henry W. Corbett died in 1903, but his younger widow outlived him for thirty-three years in her mansion surrounded by a garden and a cow pasture. This was valuable land; *Collier's Weekly* in 1917 saw an irony in the city-center pasture: "the family cow on a sixty thousand dollar plot on the family premises is in total disregard of the accepted fitness of things in this bustling and money seizing age of ours."[67]

Mrs. Corbett's step-grandsons wanted to develop it, to move her out, and to partition the block. They began in 1922 by planning a tall office block on the north lawn, the north half block on Yamhill between SW 5th and 6th. At first they intended a fifteen-story, brick and terra-cotta structure with a base of classical columns, plain walls with paired double-hung windows and a modest cornice, "similar to the earlier Pittock Block." When the Pacific Building was completed in 1926, it was very different and very much like the Bank of California. It was ten stories plus an attic. "The final design achieved the correct proportions and the overall size is slightly larger than a typical Italian Renaissance Palace."[68]

To simulate the Renaissance Palace, Doyle used, as on the Bank of California, terra-cotta imitating rusticated stone at the base. At the top there was a red-tiled hip-roof with shed dormer above an elaborate six-foot classical cornice, also like the Bank of California. Between the cornice and the rusticate base, stories four through ten are covered on the exterior with a grey/beige brick and lit with simple unarticulated steel casement windows, which tend to de-emphasize the necessary definition of the office building into floors, so that its overall appearance approximates a Renaissance Palace's three floors.

The Corbett grandsons had Doyle include an apartment in the attic for Mrs. Corbett so that she would vacate the Corbett mansion and allow the south half of the block to be developed. He topped the building with an "E"-shaped hip roof. The stem of the "E" ran along Yamhill, while the three prongs extended south. The eastern prong was Mrs. Corbett's apartment. It had a loggia on the west

In 1914 the city surrounded the nineteenth-century Failing and Corbett houses on SW 5th. On the left of the photograph is the Failings' house. North of it across SW Taylor is the Corbetts' house. Beyond are the Post Office (now Pioneer Courthouse) and, to the left or west of it, the Portland Hotel. Five of Doyle's buildings can be seen: the Northwestern National Bank Building is across the street from the Portland Hotel. The Selling Building is next door to and nearly hidden by the Northwestern Bank Building. The Meier & Frank Annex is to the right across SW 6th from the Selling Building. Notice it towers over the main store by

and to the south. The middle prong was for the elevator shaft. The western prong Doyle finished for his firm's office. Between the Doyle complex and Mrs. Corbett's apartment and around the elevator shaft there was a tiled roof garden. Under the roof of the stem of the "E" between Mrs. Corbett's apartment and Doyle's office there were a series of studios occupied by musicians and artists.[69] Mrs. Corbett refused the apartment. She retained her mansion with the Pacific Building towering above it. The area was freed up and in the final plans Doyle divided it up into more studios.

Whidden & Lewis, which Doyle would replace in 1915. Lipman Wolfe first and then the Holtz Department Store are behind Meier & Frank. (OHS 13231-B)

⇜

In his early years Doyle did classical, New York-inspired buildings. In the 1920s he built in the Renaissance Palace style. According to Felicity Musick, in an unpublished yet influential paper, Charles Greene was responsible for this change. She said he had learned to love the Renaissance on his European tour, which emphasized Greece and Rome at Doyle's suggestion.[70] Ever since credit for these later buildings has been given to Greene.[71] Certainly Greene had increasing responsibilities as Doyle was busy, absent, and ill. Yet Doyle never, even on his death bed, relinquished direction. The Italian Palace was associated with the origins of European urbanism and the growth of the first cities in Italy. Looking to the Renaissance and to Italy for urban architecture was as natural to him as finding in Oxford the model for Reed College.

Mrs. Corbett's house and carriage house were dwarfed by the Pacific Building that had been built on her north lawn. This photograph was taken from SW 6th sometime between 1926 and 1936. (OHS 87075)

The Pacific Building (520 SW Yamhill) in an early photograph. (OHS 59377)

Doyle's third Renaissance Palace, the Public Service Building (still at 920 SW 6th) replaced the Henry Failing estate, which was razed in 1924. Doyle's design has been modified significantly in the years since he built it. He had two wings of two stories extending 50 feet from the sixteen-story central mass. In 1948 three stories were added to the wings and in 1958 they achieved their present height of twelve stories. The central tower has lost some of its emphasis. The building faces SW 6th Avenue. There are two stories of terra-cotta dyed and fired to resemble rusticated stone on a granite base as on the Bank of California and the Pacific Building. Each 50-foot wing has a central arched window between a pair of balanced rectangular windows. The central façade at the base of the tower has five matching arched openings with rusticated terra-cotta voissours. The building's entry is in the center opening; the others are for windows. The attic level of the tower has nine Corinthian columns on each side to approximate a loggia. Originally the roofs were red tile.

The building opened in January 1928 as Portland's tallest building, which it was until 1958. It was a dramatic statement of the public utilities headquartered in it. Large neon signs at the top, visible throughout the city, displayed four words, one in each direction: GAS, POWER, HEAT, and LIGHT. Eighty-five percent of the building was used by the three utilities responsible for it:

This early photograph of the Public Service Building (920 SW 6th Avenue) shows the building with the original two-story wings. (OHS 52607)

Northwestern Electric, Portland Gas and Coke, and Pacific Power and Light. On the ground floor were display rooms for gas and electric appliances.

Even two parking garages affirmed Doyle's preference for the Renaissance. The Public Service Garage (now the Metropolitan Garage) shared the Failing estate block with the Public Service Building and faced SW 5th between Taylor and Salmon. It was built by the contractor for the two buildings, L. Hawley Hoffman and Company, which exists today as Hoffman Construction. Initially Hoffman built houses, but the Public Service Building and Garage catapulted him into prominence. Because he developed the garage, it was sometimes called the Hoffman Garage rather than the more common Public Service Garage.[72] The garage had six stories with space for about six hundred cars.

The garage was completed first. The ground breaking was July 10, 1926, and the garage was ready December 1. The Public Service Building began in January of 1927. The steel frame was completed in April, the exterior in October, and the interior in December. The two buildings resembled each other. There were shops along SW 5th and Salmon. The storefronts had plate glass windows with transom lights. The base was marble, with a veneer terra-cotta to look like rusticated stone on the first and second levels and beige grey brick above matching the brick on the Public Service Building. The six-story garage gave definition to 5th Avenue and emphasized the height of the skyscraper behind it. In 1962 Skidmore, Owings & Merrill removed the terra-cotta and windows and applied a concrete coat "to give the building a more streamlined look."[73]

The Corbett Brothers' Garage on SW Pine between SW 6th and Broadway survives today as the Broadway Garage. While the building has been altered somewhat, Doyle's original design is still evident. The basic warehouse structure of five stories with windows on the exterior has at its base a series of two-story shop fronts with large windows, a transom above and a stone surround with pilasters and Corinthian capitals. At the top of the building a cornice gives an impression of a Florentine Palace.[74] This was Portland's first self-service ramp garage. The first story provides ramp access to four floors above, and two below ground. Each floor accommodates eighty cars for a total of about four hundred eighty. There is a glass-enclosed staircase and an elevator to bring drivers, when they have parked their cars, to the street.

Even Doyle's one large movie theater, The Broadway, which he completed in 1926, was Italian, and Multnomah Stadium (PGE Park), which Doyle did for the Multnomah Athletic Club in 1926-1927, has a historical reference for a modern function. It recalls Roman amphitheaters, which, like the Coliseum in Rome, rise up in the midst of some southern European cities. It was built from the proceeds of a popular fund drive, chaired by some of Portland's most influential citizens. Doyle's schools, too, in this period carried the Mediterranean imprint, like the Glencoe School (825 SE 51st Avenue, built in 1924) and Nehalem Union High School (Nehalem, Oregon, built in 1925).

The one exception to the historical emphasis of Doyle's buildings in the 1920s was the Terminal Sales Building (1220 SW Morrison), one of Portland's few examples of Art Deco, a style that was more popular in other cities in the 1920s. The building was nine stories on the northeast corner of the block and a thirteen-

The Broadway Theater (now gone) was at SW Broadway and Salmon, where the 1000 Broadway Building is today. (OHS 72065)

story tower to the west. The exterior was concrete with piers from the base to the roof. Terra-cotta was used at the entry. Between the piers, there were vertical, multi-light windows and spandrel panels. "Surface articulation depends largely on the play of light and shadow over the reveals and a gathering of stylized ornament at the parapets." It was completed in 1926, the year before the Public Service Building, and was then Portland's tallest building and largest office block. It was for wholesalers. Buyers from the Pacific Northwest would came to view merchandise and hence to "advance the city's position as a commercial center." The building was designed for Stephen Hull, a Seattle merchant, but it belonged to the Stephen Mead estate, which was earlier responsible for the Holtz Department Store building. Frederick and Robert Strong, Doyle's close friends, were managers of the Mead Estate.[75]

In the early period of his career, between 1907 and 1915, Doyle's commercial buildings were along the main streetcar lines of the central city, except for the Benson Hotel, which was at SW Broadway and Oak, two blocks from the Washington Street car. After 1922, his commercial buildings were removed from the main streetcars. Admittedly some were not far removed, like the Bank of California at SW 6th and Stark, just a block from the Washington line, or the Pacific Building on Yamhill, a block from Morrison but on the Fifth-Avenue streetcar. Yet an early advertisement for the Pacific Building described the distance as detachment, even seclusion: "No street car lines operate either on Yamhill or 6th Streets, which insures the tenant freedom from the incessant ringing of bells and roar of traffic."[76] The other buildings by Doyle in the middle 1920s were farther from the central core.

His 1920s jobs, except for the Bank of California, catered to the automobile. In addition to the Public Service Garage and the Corbett Brothers' Garage, Doyle designed basement parking for the Pacific Building, the Terminal Sales Building, and the Public Service Building. There was even a gas station adjacent to the Terminal Sales Building.

There was a rapid increase in car ownership during this period, although Oregon had been slower than some states because, some advocates of good roads said, the state neglected grading, graveling, and oiling roads. In 1905 when registration of cars was first required, 218 were registered. For the next six years registration was for the life of the car, and only new cars needed to be registered. There were 142 in 1906. In each year thereafter the number doubled most years until 1911 when all cars were registered annually, and there were 6383 registrations. Of these about 2700 were in Portland. By 1914 the number for the state was

The Terminal Sales Building (1220 SW Morrison) was and is one of Portland's few examples of Art Deco architecture downtown. (OHS 62547)

16,347. Five years later, with the war intervening, it was 83,500, about one car for ten persons in Oregon. By the early 1920s about seventy-five car dealerships created new commercial districts in Portland along West and East Burnside and Sandy.[77] There was a movement to encourage tourists with improved roads and tourist attractions like Multnomah Falls, which Simon Benson gave to Portland and helped to develop. In 1925 Doyle did the lodge (still there) to resemble an English country house of split field stone, with shingle roofs, and wood windows and doors painted grey. Inside are public rooms, a restaurant, and rest rooms.[78]

Automobiles changed Portland. In 1921 there were 13,161 automobile accidents in the city; 1410 people were injured and 31 died. In December 1922 in Portland on average one person was killed in an automobile accident every four days.[79] In 1917 the Portland Railway Light and Power Company, the city's streetcar monopoly, advertised the system's safety. Over the preceding decade the system had carried "810,363,205 persons on its cars without the loss of the life of a single passenger."[80] Streets were relatively safe in the streetcar era. Old photographs of Portland as of other cities show the jumbled intermingling of pedestrians with traffic before the automobile dominated. There was a lack of concern about the proximity of people, streetcars, horses, and carriages. Streets were plazas, large areas for public intercourse, conversation, and sightseeing.[81]

The plaza was an ideal in a book on urban planning that Doyle bought as he was working on the Bank of California. Buildings should "frame" the street, which is not just "an area of land around which casual buildings may be dotted." An artist wants more than "a disagreeable hodgepodge of contradictory assertions" that may result when individual architects work for independent clients with various tastes and institutional purposes. European plazas were the model of American street architecture. Colonnades and arcades on the ground story provide "a motive strong enough to tie the different buildings together without depriving them of the possibility of individual development in the upper stories." They also opened the buildings to the plaza outside.[82] Doyle often admired European plazas during his 1906 European tour.

When Doyle pursued the Bank of California job, he was concerned about how it would relate to his U.S. National Bank; their proximity was his reason, he said, for wanting to do them both. He did not design a matching building; the Roman Temple style of the U.S. National was at least a thousand years older

Doyle did the Multnomah Falls Lodge for the city of Portland in 1925 when the Columbia River Highway was developed. (PCA A2004-002.2505)

than the Renaissance Palace style of the Bank of California. The two banks wanted architectural statements to reinforce their independence and integrity. His U.S. National Bank is next to Portland's earliest skyscraper, the Wells Fargo Building of 1907 (still at 309 SW 6th). He set his bank back so that the columns of the U. S. National Bank were set off by the blank wall of the Wells Fargo Building. There was also a correspondence between his two new banks and the older building. While their designs are very different, the arched windows of the Wells Fargo and the Bank of California are like arcades adjoining and facing the colonnade of the U.S. National Bank. The three buildings have similar cornice lines and frame the street. When Pietro Belluschi designed his Equitable Building on the southwest corner of SW 6th and Stark, he gave new meaning to SW 6th. The Equitable (now the Commonwealth) Building was innovative because it was hermetically sealed and had an aluminum and glass curtain wall. It towers over Doyle's two banks, and its detailing, color, and texture are very different from the terra-cotta Doyle used. Across the street from the Equitable, on the southeast corner of 6th and Stark, the Farwest Building (now the 400 Building, at 400 SW 6th) by Skidmore, Owings & Merrill was designed to compliment the Equitable Building. The two are almost the same height and their aluminum and glass walls define "an architectural space within Sixth Avenue."[83]

CHAPTER 7

To Avoid as Much Worry as Possible

In April 1925, Pietro Belluschi came to Portland looking for a job. He had much to offer. He had studied engineering in Rome before coming to Cornell on a fellowship as a graduate student in engineering and architecture. When he finished his M.S., he wanted to stay in America. The only work he could find was as an electrician's assistant in a mine in Kellogg, Idaho. After six months he was determined to try architecture. He talked to some Spokane architects who were friends of his employer. They recommended Doyle and wrote a letter of introduction. Doyle was busy and needed help. He had almost all the big projects downtown. The Bank of California and the U. S. National Bank were nearly done. The houses for Aaron Holtz and J. R. Bowles were well under way. The Pacific Building and the Bedell Building (now the Cascade Building, 520 SW 6th Avenue, on which Doyle was the local, supervising architect) were beginning. The Terminal Sales Building, the Multnomah Stadium, the Broadway Theater, and the Public Service Building were likely prospects, and he was working on a campus plan for Linfield College in McMinville, Oregon, and several important renovations: Oregon Life Insurance (now Standard Insurance), the Sellwood Bank, Cloud Cap Inn, and Meier & Frank. Sixty years later, when Belluschi recalled that meeting, which launched him into architecture and one of America's great architectural careers of the twentieth century, he had just one clear memory of the man who hired him and started him in architecture: A. E. Doyle was sick.[1]

It is difficult to know if Doyle (or anyone else for that matter) knew he was very ill with Bright's Disease. Probably by April 1925, Doyle's prominent Portland physician, Dr. Allen Welch Smith, who was a fellow member of the Arlington Club, had made the diagnosis. Bright's Disease, which is a general name, now disused, for acute or chronic kidney disease, was identified a century before; many people died of it. If Doyle knew in April what ailed him, he did not, to my knowledge, say so. As one comes to expect with A. E. Doyle, he said little about his health. He was too self effacing to talk about himself, too optimistic to think very long about illness, and too guarded about his professional standing to mention debility. But by the fall of 1925, he was so sick that he needed to concentrate on his illness. Dr. Smith insisted on "complete rest and relaxation," which would have been difficult for Doyle at any time because he was energetic and driven, but in 1925 that therapy was especially unwelcome. Dr. Smith and Doyle apparently came to an agreement; Dave Jack spoke of it as "a bargain." Doyle would remove himself from the business for his "health and to avoid as much worry as possible."[2] Probably a European tour was not ideally what Dr. Smith wanted, but likely he agreed to it because Doyle could never abide real rest in Portland and anything less than another trip to Europe would not attract him away from the office. For nearly twenty years Doyle had toiled in Portland. He had traveled frequently to the East and to California in preparation for some of his important projects—for example, to see modern department stores and libraries—but he had not returned to Europe since his student days, and for an architect with his predilections, Europe had the important models, and there he would be removed from Portland and worry.

There was much to trouble him. He was about to move his business from the dour, old Worcester Block to the new and fashionable Pacific Building. His suite on the tenth floor had a public reception room and a business office and a private stairway to the attic, where the main work was done in a drafting room, 35 feet by 48 feet, large and barn-like, with nineteen drafting tables. Its floors and sloping attic roof were unadorned concrete. At the

The drafting room of the Doyle office from about 1927—probably after April because Charles Greene is not included. Doyle is not either, but he was seldom in the office after 1926. Left to right are Frank Rohr, Frank Hutchinson, Sid Lister, W. H. Crowell, Stanley Gould, Mason Roberts, Bruce Kinne, Pietro Belluschi, Bob Turner. (RC)

southeast corner of the drafting room, across the landing that brought the staircase up from the floor below, was the library, an elegant room, 18 feet by 28 feet. Three windows looked east and one faced south to "one of the grandest views of the city." On either side of the south window were bookcases above "paneled storage cabinets below the sill line." On the north wall were shelves for oversized books. On the west was a fireplace "with a wood surround and marble hearth." A floor of red quarry tile had an oriental rug. All woodwork was walnut; walls were plain plaster; and the ceiling was beamed. There were prints on the walls and statuary on the bookcases.[3]

His new office was a statement about the status he had achieved. As in other aspects of his career, he modeled himself on Henry Bacon. He wrote Francis Bacon, Henry Bacon's brother and a manufacturer of fine furniture reproductions, about how the new office would be furnished: "Something quite plain, a good size table with not too heavy chairs, something the character of the furniture Henry Bacon had in his office."[4]

In 1925 and 1926 Doyle could afford the new office and he needed the space. He was busier with more important projects than at any time in his career except perhaps in 1912 and 1913. He could assume the role of the successful professional. He was a member of the Arlington Club; he and Lucie belonged to Waverly Country Club. These were conferred memberships. Neither accepted applications; prospective members awaited invitations. Lucie had her own car. She played golf frequently and lunched at Waverly. In the 1920s her bills and caddy cards were sent to Doyle's office, where they were paid and filed with his personal papers.

In the firm's library atop the Pacific Building clients discussed projects and perused the books, pictures, and plans. (RC)

Looking back on his career, the prosperity of 1925 and 1926 was more the exception than the rule. He had a very prosperous beginning in 1907 through 1913 when important downtown jobs so often fell to him. Then there was nearly a decade with only one downtown job, the first half of the U. S. National Bank. In 1922 things started looking up, but jobs were not plentiful until 1925. When William Whidden and Ion Lewis were his age in 1907, their practice had diminished measurably. Eight years later they did their last building. There was reason for concern. Doyle confided to Dave, "Expenses are on a big scale in our new office, and we can lose fast if we don't replace the finished jobs with some new ones."[5]

Doyle seems less affable at this time and sometimes easily annoyed. There were tensions, of course, with Bowles, who was dominating, volatile, rich, and powerful. Doyle cautioned his staff: "Whatever happens we cannot afford to quarrel with him."[6] But Bowles was not Doyle's only problem. Frank Ransom, for whom Doyle did a Colonial in 1922 that still clings to the crest of the hill at 2885 NW Shenandoah Terrace, was dissatisfied. When after several bills and three years he had not paid, Doyle complained, "I think you have a bully good house—so do a lot of other people. There are always some things we are sorry for and that might have been different—no more of them on your house, though, than the average."[7]

In December 1924, Doyle had something else to worry about. Some on the Women's Union board were so unhappy with Doyle that Ellis Lawrence got the job of enlarging the Martha Washington Home for Girls. Doyle had already surveyed the adjoining lot and made some plans to complete his original building. He sent no bill because his costs would be part of the final bill when the building was completed. He was taken aback to learn he had been replaced. Ellis Lawrence broke the news:

> *The Building Committee of the Martha Washington Home for Girls has consulted us in regard to the design and construction of a new wing. Our understanding of the situation is that you have no claim of any kind for services connected with the new project. I am writing this to give you the information so you may protect yourself in case we have misunderstood the situation.*[8]

Doyle replied to Lawrence with a copy to the board of the Women's Union: "Apparently the present board does not wish me to do the work, for I have not been consulted since the property was purchased. I am sending a bill to them for my services, for I think the board should feel some responsibility toward me; but I do not wish this in any way to interfere with your progressing with your work."[9] At the next meeting of the board, the secretary was directed to write Doyle and thank him for his services. He said nothing about the bill. Doyle would not let it drop. He replied: "[The bill] represents only the money I spent in your interest, and it should be paid."[10] He was sarcastic to Ellis Lawrence: "It looks to me like a polite refusal to pay the small bill I sent to them. I am very much surprised."[11]

These problems with the Women's Union, Bowles, and Ransom were in 1924 and 1925, yet in 1926 none of them figured on a list of unhappy clients. The owners of the Cloud Cap Inn on Mount Hood decided suddenly to delay indefinitely rebuilding the inn. Doyle suspected the contractors, Walter and Max Lorenz, had spoiled the deal because, when jobs they did were completed, clients were dissatisfied, Doyle said, like "for instance," and he listed five names: "Beebe, Banks, Biddle, Olmstead, Fields."[12] L. R. Banks built a house in Oak Grove (it has not been located). Spencer Biddle did a house still at 356 Kingston Ave. in 1923. L. R. Fields did a Ranch House in the Tualatin Valley, and Walter Beebe remodeled to Doyle's plans a home in Alameda.

In December 1925 Doyle was planning for Europe. To outsiders he made it sound like an extended vacation, a European tour with the family. Even with a close friend like Athol McBean, he did not disclose the trip was necessary for his health although he admitted his absence might diminish his practice: "There are a number of good things contemplated, and I should no doubt postpone the trip and get some of them nailed, but I am not willing to do it. There will probably be something when I get back, if not, I have a nice, quiet, comfortable office in which to loaf and sleep."[13] The mention here of loafing and sleeping is significant. The need for rest and longing for sleep are themes running through his correspondence in the last two years of his life.

Usually in telling friends about his plans, he spoke of the trip as a lark. When he wrote for advice about what to do and see abroad, he described the itinerary briefly. When school was out in June, before sailing to Europe, the family would go east and visit the principal American cities because the children had never seen them. Once in Europe, they would start in the south with time in Greece and then move north, spending a week to a month in each capital. He wrote for advice especially about what "a poor dad needs who wishes to give his family the best Europe has to give without going broke or doing it the way the wealthy American does, for I am far from wealthy."[14]

In January 1926 he went to California for a brief visit. Upon his return he began planning for a stay at a sanitarium at St. Helena, in the Napa Valley, north of San Francisco. He wanted "to spend time in the 'Sunshine Belt' … to get some rest."[15] He did make a second trip to California that winter but not to St. Helena. He went farther south to Pasadena. The weather, although it rained each day in early March, was beneficial: "I have had [a] headache only once and then not so very bad." However, he was anxious about being away and impatient for news even when he had been gone only five days.[16] After a week he wanted to be home. He was bored and edgy. "I find loafing hard work. This sunshine here is great stuff for me though, and I know it's doing a lot of good."[17] He was in California for about a month.

Two weeks after returning from California, he left for the beach at a time when, according to Dave Jack, "We are simply snowed under."[18] During much of April, the office in the Worcester Block was torn up in preparation for the move at the end of the month. Yet Doyle concentrated on preparing for his European trip, which he needed to finance. He would sell the Neahkahnie cottage. He advertised through the winter, but it was slow to sell. His only offer came in June. When the sale was final, he wrote the buyers with regret: "I hope that you and your family will grow to like the place as we do and that sometimes maybe we can go down and sit on your porch and watch the moonlight on the mountain."[19] Parting with Neahkahnie distressed him. He confided to T. L. Eliot, who was among the few, he said, who could truly appreciate Neahkahnie.[20]

In another break with his past, he ended the partnership with Merriam. In early February Merriam wrote Doyle because the Seattle office was losing money. Doyle did not know what to do. While Merriam was having problems in Seattle, Portland was flourishing. He was trying to reduce his commitments in preparation for the European trip. He replied, "I do not feel like dumping profits from this office into the losses in Seattle."[21] In March, when he was in California, the accounts were so bad that Dave Jack at first could not tell Doyle. He reconsidered, however,

David Jack. (OHS CN011847)

and sent them with an explanation: "You would no doubt have a little time to think this matter through and decide definitely your plan of action."[22] Doyle did nothing final until June. He concluded his letter with regret: "Things keep booming here, and there are more prospects than I want to think about, and I wish some of them could be turned over to you."[23]

Doyle could have used Merriam in Portland. There was no one to direct the large staff. In February 1926, there were twenty-four including Doyle and his son Billy, the office boy. Doyle's close friend and business manager, Dave Jack, was central; he was very effective in matters of organization and staff, but he was neither an artist nor an engineer. Charles Greene was artistic but temperamental and disorganized. William Hamblin Crowell was an MIT-trained architect from Massachusetts, who had settled in Portland in 1908 and worked for Whitehouse & Fouilhoux and for Portland public schools before Doyle hired him in 1919. He was the most likely leader of the firm in Doyle's absence. He was mature, in fact, just Doyle's age, genteel and composed. Richard Ritz remembered him as "a gentleman of the old school. He had a dry, New England wit and was well-liked and respected by everyone."[24] But he sparred with Harry Clyde Reese, an engineer, who had worked for Doyle almost from the beginning. Wilfred Frank Higgins had worked for Doyle before 1915, when he went to study in New York; he returned about 1919. He wanted to go out on his own, which he did in the fall of 1926. The superintendent was Sidney Lister. He started with Doyle in the summer of 1925.

According to Doyle, indeed, according to the public face of the firm, Doyle was the architect; all the others were draftsmen. This is what each of them wrote on the list that was compiled inside the office for the Polk Company in preparation for the 1926 City Directory.[25] However, the Polk Company canvassers contacted everyone twice, once at their places of employment and again at their homes. Apparently when the canvasser came to their homes, Higgins and Crowell reported they were architects rather than draftsmen, because that is what the City Directory said, and nothing was said about their working for Doyle. This may have been a sore point. Higgins and Crowell were architects on the state registry. A. E. Doyle in insisting on calling them draftsmen was invoking an increasingly outdated standard. In the 1920s professional status was changing. Licensing of architects began in 1919 yet until 1940 there was only partial compliance. An older practice survived for some time; that architects were independent practitioners who kept offices and advertised themselves as architects, registered or not, and the men (and sometimes women) who worked for these architects were called draftsmen whatever their training or previous experience. Some practicing architects refused to register. Wade Pipes, for example, a prominent Portland architect since 1911, delayed obtaining a license until 1926. Doyle, of course, did not go that far. He was among the first to register, in 1919, but he was the architect; it was his firm. Even when he was ill he controlled his office. The titles of his staff reflected their subordination to him. But Doyle was resisting change. Architects were people who had been appropriately trained, often in a university, and who had been licensed to call themselves architects. By 1926 there were three licensed architects in Doyle's office in addition to himself: Crowell, Higgins, and Reese, even though they were called draftsmen by the firm.

Charles Greene was the one exception. The 1926 City Directory listed him as "architectural designer" with A. E. Doyle. That designation reflected his importance. Because of Doyle's illness, Greene rose to prominence. Doyle trusted his taste; he increasingly delegated to him. For example, Greene made some of the decisions independently about decorating the new office. He went east alone and negotiated with Francis Bacon. He was increasingly responsible for design, and because he was especially Doyle's protégé and artistic and articulate, he was expected to balance the engineers in the firm by sharing Doyle's concerns for style and proportion over efficiency and technology. He was a talented artist. He was also undisciplined and immature. In a firm that often acted more like a family than a business. Charlie, as he was called, was the younger brother, artistic, unfocused, sometimes irreverent, and still adolescent at thirty-three. With Charlie Doyle and Dave Jack assumed an air of tolerance or humored reproach, because Charlie so often contravened convention. He was not a nonconformist, let alone radical or even unconventional, simply unobservant about a usual custom like numbering the pages of a letter or dating it. Dave Jack scolded him good-humoredly: "Say old top. The next thing I wish you would do and that is put a date on your letters. I sure have a hard time trying to figure out the date from the post mark. You are getting along fine with the numbering of the pages, and now please one more step."[26]

Charlie failed to pay his taxes in 1921. When the IRS caught up with him, he had a naïve excuse. "I was in Europe during the greater part of the year 1921 and didn't realize that my earning during the short time I was in the United States were such as to require me to hand in an income tax report being out of the country for several months after the time that such reports are required to be in, it escaped my attention entirely."[27] But when Doyle, Jack, and Crowell were all away, he was in charge. In the spring of 1926 Crowell wrote Jack from Washington with scarcely disguised amusement: "Did Charlie manage things all right while you were away? I sent him some advice from Salt Lake."[28]

For some clients Greene represented the firm. He and Mrs. Bowles became good friends. They traveled east together to select furniture for the new house. She even invited him to the country for a weekend. He was impressed: "It sure was a treat for me. She had quite a large house party and did everything possible to give us a delightful time. They surely have a very beautiful place. Don't know of any other place like it in the country."[29] He was responsible for much of the firm's residential design. In the summer of 1926 he accepted two clients whom he neglected and angered. In July one who had sent him some preliminary plans for a house requested them back when she heard nothing from him.[30]

Doyle worried that in his absence engineers would have too much influence with only Charlie to argue for art and aesthetics. Perhaps such considerations influenced his decision about Pietro Belluschi, who was just twenty-five when he appeared in Doyle's office in April 1925. At their first meeting, Belluschi said, he explained that "I had no experience in architecture: I had only an interest in it." Belluschi got a job, he said, because Doyle had "been in Italy and liked Italians" and put him to work "on tracing some drawings."[31] In fact Doyle may have been impressed by the letter of introduction from the Spokane architects, which Belluschi carried. It read in part: "Mr. Belluschi has studied architecture in his own country and, in addition, has had a year of civil engineering and architecture at Cornell University, receiving his C. E. Degree at that time. He is now anxious to get back into architectural work."[32]

Doyle liked Belluschi and assigned him to plan a remodel of Cloud Cap Inn, a rustic, 1889 log building by William Whidden on the northeast slope and near the timberline of Mount Hood, even before there was an agreement with the owners. Doyle later explained his haste: "There was little for Pete to do and I thought he might as well make these drawings as to loaf."[33] In September 1927, when the firm landed a theater job in Vancouver, Belluschi was given charge of it.[34] He was budding as a designer; but while he was becoming increasingly more important to the firm, he was too young and inexperienced to assume much responsibility or to contend with the older, established staff. He was a respected and a popular personality. Before departing for Europe, Doyle suggested to the young men in the drafting room that they hold a beard-growing contest. In late October Dave wrote Doyle that only Belluschi had "plucked up sufficient courage to raise a beard." They were "watching its growth daily with considerable interest. … Everyone laughs at him on the street."[35] Belluschi and Charlie became close friends. While surnames were usual for Crowell, Higgins, and Reese, diminutives were used for Charlie (Greene), Dave (Jack), and Pete (Belluschi).

Pietro Belluschi's sketch for Cloud Cap Inn, dated April 28, 1927. (OHS 39040)

Doyle's plan was to retain direction from abroad by writing regularly to Dave and to return to Portland to check on the office during the winter. The jobs were divided up. Higgins did the Terminal Sales Building. Crowell had the Bowles' house. The Public Service Building was still in design, and Charlie Greene had charge of it. The Pacific Building was nearing completion and Sid Lister was superintending it. Pietro Belluschi had Cloud Cap Inn. Unexpectedly, on May 7, 1926, as Doyle was making his final plans, J. G. Beach wrote about returning to Portland. Despite their disagreement about the Benson Hotel, Beach and Doyle had remained cordial if distant and communicated occasionally. Doyle respected Beach's abilities, but Beach was unpopular. Doyle weighed the proposal carefully and consulted, he later said, "many influential friends," and "the consensus of opinion seemed to be that it would be better for him not to come."[36] Doyle delayed, unable to decide. In the end he asked Beach to come to help with the Public Service Building. He brought experience and maturity, but he was irritable and unpopular and he added to the discord of the leaderless office.

The Doyles did not tour the East or sail from New York. They left Portland July 17 on a freighter, the *Drechtdyk*, of the Holland American Line, from Terminal 1, on the west bank of the Willamette just north of where the Fremont Bridge is today.[37] The long sea voyage without contact with the office and its problems would give him a needed period of rest. They docked the next day in Astoria, and Doyle wrote Dave Jack, giving instructions about a recently acquired camera and projector. He asked Dave to permit a Mrs. Henry to use the library. He promised to write "more from San Francisco as I have given no thought to anything around the office and will get it all off my chest before leaving San Francisco. ... [I] slept like a baby last night and am feeling fine this morning."

Two days later he wrote again and enclosed three letters for mailing. He asked Crowell to do "all possible for Bowles ... after all our grief" and "to see the thing through without any trouble even if he appears to be unfair."[38] In San Francisco they visited with Raymond Charles, the manager of the San Francisco office of Otis Elevator Company. Dave Jack cabled about a new building in Eugene for McMurran & Washburne Department Store, to supply plans and specifications without any supervision of construction.

A. E. and Lucie Doyle with three of their children. Jean is to Mrs. Doyle's right. Helen is to her left. Billy is in back with his father. This was taken probably in Europe or just before departure because on the back is written: "American Address, 437 E 23rd N, Portland, Ore., USA," which was the old address of the Doyles' home. (Newhouse)

Doyle approved the project but insisted on some supervision.[39] On July 27 in Los Angeles, they saw Athol McBean, who supplied most of Doyle's terra-cotta. August 4th, when they were two days from the Panama Canal, he wrote the office a long, newsy letter: "Everything is made just as comfortable as possible. [There are] cool refreshing drinks available at all hours." Billy wanted Dave to know it was very hot. A. E., Helen, and Billy spent their days playing shuffle board and pitching rings, "a mild form of exercise," which left them dripping, "so we kill time taking showers and changing clothes. I get 4 shower baths a day regularly. They are refreshing but not cold. Our cold water is 87 degrees." His only complaint was that they received no news. He added three items which "came to me the other day." The screw holes in the sashes at Mrs. Wheeler's needed to be "touched up," no more than a day's work. The lobby decorating in the Pacific Building should wait for his return. And the Broadway Theater needed better color.[40] He was having trouble letting go.

They passed through the canal in seven hours. There were eighteen very hot days between the canal and Liverpool, and some of the passengers began to grumble, but not the Doyles. They spent their time "gossiping" about the other passengers. They must have because Lucie Doyle began to write insightfully. She had previously had little to record except saccharine traveling tidbits about the "dear" friends who saw them off and other friends in California who entertained "in their usual charming way." There were eighteen passengers including the six Doyles. Mr. and Mrs.

Doyle wrote complementary character sketches about the other twelve.[41] After a week without sight of another boat, tedium wore on them. He wrote: "[We are] getting hungry for news from home and from the world. Have had our rest and ready for action! [We are] impatient for journey to end. [There is a] danger of this account becoming as wearisome as the journey itself."[42]

On August 24, they landed in Liverpool, thirty-eight days after leaving Portland. Doyle was expecting word from the office. There was none, although there were two cables and some letters from friends and family. Finally August 27, the accounts arrived with letters from Dave, Charlie, Reese, and Crowell. The news was reassuring despite delays on the Bowles' house because of Mr. Bowles' interference and indecision. On the Terminal Sales Building the pouring of concrete floors and walls had reached the sixth floor. The layouts for the Public Service Building were nearly complete. The ramp to the garage beneath the Pacific Building was done. The Public Service Garage stores were nearly rented. The Broadway Theater would be finished in time for an opening the end of the month. Pietro Bellulschi was going to Cloud Cap Inn to consider beginning construction in the spring. There was progress on Multnomah Stadium, the Sellwood Bank, and the remodel of the Oregon Mutual Life Insurance Building.[43]

Even a month and a half from Portland, A. E. Doyle participated in each of the projects. From San Francisco he had written about new, efficient elevators he wanted in the Public Service Building. Reese was unconvinced they were worth revising the plans. Doyle insisted: "The elevator service is the most important service in the success of an office building. These … elevators are faster and make a quicker get away and stop quicker than any others. Three will do the work of four, and they are the latest improved type being used in the best of the new buildings so by all means we should have them." As to adjusting the plan to accommodate them, Charlie "will be able to work out an architectural treatment for the penthouse."[44]

In Liverpool he and Billy spent a day finding a rental car large enough for the six of them. They finally found a "big old fashioned Napier … [with] plenty of springs and shock absorbers, and it looks comfortable." Its owner was a "disarming character," an "old Irishman" and a "charming liar." Billy thought him very funny. A. E. admitted, he "couldn't bargain with him." He made a condition that his daughter would come along as driver. "She was the best driver in England, and [because of the] rich, admiring way in which he said Josephine [her name], there was nothing left for me to do but pay the price which was more than I expected to pay and more than I could have gotten it for if I had been a harder egg." Josephine had driven lorries during the war for Americans and Canadians.[45] The car worked well although on one steep hill the family got out to push it.

They left Liverpool Sunday, August 29, driving north through Lancaster to Carlisle to Edinburgh, "a great city with a wealth of interest." He was impressed with the people and with their architecture. Questioning a traffic bobby about directions resulted in a lengthy exchange and amusement. "We always ask him to repeat slowly. He thinks we're daft. We can hardly keep Billy subdued. He thinks it is so funny."[46]

The Doyles were thrilled with their tour from Edinburgh to Stirling and Inverness then back south. Lucie Doyle wrote of lovely lunches, romantic hotels, stunning vistas, beautiful drives, lakes, rivers, and mountains. They were beginning a European adventure. They were new to travel and discovery. They were happy. Billy sent a card to Dave Jack whom he addressed, "Hon D. J. Jack." He wrote, "Having snarly time. Edinburgh is a keen place. Drove around today. I can get much of the talk but not all of it. My money is changed into English money now. I have about 5 pounds left. All well & happy. Bill."[47]

They returned to Liverpool on September 5, to leave their car and take the train to London. Doyle was anxious. There was no word from the office. He was concerned about the exterior of the Broadway Theater. He wrote to prevent any plan for stucco.

September 16, after ten days, he wrote again. He had had no word for nearly three weeks, and because of the transit time, the news he had received in Liverpool was already three weeks out of date on arrival. In effect he had heard nothing for nearly a month and a half. He wanted weekly letters.[48]

Finally on September 20, letters and reports sent on September 7 arrived. Everything was fine although Dave Jack trailed off after mentioning but not explaining a hitch on the Public Service Building. He said he would write the next day. He was delaying. He did not want to disappoint Doyle with news about a problem. The Public Service Building was to house three Oregon utility companies that had been acquired by a New York investment firm and combined into one company, Pacific Power and Light, with Guy Webster Talbot as president. Two months after Doyle left Portland, Talbot had been summoned to explain the new building to New York, who had reservations. Dave Jack delayed four days, and when he wrote, he tried to make the problem sound insignificant: "Everything is going along all right on the Public Service Building. We have not had any definite instructions yet to proceed with the work. Mr. Talbot had to leave this morning to have another conference with the New York officials. ... He is hoping to be able to wire us from New York the latter part of next week giving us the necessary authorization."[49]

Doyle was troubled and frustrated. He thought everyone had agreed before he left Portland. He replied: "A month is too long to wait between letters, particularly when there is a job like the Public Service Building in the office. I'll be glad to see the job settled and contracts let. [I] can't understand why Guy Talbot had to go east again on it, for I felt that all we had to do was to satisfy him and that whatever he recommends would be immediately approved."[50] When, finally, on September 29, word came, Dave cabled: "Talbot back received instructions proceed per original design new drawing have to be made account ten foot setback at rear from third story changing all column centers expect start excavation November first."[51]

Doyle had been waiting for this news. It cheered him. The Public Service Building was his largest project; it was worth about $2,000,000, half again more than any other job. He did not understand the ten-foot setback. Dave explained in a letter a few days later what was involved. Consulting architects recommended that the east wall of the central tower of the Public Service Building be set back ten feet from the line. They thought the Public Service Garage, which was six stories, could be raised or replaced with a taller building that would encroach upon the Public Service Building. Doyle was relieved but unconvinced. He wrote Dave: "It will be a long time before the ... garage will be replaced."[52] It is now eighty years later. Doyle is still right. The garage is still six stories.

Dave had another problem, which he skirted without explaining. When he wrote in September, Charlie had been away from the office for three weeks "at home with a very bad case of rheumatic fever" under the best care with a doctor supervising and a nurse in attendance. Charlie must remain in bed; he "could not use his hands." There was an $87.12 expenditure for Charlie in the office accounts that had been sent to Doyle. Dave gave an incomplete explanation: "Numerous expenses had to be taken care of. I have seen that these bills have been paid through the office, and, of course, these will be properly taken care of by Charlie upon his return."[53]

Harry Wentz helped while Charlie was out. He worked on the solution for the exterior of the Terminal Sales Building, and he filled in when Charlie was too ill to mollify and advise Mrs. Bowles. He helped too with the interior design and decoration of the Public Service Building. At the end of the year when the Christmas bonus list was made up, he received one in keeping with those of the important members of the firm: $150. His monthly salary at the Art Museum was $200.

However, the problem was much bigger. A Boston couple had spoken to Charlie over the summer about a house in Oak Grove. Charlie apparently told no one about the job, and Dave Jack learned of it only when they wrote to complain. He answered for Charlie: "Mr. Greene is still seriously ill at his home, where a nurse is in constant attendance upon him. Upon his recovery we will see that your correspondence is referred to him for answer." Six weeks later, when she had heard nothing more, Mrs. Roberts wrote a second time, but she addressed her letter to Doyle. She did not know he was in Europe. Dave again replied: "Mr. Greene is feeling very much better and is now able to come to the office two or three hours daily, but it will be several weeks before he is able to take up his duties in the office."[54] Dave Jack neglected to say why he, not Doyle, was writing. There was no need to publicize Doyle's illness and absence.

Neglected clients were just part of the problem. When Dave told Doyle that the firm had paid $87.12 of Charlie's expenses, he was concealing the true amount. Charlie had built an expensive house, and he had furnished it in style. It was a small fashionable Arts and Crafts house in the Alameda district of Portland on a bluff looking west with a view of the city (it is still at 3401 NE 34th).[55] Well before he became ill, he had only been keeping ahead of his creditors by paying a few dollars on account. Dave Jack had actually paid fifteen separate bills for Charlie for a total of $365.69. That was on a Tuesday. By Friday seven more bills were paid for a total of $1,056.87. Dave Jack took Charlie's salary for that month against the account, which left a balance of $781.87, but he did not tell Doyle. Charlie's monthly salary was then $275; his annual income was almost doubled by profit sharing. Charlie was living on credit, well beyond his means, and Dave Jack quietly paid the bills.[56] Dave even wrote learn what payments on Charllie's car loan were delinquent and when future payments were due.

Doyle suspected unpleasant news was being kept from him or purposely delayed. He complained but Dave did not immediately reply. Eventually he explained:

> *I have been reminded in so many of the last letters about not having written that I feel an explanation will have to be given because I hope you will feel a little differently after reading the following:*
>
> *I had not intended to tell you anything about what was holding up the Public Service Building until it was settled. You are on your vacation—primarily for your health and to avoid as much worry as possible—and I have that in mind. You may rest assured that matters of vital importance would be cabled to you as the rates are so reasonable.*[57]

⋘

The first week of October the Doyles rented a car with a driver and set out for Oxford, where A. E. did a sketch of St. John's College. Mrs. Doyle wrote "St. John's garden is very beautiful and the architectural interest is great having been the inspiration for Reed College." His postcard collection, now at Reed, has many of Oxford colleges. Two are of St. John's. One is dated November 1, 1906. He bought it on his first day in Oxford during his first trip to Europe. The second is dated October 2, 1926; he bought it on this second trip.[58] They are the same view of the building at St. John's on the garden and it is indeed very much like Eliot Hall as seen from the south. From Oxford they went on to Stratford, Kenilworth, and Tewkesbury, then into Wales to Cardiff so that he could see a new museum he described in a letter to Anna Belle Crocker. Portland's "old" museum was just twenty-one years old; it had been built in 1905 in time for the Lewis and Clark Exposition. Crocker said it "is dingier and more inadequate than ever." Plans were beginning for a new art museum, which Doyle would not live to design.[59]

Doyle did this drawing October 2, 1926, of St. John's College from the garden. (RC)

Shortly after returning to London, Doyle received a long letter from Dave about progress in Portland. Among other things, Dave reported on experiments with different exterior paints on the Terminal Sales Building, "We are considering a light cream but are having trouble determining the best kind of paint to be used."[60] Doyle replied in annoyance; he had given instructions about the building's exterior. Perhaps he thought he was being ignored. He wrote, "You all know that I hate *paint* [his italics] on concrete. It must be stain or a cement wash." He had seen a cement wash "applied very thinly with a bit of color in it" in London. He wanted a "pinkish gray color."[61] His irritation was unnecessary. Probably Dave had written "paint" in haste. Everyone knew Doyle's preferences. October 14, the day Doyle answered in anger from London, Wilfred Higgins wrote Doyle to explain their experiments. Doyle's and Higgins' letters crossed. Higgins had tried and rejected paint. Independently he had decided for "a wash with some grinding."[62]

There were tensions in the office. Dave reported: "Reese doesn't like to work with Crowell." If they worked better together Dave could cut some staff and reduce expenses.[63] With Charlie out, Doyle worried the engineers would dominate. "The engineers are very much in the saddle; and with the best intentions in the world, the important matters of design and architectural details can be overlooked."[64]

From Wentz he heard that Charlie was "on the mend because he seemed 'peevish.'" Doyle wrote: "I hope he gets peevish with the engineers and tells them where to head ... if they disregard architecture too much."[65] J. G. Beach was a special problem. Doyle asked Robert Strong to check on the office. He did and reported back: "I went over one morning and in the same manner that I do when you are here, sat around on the high stools talking to Beach and some of the boys and gossiped with Dave Jack."[66] As he left, he told Dave he would help with the conflicts in the office, "to sit in at any meetings or help in any way."[67] Doyle understood the difficulties. He wrote Dave: "I appreciate, Dave, what you are doing. It's not an easy job. I wish our fellows were better team workers but it is perhaps too much to expect of engineers and those in an artistic profession."[68]

More was troubling Doyle. The trip was not working out as well as he had hoped and as well as it had seemed to be in the first few weeks. Travel was costly. A car and a driver were six to eight pounds a day (thirty to forty dollars). Theaters "are the worst."

Balcony seats for the best shows were three to four dollars. He had to "limit the crowd to two major shows a week." The movies in London they had already seen at home.[69] He could do little more than worry. Everyone had sacrificed for the trip. While some economies were required, he would not be stingy: "For the sake of a few dollars, I am not going to make the trip uncomfortable for anyone, and we may not be over again so we will make the most of it while we have the chance. Good hotels are as high priced as in the U. S., and nothing is cheap for the American traveling with his family. We are all supposed to be wretchedly rich."[70] He had to arrange all his family's activities. He protested: "Unless I plan something for them or suggest places to go, they do nothing but hang about the hotel. They are a helpless lot, but I suppose I have spoiled them and must take the blame." Helen was an equestrian. Finding her a horse fell to him as did arranging for Jean's violin lessons.[71]

Another of his worries was that the office needed work. He hoped the staff could find new jobs. He explained to Dave:

> *I don't care to be as busy as we were, but there seems to be very little besides the Public Service Building, so I recommend that you have a meeting with the fellows to discuss pulling for the shore and affecting whatever savings in operating expenses that can be made if you have not already done so.*[72]

Dave thought they were finding work, at least as much as they needed. Doyle recognized he had to find the new jobs. He wrote Dave: "I will be very glad to get back for a month or so and see if we cannot get some new work. It is time though I did not wish the office to be as busy as it has been the last year or two, but I did not expect it to fall off entirely."[73] He was already anticipating his return to Portland in December.

⇜

Doyle hardly mentioned his health after he left Portland. Dave worried. Probably he feared Doyle's irritability was a symptom of stress. When Dave saw Dr. Allen Welch Smith, Doyle's Portland doctor, he had an opportunity to ask. "He [Dr. Smith] is wondering whether you are still fulfilling your part of the bargain. Advice, of course, is easily given, but he feels just as strong as I do on this subject, and I do hope that you will take things a little easier." Dave concluded his letter by suggesting that in December Doyle return to Portland by freighter to benefit as he had in the summer from a long voyage through the Panama Canal.[74]

Doyle was less than candid. He would not admit that there had been a relapse. "Things are so intensely interesting, and I have so much detail to look after in arranging for our trips ... that I have very little time to do the thing I would like to do and have had no rest to speak of. About ten days ago, I took a cold and got down. [I] had a doctor check up. I felt about like I did six months ago but there's no new developments."[75]

This letter was written in early October. The next day Doyle was out of sorts. He was too early for breakfast because he had forgotten clocks were to be set back at the end of daylight saving time. He did not feel like writing any of the letters which he owed: "[I] haven't an idea in my head though and am in no mood for it." Still, he wrote to Dave again, but said nothing about a relapse.[76]

More than two weeks passed before he admitted that he was in great pain with "terrific headaches and weakness just dragging myself around." Without saying anything to anyone in Portland, he got from the London office of the Otis Elevator Company the name of a general practitioner, who referred him to a series of specialists. The consultations and tests were inconclusive. He wrote Dave what the doctors said:

> *[There is] some blood pressure, thickening arteries as they called it which should not come at my age. ... Kidneys [are] not as bad as they were in Portland (but I have been very careful of diet). Also [I] had eyes tested again but no change of glasses is required. The vision is o.k. but the veins are affected as in the arteries. When they were all through, I asked for the answer. They said "poison in the blood from some unknown source. It may be teeth, tonsils, kidneys or any number of things."*

The doctors said he had "a tired nervous system" and "nothing functions properly with tired out nerves." They recommended rest. "I should let the family look out for themselves, get away alone at some hot bath establishment in France for a couple of months. ... (One doctor's) big theory is plenty of hot baths and sweat to help the kidneys." This news was for Dave and a few others. Certainly Doyle did not want it outside the firm. As for inside: "You must use judgment in telling anyone, perhaps Reese, Beach, and Crowell are the only ones who should know at all." He reported this discouraging news because he wanted "to be square," Dave should do the same, always convey bad news. Doyle still smarted from the long delay about the Public Service Building. He concluded: "I want you to tell me the worst, always."[77]

The last weeks in London were hard. He wrote little about their stay; he explained later: "I was miserable so much of the time that I had little interest in anything that was not entirely forced on me."[78]

Things were looking up in Portland in October; the Public Service Building was going ahead, and Charlie was on the mend. His first day back to the office was October 4. Dave suggested he write Doyle. It was an upbeat letter about the just opened Broadway Theater. Charlie was "quite wild about it; the color is perfect." Visiting it was all he managed his first day after "six weeks on my back."[79] Dave thought it would be ten days before Charlie "is sufficiently strong to be down to the office all day."[80] In November Charlie was well enough to travel to San Francisco and to Los Angeles to see "the latest work that is being done down there."[81] He went on to Mexico. The trip helped; he was cheerful when he recrossed the border to San Diego. He wrote Dave, "[I] am in the best of spirits. ... [I] am feeling great and think I will be able to do something to amount to something."[82]

The Doyles left London October 20. The next day, Amsterdam seemed prosperous and clean after London. A. E. felt better on the continent. He was following a new regimen. He took it slower, and he worked only "a few hours in the day." Finances too were better; England had been expensive, at least no cheaper than the States. The Belgian franc was depreciated and prices were very low. On October 25 in Brussels he sent the family to see the battlefield at Ypres. He stayed behind to rest. On their way to Paris from the train they saw more of the war. Mrs. Doyle recoiled from the sight of "many trenches, shell holes and ruined buildings."

In Paris there were museums, galleries, and concerts. On October 28, returning from the Louvre in the rain, Mrs. Doyle "got very wet" and came down with "a bad cold which developed into tonsillitis." She was confined to her room for ten days, and he went off on his own to Berlin, Dresden, Nuremberg, and Munich. By himself he did much better: "I visited the museums in the morning having a late lunch and then a rest in the afternoon with an auto drive before dark. [I saw] a show at night but not every night about every other night."[83] He thought he was fulfilling his doctors' orders with an afternoon nap and theater every other evening.

In Berlin he received an urgent telegram. Dave wanted him home between December 15 and January 1. Doyle cabled immediately that he would sail from Naples December 11 for New York and arrive in Portland by train after Christmas. There was an almost immediate, nearly explosive, cable from Portland: "Dr. Smith insists on complete rest and relaxation. This prompted our previous cable stop recommend again direct ocean trip."[84] Doyle did not comply.

He returned to Paris and arranged for a car in which the family toured France, arriving at the Mediterranean on November 24. The next day, Thanksgiving, they met his mother's sister, Elizabeth (Mrs. C. A.) Vanderhoof, who was a painter and then living in the south of France. She stayed with them for two days in Nice. The following Wednesday, December 1, they arrived in Florence at their home for the winter on the edge of the city, the Villa Christina. Mrs. Doyle was happy with the "lovely place ... We have a fine suite of rooms ... charming." A. E. was so pleased that he did a floor plan of the three large rooms with two baths off a gallery and stairway. He also sketched the long, wainscoted and lofty living room.[85] Since Kathleen and Helen would be going away to school and Doyle would be returning to Portland, Mrs. Doyle, Jean (aged sixteen), and Billy (aged fifteen) each had a room for the winter.

Doyle's sketch of the sitting room of the Villa Christina. (Newhouse)

On Saturday December 4, the Doyles contacted the headmistress of a school for Kathleen and Helen. Mrs. Lucy Dodd Ramberg was originally from Portland. She had studied a year at Wellesley and then traveled and studied painting in Europe, where she met and married a German aristocrat and classicist, Walter Ramberg. They lived in Florence in a large fourteenth-century villa until World War I broke out, when they returned to Germany with their children. He was commissioned in the German army but was killed by accident within a few days during target practice with his troops. She and her children remained in Germany with her husband's family. At the end of the war, because their villa had been confiscated by the Italian government, she returned to Portland, where her children attended school and then Reed. In the early twenties she regained her Florentine villa and opened it as a school for American girls, juniors and seniors, whom she and her staff taught French, Italian, art and history.[86]

Two days after Kathleen and Helen started at school, A. E. Doyle left for Genoa and his boat. He had a bad cold. He wrote Mrs. Doyle before sailing that he had "pleasant quarters and [was] feeling better." In New York when he landed, accounts and plans for the Public Service Building awaited him. He wired Dave that the voyage had been "splendid." He was then on his way to Boston to spend Christmas with friends and to see the Boston School of Design (now the New England School of Art and Design, part of Suffolk University in Boston), which Francis Bacon had recommended for Kathleen and Jean.[87] But Doyle did not stay

Kathleen Doyle at about eighteen. (Newhouse)

for Christmas in Boston; the office cabled Christmas greetings, but the telegram was returned undelivered because he left before December 24. He wrote Kathleen from somewhere in Montana, the day before his train was due in Portland, about Boston, the school, and the Stewart Club. He ended: "The train is on time. If the good record is kept up, I'll be home tomorrow night at 7 o'clock New Year's Eve. It will be an eveless New Year's Eve though with Mother and all of the rest of you so far away. It seems very strange to be going home when there ain't no home without you."[88] In Portland, because the family house was rented, he took a room at the Arlington Club.

Mrs. Doyle's holidays were no happier. December 19 was their twentieth wedding anniversary. He was on the Atlantic. She wrote in her diary: "K[athleen] and H[elen] came for dinner at the Villa and helped to celebrate the 20th wedding anniversary of Bert so far away." Then Kathleen and Helen were off to travel for twenty-one days with their school. Christmas morning, Mrs. Doyle, Jean, and Billy were together. They exchanged "gifts at breakfast with as much joy as possible with the family so separated."

Portland seemed "busy but dull after Europe" with more snow and cold than Doyle could remember for years. There was flu but he avoided it. He promised Dave to work mornings and to rest afternoons. He did not keep to it. After two weeks he wrote Kathleen that half the time he was traveling to Seattle, Boise, and Eugene. There was no let up. A few weeks later, he wrote, "[I] am working like a horse to get away on Monday night (Feb. 14), and there'll be very little rest night or day. It would be the same though if I stayed another month." Even his evenings were busy with dinner parties, which ended for him at ten o'clock when "Dave called for me and dragged me off … so that I'd get proper sleep! He looks after me like a nurse." He claimed he was getting better. January 26, he wrote that he had gained four pounds, and he felt better than he had "for a very long time." February 9, he said he was even better: "[I] have been feeling fine most of the time and have gained 8 pounds since I came home. [I] think what I needed was to quit loafing and go to work." As always, there is reason to be suspicious about his optimism; rapid weight gain may indicate edema, which can accompany nephritis.

Kathleen was having a wonderful winter. She wrote Doyle about her travels with Mrs. Ramberg. He was pleased with her interest and accomplishments. He suggested she might stay on in Europe after the family returned to Portland to see and do more. But he wanted her to go the Boston School of Design. When the school catalog reached Portland he wrote her, "I am as excited about it as if I was going to go and start all over."[89]

Jean and Billy were with Mrs. Doyle. Jean was too young for Mrs. Ramberg's school. She was studying violin. Billy was in school and got a chance to travel and to see things on his own. He wrote four pages to his father about a trip to Pisa. It was a "good letter, well written, no blots," A. E. told Kathleen. Billy reported with triumph that he "leaned against the leaning tower and climbed to the top and no catastrophe. [It is] all baloney, he says, not being allowed to go up." Mrs. Doyle's winter was apparently less happy. Her diary's frequent dated entries ended January 2. She wrote her account of these two months at one sitting. Her days were too joyless to be recalled individually.

Doyle left Portland February 14 on a train to California to talk to Athol McBean about the terra-cotta for the Public Service Building. Then he headed east. In New York Anna Belle Crocker asked him to interview an artist, a possible replacement for Harry Wentz, who wanted to take time off from teaching. Then he went to Boston to see about school for Kathleen. Before he sailed, he wrote optimistically: "Weather is fine here though cold and prospects look good for an easy trip. I don't mind the high seas if they don't get too high."[90] He was ill and miserable, however, on a rough crossing. The last day out he wrote: "I came to after two days of violent sea sickness. It's been heavy weather the whole trip; with a gale for two days. Almost everybody [is] sick. [We are] a whole day behind."[91]

Obviously he had little rest on the crossing and two weeks after he had returned, on March 24, he, Mrs. Doyle, Billy, and Jean left Florence in a rented car with a driver for Rome and Naples.

He was disappointed. Rome was changed after twenty years and crowded with Easter pilgrims. He wrote Anna Belle Crocker: "The buildings were built for giants, but the streets were not, and with the great increase in traffic and autos, particularly at this time of the year, it is much more difficult and tiring than in Florence." He was so exhausted that he dropped his usual cheerfulness and admitted discomfort and frailty: "My original idea was a trip to Italy. I had a vague kind of dream that it would be a fine place for a rest, but when I arrived in Florence last December, I had to leave immediately for home. Now on my return I have to travel, keep on going, Sometime I hope to meet someone who can do the things he plans to do or that he thinks he can do."[92]

There was a brief visit to Naples, especially for the National Archaeological Museum and to a nearby foundry where he ordered copies of some ancient bronzes, before he sent Mrs. Doyle and the two children to see the Amalfi coast, which he had walked in delight twenty years before. Even in a chauffeur-driven car on improved roads, the trip was more than he could do. He returned by himself to Florence, where he was alone for several weeks because, when the family returned from Amalfi, they left again almost immediately with Kathleen and Helen for Ravenna, Venice, Milan, the Lake Country, Switzerland, Munich and Vienna.

On April 12, after his family had gone, Doyle visited Bernard Berenson, at the Villa I Tatti, a forty-room classically styled house with formal gardens that Berenson had fashioned from a simple farmhouse he had bought in 1902 on the hills of Settignano, not far from Florence. Berenson was generous with his time. And Doyle wrote glowingly of the visit, of his warm welcome, of the delightful weather that day, of the beauty of the Villa I Tatti, of its library and paintings, and of the garden where the wisteria was in bloom: there was "a mile or two of it," and "several miles of iris," and "thousands of cypress and olive trees." It was a warm early spring afternoon, and they sat for much of it in the garden. They talked of matters on Doyle's mind: Kathleen's application to art schools; the work of and plans for the Portland Art Museum and Reed College; and his interest in finding some art to take back to Portland. Berenson was interested and helpful. He did not recommend art school; he thought artists are better trained in the studios of practicing artists. He liked what he heard about the Portland Art Museum and Reed and asked to have the museum's annual report and Reed's catalog sent to him. He suggested that Doyle visit Harvard to see the Fogg Museum for an example of an especially successful plan. And as to Doyle's art collection, he recommended a Russian émigré, Nicholas Lochoff, a brilliant copyist of early masters.

Doyle wrote excitedly to Kathleen and to Anna Belle Crocker. He was pleased by Berenson's interest in the Art Museum. He respected Berenson's ideas about art school yet he would only "go so far" with him, uncharacteristically in view of his preference for office training. He was much impressed with Berenson's recommendation of Lochoff for "painting the old stuff as he imagines it originally existed." Berenson knew him well and "heartily approves of this kind of copying by one who is enough of an artist to get away with it."[93] With a note of introduction from Berenson, Doyle visited Lochoff's studio and "saw and admired his amazing things," especially copies of two paintings by Piero della Francesca, of the Duke and Duchess of Urbino. Doyle tried to get a price, but Lochoff declined: "He smiled it off."[94] He would eventually sell them to Doyle, but not without effort and prodding from Portland.

To Kathleen Doyle bragged: "ain't I the clever one." To Crocker he was more restrained, yet so eager was he to tell her about Berenson and Villa I Tatti that he neglected to ask her to send the museum's annual report. Therefore a day later he followed up with a postcard. Her short letter to Berenson that accompanied the requested annual report acknowledged Portland's isolation and insignificance before such greatness: "I am afraid our work, meeting as it endeavors to do a variety of needs and points of view, has value only insofar as it is able to aid rather than cut off growth and so lives for its future. We have, of course, long known your books and are honored that you should feel an interest in our small institution."[95] Like Doyle, Berenson had transcended early obstacles. He had immigrated to America at age ten; he was the son of a Latvian Jew, who, as a late nineteenth-century pushcart peddler, supported his family in Boston's North End. He had a superb education. He attended the Boston Latin School, then did a year at Boston University before Harvard, where he studied the classics, philosophy, and literature. After Harvard he traveled and studied in Europe. He ultimately settled in Italy and devoted himself to Italian Renaissance art. He hunted down the works of the masters and developed a reputation for identifying and authenticating paintings. Like Doyle, Berenson had patrons.[96] For Doyle and Berenson and for their patrons there was an identification between America and the Renaissance. In the 1920s Doyle emphasized the Italian Renaissance, which Berenson said prefigured America: "The spirit which animates us was anticipated by the spirit of the Renaissance, and more than anticipated. The spirit seems like the small rough model after which ours is being fashioned."[97] They admired the Renaissance and the adherence to timeless classical principles, and they could appreciate too the careful reproduction of old masterpieces of Nicholas Lochoff, whose copies were, Berenson said, "very different from all other reconstructions." They were "such faithful, such scrupulous" recreations "down to the minutest speck which in the course of centuries had adhered to the picture, everything was there."[98]

Berenson, Lochoff, Doyle, and Mrs. Ramberg were beginning to appear out of date, like characters from the novels of Henry James. Berenson lived until 1955 in Italy, even during World War II. Despite being American and Jewish, he evaded incarceration, internment, and deportation. He was "the last great representative of a type, the connoisseur dealer."[99] The European past was becoming less important to American art and architecture, and while, of course, there would still be Americans interested in the history of art and architecture, they were increasingly dealers or academics. Lochoff early experienced the intolerance of some moderns for copying the past. He was sent to Florence in 1911 by the Moscow Museum of Fine Arts to reproduce Renaissance paintings and send them back to Moscow. The Russian Revolution ended his appointment in 1917. He stayed on in Italy doing his work for American collectors and museums. He died in 1935. Mrs. Ramberg lived one year longer than Doyle; she died in 1929. Doyle's time was shortest. Frail, thin, and pained in the spring of 1927, he had just ten months to live. They all lived long enough to know how modernists derided copies of ancient paintings and buildings, but only Berenson lived to see how influential modernists became.

With the family traveling, Doyle rested and consulted a doctor he liked. He wrote Dave: "I'm kind of hibernating and saving money, not buying much and am trying to get along without the extra $1000 that I thought I would require. Things are so frightfully expensive here." He was not too tired or too involved in his health to neglect business. He concluded this letter with instructions about completing the Public Service Building.

He also asked Dave to arrange for the sale of his stock in the Morgan Building so he could buy a collection of scarabs, beautiful and ancient Egyptian amulets in the size of and resembling beetles and carved from a variety of substances like glass, terra-cotta, limestone, and basalt. The collection belonged to an English Egyptologist who had them on permanent loan to the Ashmolean in Oxford. He had decided on the souvenirs from the European tour, an expensive, varied collection of European art. He had already ordered six bronzes from Naples. They were to be shipped to Portland. I do not know what he paid for them; he paid twenty-five dollars to have them packed. The scarabs, I know, were expensive although I do not know the price. He paid a number of installments of two hundred pounds (about a thousand dollars) each. Lochoff's portraits, which he eventually got, were four thousand dollars plus another eight hundred dollars for duty. In other words, while I cannot put a precise figure on the total, these treasures accounted for much more than the price of the Neahkahnie cottage, which he sold for thirty-five hundred dollars and which today would be worth over five hundred thousand dollars.

He spent Easter, as he had Christmas, away from his family. Soon after, he was on his way to Budapest to meet them, with stops in Ravenna and Vienna. He had another bad cold. From Budapest he wrote Dave about "the most elaborate Turkish bath establishment." He paid a little extra for a room and bath to himself. The baths helped. He expected the crossing "will set me up and I am glad to be on the way home again where I'll be content to stay for a while."[100]

The family took the train May 1 to Trieste. They spent the next day with Mrs. Ramberg and Jean, who would remain behind and accompany Mrs. Ramberg back to Florence to attend her school and to study violin. The rest of the family sailed for New York May 3.

Doyle sacrificed his beloved Neahkahnie cottage and many of his investments for this tour. He also lost out on the last phase of Portland's early twentieth-century spurt of growth, and he left to others responsibility for some of his most important buildings like the Public Service Building and the Terminal Sales Building. He abandoned his office staff to strife. And he impaired his health with fatigue and worry about reservations, expenses, the family's entertainment, and the office. The idea was that travel would free him from stress and permit him to rest. It did not, nor did he learn much from it. He saw ideas for houses and techniques to try. But his notes were casual and hasty; there was no breakthrough and no systematic tour of study as there had been in 1906. But he was proud of his family's exposure to art and the sites of great events. His daughters went to a school with the daughters of American millionaires. Probably today a European trip seems insufficiently important to risk career and life but in 1926 some still thought a leisurely and luxurious tour of Europe was a lifetime's goal.

A. E. Doyle was twenty-nine in 1906 when his own training had culminated in a grand tour. It was a measure of his success that his children saw Europe when they were young. Their experience justified the trip, he told Anna Belle Crocker: "The children particularly have been so appreciative and have absorbed so much. You won't know them."[101]

I suspect that Doyle was not much convinced by this justification. Europe did not appeal as it had: it was expensive and crowded. He ended his last letter to Dave with a promise; he would be content with home and work. Europe was becoming less important. America and even Portland were looking elsewhere for ideas. In the previous year Doyle had gone to California three times. He had sent Charlie twice and Wentz once. They wrote excitedly about rapid expansion and new ideas in San Francisco and Los Angeles.

CHAPTER 8

Dwindling

The Doyles landed in New York May 19. There was a letter from Dave Jack with terrible news; he had fired Charlie Greene. No copy of this letter survives; probably none was saved. It did not explain why. Doyle could not learn the reason until he returned to Portland. He was upset that someone who had worked so closely, so long, and so well should have been summarily dismissed. He cabled Dave almost immediately. The stilted prose of a telegram shows concern and perhaps even suspicion: "Sorry ruckus with Charlie could not await my arrival but withhold judgment until I know facts." A week later Doyle still did not know the story. He wrote from Boston; "I feel very badly about Charlie and cannot imagine what has happened." He wanted to be home. He was weighed down with fatigue, illness, homesickness, and now crisis, but the family insisted on completing their tour. Everyone wanted to see Boston, Washington, and New York, and the women wanted to shop for clothes. "They were in rags," they said. A. E. contented himself with reconsidering plans he had for Portland's Union Station: "I'll be able to see some railroad stations that I would like to see. I have a scheme for the alteration to the present station that I would like to try as soon as I get home, and I hope to be able to stir up something for the fellows to do."[1]

For sixteen days Doyle had been ship-bound between Trieste and New York, without knowing that something terrible had happened in the office a week and a half before he left Trieste. It was so displeasing that Dave Jack took the train to Seattle to convey the news in person to Merriam, who had worked closely with Charlie for years, perhaps to soften the blow and probably too to avoid committing to paper the name of what at the time was thought to be a crime and a sin.

Charlie Greene's fall from grace occasioned Pietro Belluschi's rise to prominence. Belluschi explained his promotion from his initial assignment to the "design department" to Meredith Clausen when she interviewed him in 1983:

This portrait of A. E. Doyle has been frequently published. It was done in 1927, the year before he died. He was very ill. His face is thin and drawn; his eyes are vague. He has lost his youthful vigor. (OHS 53703)

> *The man in charge of the department had been raised from an office boy to head designer. His name was Charles Greene. He started as a poor boy with no education in architecture. He had some talent, but he was a homosexual, and a very obvious one. He was not a closet one. (chuckles) He was there trying to be a good designer and was much taken with Italian styles. Then a piece of luck came my way. Luck has been a recurring thing in my life. Charlie Greene was always giving parties at his house and inviting young boys from the nearby high schools. Of course, he was very obviously a homosexual. The school board became aware of the problem of orgies, and they gave him 48 hours to get the hell out of town or he'd go to jail. So he had to leave very quickly, and I became the head of the design department.*[2]

Belluschi characterizes Greene as the supervisor. He emphasized a distance between them, perhaps out of a false modesty, likely too out of a lifetime's habit of repressing a scandalous incident. In fact, Greene and Belluschi were colleagues; Dave and Doyle spoke of their work together. They were also housemates. The City Directory for 1927, whose information was collected before Greene left Portland, listed the two men as residing at the same address, 717 Beakey Avenue, Charlie Greene's house (now 3401 NE 33rd Place).[3]

The immediate reason for Greene's dismissal was not "orgies" with high school students. Something happened with four members of the firm. The information is incomplete and purposely vague, but there can be little question about the outline of the story. A professional detective investigated April 25, 1927 and recommended dismissal. His report reads in full:

> *Today the client [presumably Dave Jack] called at the Agency Office and requested that I personally question some of his employees relative to the general character of their foreman, Charles Green [sic]. During the day I arranged and questioned four employees in the presence of the client and obtained statements from them which showed Charles Green was not a fit person to be employed by our client.*[4]

Greene left Portland soon after this investigation. He drove to Los Angeles, applied for several jobs, received three offers, accepted one, viewed several apartments, and leased one in time to send an undated letter to Portland before May 20, when Dave Jack replied to it.

Greene's letter was long, rambling, self-absorbed, and defensive, and he asked to have it destroyed. It was not. It was folded and filed with other papers and bills, the scattered remnants of a man's career that ended suddenly and disgracefully. He protested, perhaps too much, that despite his exile he was prospering. Jobs paid well. One was as a set designer at Universal Studios. "The salary offered was like a movie actor's." He decided to take another, very attractive, although not as well-paid, position, because it promised regular work. His apartment was "the most charming thing" in Hollywood. It had "a large studio on the street with a circular staircase leading up to an upstairs sitting [room]. Each [floor has] … a fireplace, a bath and kitchen." Charlie was his most effusive probably because he was deeply hurt, angry, and self-protective.

He was so upset that he postponed starting work. He wrote, "My nerves are pretty rotten so I thought I would rest up a bit before starting in." He was still smarting from the accusations that were made about him. He blamed the detective. "If he gets to me down here, I'll simply fight. I've heard some things which don't sound good to me. And if it is not going to be kept quiet, I'll go back and have it out. There was nothing wrong as far as the evidence they have is concerned—nothing they could convict me of—it was all a frame up." It also seems clear that he was not accused, or at least he did not know he had been accused, before the school board, of orgies involving high school students. According to Charlie, everyone involved was a consenting adult: "The advances were not made by me and no minors were involved."

The one person Charlie missed, indeed the only person in Portland he mentioned, was Belluschi. He did so twice. The first time was when he described job opportunities. He interjected: "[I] wish Pete would come down, and we would make a killing." He mentioned Belluschi again in closing. He ended the letter, wrote his address, signed it: "as ever, Chas," and then added a postscript: "Will you ask Pete to write me?"[5]

Everyone was vague, even evasive, about what had happened. When Dave replied to Charlie, the specifics are lost in ambiguity: "I have not heard of any comment that has been passed since you left the office but you may rest assured that the whole matter has blown over." The investigator was indirect. He did not name the offense; he wrote, "Charles Green [sic] was not a fit person to be employed by our client." Charlie was nearly as oblique, although he hints that the offense was sexual: "The advances were not made by me." Everyone was troubled; they wanted to forget Charlie and what he had done. As to having Belluschi write, Dave was reserved: "I gave Pete your message and he said he would write you in the near future."[6] Sixty years later, a lifetime removed, Belluschi put a word on what Greene had done when he said that Charles Greene was a homosexual, but he said nothing about a private investigator asking about "advances" (Greene's word) inside the office to four members of the office staff.

Dave Jack had an unenviable responsibility with the worst problem in Doyle's absence. On the one hand, Charles Greene was Doyle's important colleague; they had worked together for nearly two decades. Doyle had supervised Greene's education, paid in part for his travel and training, nurtured the development of his artistic ability, and promoted him for his talents. He was essential to the firm; in Doyle's absence he was the experienced "artist." But, on the other hand, in early twentieth-century Portland, homosexuality was a very serious charge; even the word was only beginning to be used. Those who wrote or spoke about such an unpleasant subject were more likely to say *perversion* and *depravity,* which were the terms employed for a celebrated scandal, fifteen years before. On November 15, 1912, the *Portland News,* a newspaper with labor affiliations and anti-establishment inclinations, broke a story about a group of homosexual men, some of them significant professionals and all of them respectable members of the business community, who were arrested at the Portland YMCA for "the lowest offenses against manhood that depravity in 3000 years has devised and that nations have withered of dry rot and blown away for less offenses." Other newspapers considered the issue less newsworthy, indeed offensive. Some of the accused committed suicide; some fled to avoid arrest and indictment. Careers, reputations, and lives were destroyed. The YMCA lost members and financial support. The outrage was not just that men had had sex with other men, although that was considered odious. The real concern was they were corrupting boys. According to the *News*, "The evidence shows that wherever boys gather, there do degenerates gather to prey on them."[7]

Doyle frequently employed boys. They came to him for training and experience as he had gone, at fifteen, to Whidden & Lewis. By 1927 secondary education was normal, and most boys would have finished high school first. Ernest F. Tucker, for example, graduated in 1919. He was eighteen and considering possible professions. He went to Doyle to ask about architecture and was hired as office boy. By 1927 he had not only worked for Doyle, he had done two years at Stanford, earned his degree in architecture from Pennsylvania, worked several years as a draftsman, and opened an office down the hall from Doyle's in the Pacific Building. He wrote fondly about the encouragement and training he received from Doyle. At their first meeting, as they talked, Doyle had explained something to Tucker about the firm and teaching: "I want you to feel absolutely free to use my library at any time and don't ever feel that you are wasting office time by just looking at pictures."[8]

Wyman Bear also started after high school as an office boy; he was a draftsman in the spring of 1927, when he was twenty-one. His good friend Stanley Gould was sixteen and a student in a Benson Polytechnic architectural course in 1923, when his father became too ill to work. Doyle hired him at six dollars a week.[9] Doyle's own son Bill, at the age of fifteen in the spring of 1926, before the family set out for Europe, was the firm's office boy. For Doyle mentoring the young was one of his responsibilities. A number of Portland architects began their careers with him as young men and boys.

Charles Greene's presence in the office, after so serious an accusation, was embarrassing; it could result in scandal, but firing him only diminished the awkwardness. Disentangling him from the firm was complex. He left Portland hastily without settling his affairs. His brother, Fred Greene, would sell his house, but nothing was decided about the contents. In his letter to Dave, Charlie asked to have everything sent down, even his drawing instruments, which in his haste he had left behind. He could not begin work without them. As for his furniture, clothes, and household goods, he wrote: "I will want everything for I have practically the same layout I had at home, only, of course, ever so much grander."

There was also a problem with Greene's many debts. When he left Portland, he still owed the firm $779.05 from the bills paid the previous September during his convalescence. Nothing had been repaid through the winter, and other bills were owing. After he moved to California, the mortgage company demanded payment; and after "two or three" requests, Dave paid them, as well as the car loan and several other bills that brought the total to $1,110.11. In addition, "There have been numerous other bills coming in, and we are getting them together and will send you a statement of them."[10] Over the next few weeks, there were more bills from Meier & Frank, J. K. Gill, a grocer, doctors, nurses, and the hospital where Charlie had recuperated from rheumatic fever. The total became $3,034.28. When Charlie's letter arrived with word about a lavish Hollywood apartment, Dave was watching the bills accumulate. When he replied, he assumed a pitiless, avuncular tone:

> *I do not wish to make any word of criticism as to the apartment that you seem to have taken, but I do sincerely hope that you have considered the question of income and outgo as these two items are very closely related, and when not so considered then times come when one has to do some very hard thinking to prevent getting in trouble. I most certainly do not want to see you have any financial problems to settle. It seems to me with the fine qualities you have and with the large salary that you should be able to secure that you ought to be able to live comfortably and put a little by so that in four or five years you can take your contemplated trip to Italy. This is not hot air but a pure statement of facts of what can be done if you will get down to bed rock and snap out of it.*

Dave was concerned about being repaid. He thought there was enough equity in Charlie's house to cover the outstanding bills, but it was slow to sell. Fred Greene had advertised and showed the house to about twenty people by May 20 without any offers.

In the summer Fred Greene found a buyer, but instead of repaying the firm, he kept the proceeds. He explained that he had loaned Charlie more than three thousand dollars several years before. Dave was angry and stern when he wrote Charlie:

> *Before you left Portland it was definitely understood that the money received from the house, that is the balance received over and above the first and second mortgages was to go towards the payment of the enclosed bills. Your brother Fred agreed that this would be done, and we just recently discovered that he had sold the house and kept the balance of $3,000 himself, saying that this money was due him on account of you having borrowed more than this amount from him many years ago. We don't wish to question this at all but wonder if you think you are doing the right thing by Mr. Doyle, and by those who have done everything possible to help you out.*[11]

Dave also sent Fred Greene a list of the outstanding bills and reminded him of his family's responsibilities: "Some of these people are getting very impatient and insist on receiving payment, and anything you can do to assist in the settlement of these accounts most certainly will be appreciated because it has caused in the office considerable annoyance and embarrassment."[12]

The debt remained unpaid. The following winter Charlie added deception to his other shortcomings; he got the story back to Portland that he was dead.

The Doyles spent three weeks in the East and on the transcontinental train. When they arrived in Portland the evening of Friday June 10, Dave Jack was waiting to collect the luggage and to deliver the family home. Then presumably, he told Doyle what Charles Greene had done. If A. E. Doyle ever thought the matter was handled precipitously or incorrectly, there is no record of it. Indeed, there is no evidence he ever wrote or said anything about Charlie again.

Another of Doyle's young men suddenly resurfaced. No one had heard from Donald Stewart for a year. In 1925 and 1926 he and his wife, Elizabeth, traveled in Europe, and he kept in frequent touch with the office. He wrote often to report on his travels and to ask to have money sent or something done at home. He had written last just before the Doyles left on their European tour. He asked for a loan. Doyle had already advanced them $546. Nevertheless, he sent another three hundred dollars. There was no acknowledgement and no news from Stewart for over a year until June 12, 1927, when he finally wrote Dave. He wanted furniture and dishes in storage in Portland packed and sent to New York, where he was working. He was repentant: "All the things you have thought or said of me are quite true. I hope in the future I can reestablish my standing in Portland."

He explained, "Expenses are terrific." Rent was sixty-five dollars a month for a basement apartment in Greenwich Village. "It certainly has been an experience." He was working for the nationally known and Portland-bred architect, Benjamin W. Morris, for seventy dollars per week. He and his wife had many expenses, especially doctors' bills, which they had nearly succeeded in paying off. Work was going well; "Mr. Morris' office seems much like Mr. Doyle's and I'm getting along fine. [There are] mostly young fellows ... [who are] very congenial."[13]

Dave replied in a half-serious mocking tone: "I was very glad to get your letter ... and to know that you are still in the land of the living. We were beginning to think that New York had swallowed you up, and the Pacific Coast did not exist nor any of its people."[14]

Some months passed before Donald Stewart wrote again.

There were more serious problems. Portland's building boom was over; there were no large jobs to keep the office going. Matters became complicated July 19 when Doyle entered the Portland Convalescent Hospital, a private hospital that is now an apartment house at 2566 NW Marshall. The office was concerned about disclosing the seriousness of Doyle's illness. Dave was guarded even with Merriam: "This information about Mr. Doyle being away from the office we would appreciate your keeping confidential as it is necessary for him to go to a nursing home for this period."[15]

The confinement was expected to be six weeks. However, except for a brief period on some days in the fall when he was permitted to spend a few hours at the office, Doyle remained at the hospital until the end of his life. Dave came to the hospital every morning with the day's correspondence, with office problems, and with a pad to take dictation. He was almost a member of the family. Billy Doyle enlisted him to take his side in disagreement with his father about school. Billy wanted to attend the Oregon Institute of Technology, a business and college preparatory school on SW 6th Avenue connected to the YMCA. A. E. wanted him at the University studying architecture. Billy asked Dave to intervene:

> *When you go up and see Dad, he will probably ask you to find out about the O.I.T. I want to go there and I approached him and he wants to find out what kind of teachers they have. Please talk it up as much as possible. I think the teachers are as good as any anyway. I'll probably be down tomorrow. Doggedly yours, Bill*[16]

A. E. wanted his son in college as he had wanted Kathleen in school in Boston, not as Bernard Berenson recommended, apprenticing in a studio.

Throughout his career, Doyle emphasized office training. In his last year he seems to have changed. As a protective parent he wanted the best for his children. Perhaps he had come to realize the importance of college. In 1922 Charles Carey prepared short biographies of Oregon worthies. Doyle said something he had never, to my knowledge, said before: he had taken special courses at Columbia University.[17] The term "special" was equivocal. Columbia had stopped accepting "special" students nearly twenty years before. Few in Portland could have understood that the term referred to an unusual practice at Columbia phased out in Doyle's last year in New York. "Special students" audited courses; they were not enrolled in the university. Apparently A. E. Doyle was coming to accept the importance of university training. In the same year, Charlie Greene was barred from the American Academy in Rome because he had no scholarship, and Doyle hired Donald Stewart, a "college man"; perhaps most important of all, the University of Oregon's School of Architecture and Allied Arts was in its eighth year and W. R. B. Willcox, a dynamic teacher, joined the faculty to develop "probably the most progressive architecture school" in the country.[18]

At the end of August, Donald Stewart's wife, Elizabeth, wrote Dave to tell him that their furniture had arrived, to thank him for having it sent, and to explain that Donald "might write to you most any day." She was embarrassed by her husband's failure to write, fearful that he seemed to show lack of appreciation, and wanted to express the depth of her appreciation. She wanted to begin making payments on the debt. She explained, "the proportionate salary and expenses of living in New York had us pretty well upset, and we are just beginning to feel adjusted."[19] Donald Stewart wrote in October to say he would begin repaying soon.

When Dave replied, the anger and sarcasm he had exhibited in June was gone. He accepted Stewart's proposal of repayment. He used this opportunity of contact with an old friend to suggest how serious matters were in the office, which he admitted, was "more quiet than it has been for many years." He blamed the economy: "This condition does not only exist in our office but also in the majority of architects' offices." While agriculture was doing well, "The lumber industry is in very poor condition and that is one of the main reasons that things are poor in the Northwest." Dave Jack mentioned Doyle's health vaguely without revealing the seriousness of the illness or the hospital: "As you no doubt know, Mr. Doyle's health has not been particularly good since his return from Europe. He tried to do a little too much while over there, and the result was that he had to lay off and rest up, which he has been doing for the past two months."[20]

In September with Doyle ill and business slow, two of the young draftsmen, Wyman Bear and Stanley Gould, left to find work in San Francisco or Los Angeles, where they could do night courses. From the hospital Doyle wrote letters of introduction. His evaluation of Stanley Gould was supportive but restrained: "Stanley is anxious to get experience in other offices away from Portland, preferably in California, and I am encouraging him in his ambition. While he is not a designer or experienced draftsman, he makes good drawing and is not slow."[21] At first they were unsuccessful. They wrote home about their disappointment: "there isn't any more work than in Portland."[22] Doyle replied with a list of leads. Then by "shear luck," at the end of September, Wy "ran into" and was hired by Marbury Somervell, an architect who knew Doyle well because he had worked in Seattle and Vancouver BC before Los Angeles.[23] In time Stanley too had a job in Glendale for an architect whose practice was limited to doing houses. Stanley did not much like it. He wrote Dave, "I would have been farther ahead in experience [architectural] if I had stayed put. It takes so long to get into L. A. that it is practically impossible for me to go to school." He did not, however, regret his move. He felt he had learned a lot: "The main thing I have come to realize is that if I expect to succeed I must appreciate a good job when I have one. I certainly didn't do it with Mr. Doyle."[24]

By the beginning of the year, Stanley's prospects brightened. Somervell would hire him too, but for less money. Stanley liked to work for "a very good architect," but he would earn less money and he was saving for a tour of Europe. He wrote Doyle for advice. Doyle was blind and too ill to read his letter. Dave read it to him. Three weeks from death Doyle considered the question and discussed a response with Dave, who replied, "Mr. Doyle was very glad to get your letter this morning, and he felt that you should accept the position with Mr. Somervell because, even though you are making more money where you are at the present time, you never know how long it will last, whereas Mr. Somervell is a very good man to be with, and you will be improving and learning all the time you are with him."[25]

In his last few months, Doyle thought about the lives and promise of the young people around him. He was by temperament and habit a teacher, and he advised and encouraged. He relished the achievements, the prospects, and the energy of the young.

Kathleen left for Boston a few days after Wy and Stanley. Confined to his hospital bed, Doyle could not see her off to the school he had chosen for her. He wrote her the evening she left; his letter, he expected, would arrive on Monday, "a day of beginnings, beginning of school, beginning of the week." He shared her excitement. It's a great life, he said. She should take what she could. He contrasted his age with her youth, ends with beginnings, and accomplishments with prospects. He did not protest against his illness, confinement, or impending death. He contrasted his infirmity with her vitality, and he recalled wistfully his youthful enthusiasm.

> *When we are young, we can be attached to life by ambition, by our own personal interests often merely by the sheer joy of being alive with the future stretching out before our mental gaze, one glorious promise of what one day might quite easily come true. When we are young we are content to take what life gives us. Perhaps content is not the word. But we seize what we can get with both hands. And it should be so as I said the other evening—for the time comes all too quickly when we must give and if we have not taken when we had the chance we will have very little to give later on. It's the way also to grow old without becoming sour, disappointed and embittered as the younger generation pushes us slowly but relentlessly over the edge of activity into the abyss of oblivion below.*

Then, apparently realizing how bitter he might seem, he added: "This doesn't sound cheerful does it? I don't mean it to be otherwise though." He explained: "You have just left on the U.P. Train. It's now 9:45 and I'm here thinking about you and sorry I could not be at the train to see you off."[26] A few weeks later he wrote her on her birthday. He concluded a brief congratulatory note with an observation about his life: "Youth is so much like a fly, buzzing about in a bottle. At every movement it hits itself against the sides; and when at last it does get out, it usually has little or no 'buzz' left. That's me, but my heart is warm, my head is clear (not so very) but my body is unequal to my desires."[27]

⋘

He fretted about the arrival of his art from Europe. He wrote the director of the National Archaeological Museum in Naples about "the little bronzes that I purchased from the little shop near your museum." He was disappointed, angry, and sarcastic: "No doubt it was easy to take the money and forget to send the goods."[28] Perhaps his plea helped. They were in Portland at the end of October, when he did a sketch of one of them, Hypnos, for Kathleen. He asked her not to be too hard "in judging it. … Hypnos has given me a lot of comfort and amusement and has more than justified herself."

In the autumn before he died, Doyle did this sketch for Kathleen of Hypnos, one of the bronzes he had ordered from a foundry in Naples. (Newhouse)

He told her too about the scarabs: "Kathleen, you should see the scarabs. They are all beauties. Dorothy [the office secretary] has them all properly placed in the cabinets and I verily believe that they are the finest I have ever seen. It's too bad they did not arrive before you left, for you would have had such a good time arranging them."[29]

Lochoff remained a problem; he had not yet agreed to sell the paintings to Doyle, who appealed to Mrs. Ramberg: "I feel horribly guilty in adding to your troubles, but it would be almost impossible for me to deal directly with Lochoff. Please keep account of all of your expense in connection with the pictures and add a commission if you are unable to obtain it from Lochoff."[30] He even wrote Bernard Berenson ostensibly to send a Reed catalog and to report on visiting the Fogg Museum, which Berenson had recommended that he study in planning the Portland Museum: "Perhaps he [Lochoff] has changed his mind. If this interests you at all and you happened to see M. Lochoff, you might find out something for me. It will be fine to have those paintings for our Art Museum. I have the right place for the pair of them and will be disappointed if I don't get them."[31]

When Lochoff finally agreed to sell and was arranging to have them sent, Doyle regretted the financial commitment. If the Museum bought them or helped with the purchase, there would be no duty. He asked Anna Belle Crocker if she would receive them and consider paying in part for them. He explained, "I was probably foolish to make the purchase for I can't really afford to do it or shouldn't do it at this time."[32]

The doctor, he thought, tested him. He would talk "about everything and everybody," to see "how I react." The doctor wanted him to rest, especially for his too-active mind, because his "nerves are shot [which is] the principal reason my stomach will not get used to the new diet." Doyle said, "Bosh. What I want is some food that has some pep in it. I'm too weak. Told him that there wasn't a smile or a bit of pep in a barrel of the stuff they were feeding me." The doctor chuckled and advised: "Just have a little patience and you'll get used to it."[33] By the beginning of November, Doyle was allowed two trips to the office a day. He dressed for work in the morning and returned to the hospital in time for lunch and a nap before going back to the office again in the afternoon. He was gaining weight, although, he admitted, "My food upsets every once in a while and I get a set back." He would remain in the hospital because, "[I] am less worry to Mother here than I would be at home." November 7, he told Kathleen that he would be home for Thanksgiving. He ended a brief note: "I wish you might be also. I don't dare let you know how much I'd like to see you. We'd both cry." On November 13, he wrote Kathleen for the last time; he was upbeat: "[I] Am getting fat, round cheeks and should be released. I go to the office every day of course."[34]

There was a pronounced deterioration after November 13. On December 10, Doyle had "another bad turn." There was no improvement, and the next week Dave wrote Vera Pooler, a client who took a special interest in him: "His condition has not improved. ... Some days I am only allowed to see him for two or three minutes. His head has been bothering him, and he has considerable difficulty in speaking. He still, however, is very optimistic." They hoped he would be home for Christmas.[35] Pooler visited during the early part of December; he was depleted, discouraged, and blind: "I don't think I ever felt so sorry for anyone in my whole life. Just the thought of being in that room alone all day and not being able to read or even see is too dreadful for words."[36]

Two days later, December 15, his condition was so serious that Kathleen and Jean were called home. The office sent telegrams signed by Mrs. Doyle to Boston and to Florence. The telegram to Florence understated the gravity of his condition: "Mr. Doyle not so well think it wise for Jean to return January first no immediate worry cable sailing date."[37] The next day Jean cabled Dave: "Cable Dad's exact condition is my return necessary?"[38] Seemingly she was unprepared for the gravity of her father's illness. Dave answered immediately: "Dad advanced Bright's Disease condition serious make own decision."[39]

Mrs Ramberg replied; she would accompany Jean to Cherbourg for the December 21 sailing of the *Mauretania*. Dave arranged for A. J. McComb at the New York Otis Elevator office, a long-time Doyle friend and supplier, to meet the *Mauritania* in New York and to see Jean aboard the Chicago train in the evening. In the course of these arrangements, on December 23, while Jean was at sea, he explained to McComb that Doyle might "not last until Jean arrives."[40] She arrived home Saturday morning, December 31.

As Doyle became worse, the firm, which had been solely his, became A. E. Doyle and Associate. As of January 1, 1928, all money coming in was deposited in a partnership account, to which Jack and Crowell had access. Sid Lister was the other partner. A draft of a deposition survives explaining the partnership. Doyle was deposed and he swore under oath that W. H. Crowell had worked for him as an architect for ten years. For the past three years Sid Lister had been superintendent. And for twelve years, David Jack had been business manager. During that time Doyle had been the sole registered architect. For the last four years, illness had restricted him, and these three "with the assistance of sundry minor individuals" have been "responsible for practically all the work turned out of the office." He swore: "My health has not permitted me to give more than supervisory advice throughout these years, and I wish it to be known, as an act of simple justice on my part, that these men could have dispensed entirely with my assistance insofar as efficiency in the various branches of my business controlled by them is concerned."[41]

The years of service Doyle swore to are excessive, except for Dave's. Crowell had been with Doyle eight years (since 1919) and Lister for just over two years (since the summer of 1925). The description of the relationship between Doyle and the others is also inaccurate. Crowell was, in fact, a registered architect but his title was draftsman; and Doyle had been in control until the last few months not the last four years. There may have been some recognition of how the firm needed to change the winter before when the City Directory for 1927 was prepared; Reese, Beach, and Crowell were for the first time all listed as architects with A. E. Doyle. The firm's practice of calling them draftsmen apparently ended. The three were, of course, registered Oregon architects, but Doyle had not previously accorded them that status within the firm. There is no record, to my knowledge, of what happened. Perhaps, in Doyle's absence, they began to call themselves architects or perhaps Doyle simply recognized that times were changing and that his men were architects and deserved to be so called.

Three key players were not mentioned in the deposition. Charles Greene had been banished in the spring. Harry Clyde Reese had died unexpectedly after a hunting trip two months before, in October 1927. George Beach, too, was left out. When he returned to Portland, he expected a close relationship with Doyle although he seemed unaware of his illness. On December 22, the day before Dave Jack told McComb that Doyle might not last until Jean arrived, Beach wrote Doyle a long letter and said nothing about

Doyle's condition. He assumed Doyle could travel: "Mabel [his wife] and I are planning to go to California for a few weeks with no special time set for the trip, but we were thinking that it would be great if we could all go at the same time." He also had much to say about the Public Service Building, which would open the first of the year: "Everybody is enthusiastic ... bubbling over," especially about the engineering, which was Beach's responsibility. The heating and ventilation system are "perfect," and the exterior lights on the roof "are a thousand to one shot for beauty." He seemed to think he had a future in the firm. He wrote that job prospects "are many and varied, and in due course some one of them will go over. Probably the hotel first." Doyle hoped to do an addition to the Benson Hotel. He had made some preliminary plans. Beach suggested revisions. He saw no need to match the architecture of the addition to the original building. He advised "the same floor levels, of course, but not the same column centers and exterior, as these column centers do not give a small hotel room, which seems to be what is wanted now rather than the large rooms." Doyle did not like these ideas. In the margin is written in Dave Jack's hand: "A. E. said no."[42]

A week later, on December 30, Doyle in his morning consultation with Dave "brought up the subject about Beach." Dave kept detailed notes. Doyle "regretted that Beach had not left the organization a long time ago because he did not fit in." He was glad Beach was leaving the end of the month. Many friends had advised against Beach returning. "However, Beach was so insistent on coming up that he was given the opportunity to help out on the Public Service Building, but Mr. Doyle said there was absolutely no understanding" that he would stay on after Doyle returned from Europe. Beach wanted an interest in the company, but "Mr. Doyle was very much opposed to it." Beach was to leave at the end of 1927, and Doyle "would not consider in any way having Mr. Beach as a part of the firm and was very emphatic that everybody would be better off if he [Beach] left."[43]

⋞⋞⋞

Doyle had good days and bad days. He was too ill to see William Whidden, who called at the hospital Christmas day, but was turned away. Doyle was disappointed. He dictated a letter to Whidden to express his regret at having missed the visit, to thank him for coming, and to assure him of what, Doyle must have known, was not true, that soon "they will let me out and I can return the compliment and call to you." He apologized for dictating: "My eyes are not well enough to see to write a personal letter." Since he had so little to do he had been thinking "about the old days." They were "very happy days" and now thinking about them is "always happy." He learned "the best lessons" of his life then. He learned to draw. He "always loved to draw."[44] A few days later Henry Ladd Corbett, too, was not allowed in. He wrote a newsy letter about downtown developments. Doyle was delighted and alert on January 9 when he dictated a cheery response: "Thanks lots for the bully letter. It was a delight. I will not attempt to answer it but hope to be out in a short time to see you. The eyes are stubborn and slow but my 'witch doctors' and others tell me that I will be let out before long now."[45]

Dave Jack confirmed there was a noticeable but temporary improvement January 9. He thought Jean's return was responsible.[46] The next day Doyle dictated a letter to Major R. G. Anderson, from whom he had purchased the scarabs, to report on the safe arrival of the last shipment and on his plans for displaying them. Dave saw real deterioration that day: "Mr. Doyle did not seem so bright today, in fact, he seemed to be a whole lot weaker and far more weary looking. ... His condition seems to be getting weaker and weaker."[47] Two days later he was still worse. Dave was resigned: "Mr. Doyle to me today seemed to be quite a little weaker, and he seems to feel that it is a wonderful thing to have had the children come because he feels the expressions of love that came from them and that he returned could not help but have an effect upon them in their lives. He does not seem to be suffering so much pain these last few days. For which we are very thankful."[48]

Doyle continued to conduct business. When Merriam wrote him about a problem with the IRS, Doyle replied and spoke as if his illness was a temporary inconvenience. "I am still lying on my back here in the hospital, and I certainly expected to be out long before this."[49]

In these final days Donald Stewart wrote to make amends. He apologized for the continued delay in repaying his debt. He wrote Doyle: "Surely you must think I'm an ungrateful wretch, but I assure you that if good intentions were letters your desk would have been littered with them by now." He explained that medical and "another" debt had "kept" him "broke." They were now paid, and he promised to begin payments the next month. He added a gracious tribute: "To my grief I have learned there are few people who are as generous and altruistic as you have been. New York is a continual struggle; and I hope to return to the northwest someday where life is a little easier."[50]

Doyle continued to have bright periods. On Saturday, January 21, he dictated a note to the editor of the *Spectator* about a recent piece: "Some days ago my wife read me a paragraph from the *Spectator* referring to my illness. She was much pleased with the article but I thought I didn't deserve all of it so I have been looking forward to the time when I would meet you at the Club or elsewhere and tell you just what I think of you." He concluded by promising to submit an article on art museums.[51]

Two days later, January 23, 1928, Monday morning, Dave was going over the daily business. Doyle was "very bright" when he suddenly lost consciousness. Dave stayed with him. At three in the afternoon he died.[52]

CHAPTER 9

Carrying On

Tuesday morning, January 24, the day after A. E. Doyle died, *The Oregonian* had a front-page obituary for "the designer of Portland's skyline." The city's "most beautiful and substantial business structures stand as monuments to his skill and ability ... which played an important part in making Portland the beautiful city." In the afternoon, *The Journal* was as generous: "The skyline of Portland's business district might almost be called a monument to Mr. Doyle for many of the most prominently appearing of these structures are the product of his artistic genius." The next day, *The Oregonian* had an editorial tribute: "He dreamed of a city wherein would be no ugliness, no harshness of line, no incongruity of details. He dreamed as the Greeks dreamed when they believed in beauty, and were serf to her." Jamieson Parker, a former student and draftsman and in 1928 a rising Portland architect in his own right, wrote a tribute for the weekly (Portland) *Spectator*: "Visitors have remarked on a certain harmony of character in our business district, caused by the design and color of the large buildings. To Albert Doyle is due a very large share of the credit for all that is good in our architectural atmosphere."[1]

It was characteristically cold and wet on Thursday, January 26. The Portland Art Museum closed in honor of A. E. Doyle, who had been president of the Portland Art Association. His funeral was at 2:30 in the afternoon at NE 17th and Schuyler in Westminster Presbyterian Church, where the Doyles had been members since moving to Irvington. The church (still there) was designed by Ellis Lawrence when Doyle was the chairman of the building committee and had declined to be considered for the job because of the conflict of interests. The pallbearers included both Dave Jack and Harry Wentz, who had twenty-one years before been the best man at the wedding of A. E. Doyle and Lucie Godley at another Westminster Presbyterian Church in Chehalis, Washington. The funeral was followed by concluding rites for the family at the Portland Crematorium. A. E. Doyle's ashes were deposited in the family plot he had established at River View Cemetery. The

Lucie Doyle as a young widow in 1929. (Newhouse)

office of A. E. Doyle and Associate had his gravestone match the stones of his father, his mother, and his father-in-law. Someone in the office did a rubbing of his mother's to make sure. A stone was done at the same time for Sarah Godley, Mrs. Doyle's mother, who had died two months before.[2] After the funeral Kathleen returned to Boston and Jean to Florence.

Two weeks after Doyle's death, the telephone company changed the listing for the office of A. E. Doyle, Architect, to A. E. Doyle and Associate Architect with separate numbers for W.H. Crowell and S. M. Lister.[3] Dave Jack increasingly found the jobs and made the contacts; in March he was elected to the Arlington Club.[4] Crowell took responsibility for the drafting room and the working drawings. Pietro Belluschi was the designer.

On May 7, 1928, the annual meeting at the Art Museum of the Portland Art Association coincided with the opening of an exhibit of A. E. Doyle's art collection. There were Nicholas Lochoff's copies of the Piero della Francesca portraits of the Duke and Duchess of Urbino, the copies of ancient bronzes from Naples, the Egyptian scarabs, photographs of Doyle's buildings, some of his drawings and some of his books and brocades. His former draftsman and protégé and by 1928 an established architect, Jamieson Parker, succeeded Doyle as president of the Art Association.[5] After the exhibition, Mrs. Doyle gave the Lochoff copies to the Art Museum, and later in the year a group of friends purchased the scarabs for the Art Museum.[6]

In the summer of 1928 Belluschi took the state examination. He passed brilliantly and became a certified architect.[7] In December he wrote the telephone company and asked to have his name listed as an architect in the directory and under "Architects" in the classified section.[8] In 1933 the firm was reorganized and Pietro Belluschi and William Kemery, an engineer, became partners.

Business was slow, but architecture was changing. Modernism was taking shape. In 1927 in Germany on the Weissenhof Hill overlooking Stuttgart, an international group of architects, some of the founders of the modernist movement, built an exhibition housing settlement. Participants came from several European countries and included Ludwig Mies van der Rohe, Le Corbusier, and Walter Gropius.[9] In a Paris suburb that year, Le Corbusier completed Villa Stein. His ideas were being read in America with the publication in English of his *Towards a New Architecture*. He denounced tradition, ornament, and style, which he called "obsessions" that no longer have a place in architecture. He advocated modern construction materials without decoration. "The styles no longer exist, they are outside our ken; if they still trouble us, it is as parasites." Architects must set themselves "against the past" and find "novelty" and "rhythm" in new methods and materials. The "old architectural code," which evolved during four thousand years, "is no longer of any interest; it no longer concerns us."[10] In 1927 Frank Lloyd Wright, who had long been silent and thought dead by some, was preparing a series of articles for the *The Architectural Record*. He urged architects to value originality, to create with materials at hand from their own vision, and to eschew historically dictated patterns. Architecture was about "scale, materials and building methods."[11]

Doyle was too blind and ill to read Wright's article when it appeared in January 1928. On his extended, almost year-long tour of Europe in 1926 and 1927, he did not visit the Villa Stein, although he was in Paris, and while he was as near Stuttgart as Munich, he did not see the Weissenhof exhibition. He saw some modern work, but when he did, it was by accident. From Amsterdam, for example, he wrote, "The modern houses, buildings, and paintings are all very interesting. There are a host of modern artists and architects breaking away from the traditional things and are doing some very interesting serious work. Whether it will live and contribute anything toward progress, time alone will tell."[12] In Antwerp, he was less impressed: "The new houses some of them are screams. The old stuff looks better than ever by contrast."[13]

Usually Doyle described attractive old cottages, manor houses, and villas or museum collections of the old masters and ancient sculpture. His souvenirs were some ancient Egyptian scarabs and copies of Greek and Roman bronzes and Renaissance portraits. Upholding traditional standards endeared Doyle to Portland conservatives like Bob Strong of Strong & MacNaughton, who blamed some architects and builders for "cheesy things" that "cheapen our town. ... [They] have destroyed a lot of character that Portland once possessed."[14] Doyle is, depending on the point of view, credited with or blamed for Portland's conservatism. Some have suggested Art Deco is scarce in Portland because Doyle, "a classicist to the end," dominated Portland in the 1920s with "the Classical Revival Style in his commercial buildings."[15] Doyle worked for important—and often conservative—people; he respected their tastes and judgments. He did not impose himself on others. On the Corbett Brothers' Garage, for example, he had ideas for the storefronts like "many beautiful store fronts" in California but, he said, "They are mostly wrought iron, and I don't think Mr. Corbett cares much for iron."[16]

Louis Sullivan's *Autobiography of an Idea* appeared first as a series of articles in 1922 and then as a book just before he died in 1924. In it, he denounced current architecture and the popularity of classical forms, especially after the 1893 Columbian Exposition. The reversion to classical tradition and respect for history was really, Sullivan said, "feudal thought." Only when feudal thought is overcome and "the democratic idea" prevails will the past no longer have any sway over the present. The advent of democracy has changed the condition of humankind and abolished history because "history is no longer natural or automatic." Change comes from a "totally conscious effort." History could do nothing about "the problems of a modern technological democracy," Concern for history, style, and decoration is a "pedantry" and "the artificial teachings of the schools" and "the thoughtless acceptance of inane traditions, of puerile habits of uninquiring minds." According to Sullivan, "utility should be paramount as basis of planning and design;" and "no architectural dictum, or tradition, or superstition, or habit, should stand in the way." Architecture should "be plastic; all senseless conventional rigidity must be taken out of it; it must intelligently serve—it must not suppress." Architects who popularize traditional and historical styles conduct "a selling campaign of the bogus antique." It is "remarkably well managed ... through skillful publicity and propaganda."[17]

Sullivan made an impact in Portland and Eugene, where in 1915 Ellis Lawrence had established the University of Oregon's School of Architecture and Allied Arts. In 1922 he brought to it W. R. B. Willcox, a Sullivan disciple. Together they severed the university's ties with the Beaux-Arts Society and introduced "newer methods of architectural education."[18]

Another protégé of Sullivan and especially of Frank Lloyd Wright, William Grey Purcell, a prominent Minneapolis architect, suffered from tuberculosis and moved for Oregon's mild climate. In the 1920s he wrote and lectured in Portland and at the university and worked closely with Lawrence on the reforms at Eugene. He was a president of the Oregon Chapter of the American Institute of Architects, which gave his views prominence. In popular and persuasive lectures, he reflected his loyalty to Sullivan and Wright. He advocated "indigenous American traditions" as opposed to European imports. "His lectures did much to undermine confidence in academic classicism, especially among younger Portland architects, and to introduce them to a new way of thinking."[19] He insisted that "Architecture is not a visual art. It is an art of facility and of operation, and its practice has nothing to do with esthetics which is solely the science of appraisal."[20] Purcell remained in Portland until about 1931, when he retired to California after inheriting a small fortune. Despite his illness he lived until 1965. While his Portland stay was brief and by 1965 he had been absent for thirty-four years, his importance to Portland architecture was recalled at the time of his death.[21]

Of these three architects only Lawrence built much in Portland, and even he never had a downtown job. He had many Portland houses, Westminster Presbyterian Church, and the campus of the University of Oregon Medical School, now OHSU, and many other important buildings in the Northwest, including Whitman College and the University of Oregon campuses. The other two did very little: Willcox was a teacher. Purcell's stay in Portland was short and until 1927 the City Directory did not list him as an architect; he was the president of Pacific States Engineering Corporation from 1923 until 1925 and then the vice-president of Guaranty Trust. He did a few houses. There are two on Vista Avenue (2660 and 2666 SW Vista). And he did much of the Third Church of Christian Scientists at SE 17th Ave. and Madison.[22]

Doyle owned a copy of Louis Sullivan's book[23] and for all of his reputed conservatism, often wrote as if he subscribed to Sullivan's ideas. He too scorned ornament: "I think the biggest problem ahead of architects in this country, on account of the high cost of all building materials, is to get good buildings in a much simpler fashion than we have been doing, and it will likely result in better architecture. I think the public is getting sick and tired of several layers of useless ornament done after a bombastic and decadent Roman Style, and they welcome the simpler things that have real style."[24] He said he sought simplicity not encumbrance which must be avoided at all cost: "Life, you know, is getting very terrible, and very complex, and Art should not be that. I have a scheme in my mind for a building that will not contain a single frill." He was quoting the American architect Bertram Grosvenor Goodhue and applying his maxim to the Bank of California, which Doyle said achieved "extreme simplicity and strength."[25] In England in 1926 he disdained English architecture as "fussy and ornamental."[26]

Doyle appreciated and experimented with concrete. When he was traveling in California in the winter of 1926, he wrote home from Pasadena about some impressive concrete houses: when the "forms [were] removed," the surface was "painted with oil on the rough concrete [although it was] not too rough." His interest in this material developed in the course of 1926. He later rejected paint in favor of stain and weathering. The Broadway Theater, which was completed after he left for Europe, he wanted left to weather. After the forms were removed, nothing was done to it before the theater opened. Initially the manager thought it looked unfinished. He asked about stucco. Doyle was in Europe and Dave discouraged the idea; he "strongly recommended against any change being made.[27] Doyle wrote from Europe asking that the theater be left to "weather at least until I get home. I don't like to stucco the exterior if we can avoid it."[28] Because of the long delay from the mail, he wrote even after there was the manager warmed to the technique. He came "to like the exterior of the building, and he felt that other people were beginning to feel the same way."[29] The Broadway no longer exists. R. E. Ritz liked it: "the concrete was formed with ship-lap forms, allowing the fines to squeeze through the joints, giving texture to the wall as decoration."[30]

Doyle in talking about his buildings emphasized how they functioned. His Central Library is impressive for its Georgian style with arched windows in an ordered, symmetrical façade rising to a balustrade. He appreciated the style, said he liked it, but he did not boast of the style when he talked about the building. He spoke of how inexpensive it was to build and how efficient it was for the work of librarians. Style could be completely unimportant to him. When he proposed a house plan for Westover Terrace, he concentrated first on giving every room a view, because an interesting vista is the "vital thing in planning a house." He was also concerned about how the house functioned. The kitchen and pantry were on the cool side away from the sun. And the outbuildings were shielded from the house. As to the architectural style, he ignored it: "The exterior is unimportant as it would be possible to make a fine exterior in any one of a number of styles to suit this plan."[31]

He was not particularly interested in the classical style of the Roman temple he designed for the U. S. National Bank. He talked not about its grandeur and pedigree but about its efficiency and its pleasantness. When he applied for a bank job, he never emphasized his ability to make temples into banks; he talked about his understanding of the working of the banks and their needs for technology. When he applied to do a department store, he did not brag about his white terra-cotta, classical department stores. In one such application, he wrote: "A modern department store is so full of pipes and wires and utilities of service and problems that should all be carefully worked out before starting, that an experienced architect in this class of work can save many times his commission for you in mistakes avoided and economy of building and at the same time get the utilities that make for good service and economy of operation that are so essential in these times of high labor costs."[32]

He also understood hotels. His Oregon (now Benson) Hotel was successful, he explained, not because of its compelling French Renaissance architecture; its green mansard roof even today is an easily seen feature of Portland's skyline. In explaining the new hotel, he talked about the business model. The opportunity for the architect lies, he said, with providing something new: "Efficient business management in the past has been the life of the hotel industry, but like many other undertakings, it now feels the force of competition, and is compelled not only to continue maintaining the highest efficiency in management, but it must reach out after something distinctive in the opinion of its patrons. It must justify its existence by supplying something in a special way for a distinctive division of society."[33]

The one building in downtown Portland that shows the trend toward modernism in the 1920s was by Doyle. The Terminal Sales Building has a concrete exterior with some terra-cotta for contrast, and "vertical emphasis and massing for architectural effect."[34] It was one of Portland's few Art Deco buildings, and it was "unabashedly modernistic." It "expressed the firm's latent modernistic impulses and, more than any other building in its time, pointed the way toward the crisp lines of the 1930s."[35] People knew it was innovative. Wilfred Higgins, who was responsible for much of it, was very proud. He wrote Doyle about favorable comments. One of the developers was especially pleased. "He said that he feels that the concrete feeling is maintained and that it is smooth enough so that none of the skeptical would take offence. He was particularly pleased with the color and expressed the belief that it would wear well." Harry Wentz was enthusiastic. Higgins continued: "He felt that it had great strength, was not overdone, and soared up into the sky, and that generally it was picturesque, and it looks so much better than the original drawing."[36]

Doyle was modern within his own time. A Norwegian professor asked for some "drawings of modern American work." Doyle suggested the U. S. National Bank, the Pacific Building, the Terminal Sales Building, and the Public Service Building.[37] Doyle was friends with modernists. He and Ellis Lawrence were cordial. He had an amiable relationship with W. R. B. Willcox. They communicated warmly. Doyle accepted students of Willcox in his office, and he wanted his son Billy to attend the University of Oregon. He wrote Lawrence, who was Dean of the School of Architecture and Allied Arts, about his plans for Billy.

> *I am anxious to talk with you and Willcox soon about my boy Billy. He will be ready to enter college in the fall and he wants to go to your school at the University. I am in sympathy with it because there is no one whose influence I would rather have Billy have than Willcox. I think he is a great chap. I am not sure, however, that it is entirely fair to your school because Billy is not sure that he wishes to be an architect but he thinks it would be better to take the special course in architecture than anything else.*[38]

But often traditionalists and modernists chose sides in vituperative public disputes. In April 1927, when Doyle was in Florence preparing to come home, the Portland Art Museum had an exhibition of the Blue Four: Wassily Kandinsky, Paul Klee, Lyonel Feininger, and Alexej Jawlensky. The catalog for the exhibit talked about the novelty and innovation of artists who rejected "technical skill and realistic imitation of nature" as "the sole end of the painter's effort." They were interested in "the abstract qualities of underlying rhythm, form and color to express emotion."

Portland was surprisingly receptive. According to *The Oregonian*, there was a little carping. "One or two visitors have hissed 'Scandalous!' Some shook sober heads and said 'It is bad for the young people to see.' But no one has called out the national guard." The museum admitted to being surprised so many people "liked it." Portland was changing. Three years before, in April 1924, Portland had been less receptive to an exhibit of French and American modern paintings and African masks. *The Oregonian* had as its review's headline: "One Picture Looks like Egg with Dubious Mouth and Suggestion of Shingle Bob." It quoted a comment: "All the crazies aren't in the asylums." That was mild compared to the response to the museum's first attempt to introduce Portland to modernists in the autumn of 1913, when Marcel Duchamp's "Nude Descending the Stairs," was shown just after it had been in New York. Both *The Telegram* and *The Oregonian* reported a New York critic who compared the painting to an "exploded shingle mill." *The Telegram* was particularly acid: "The picture is done in tones of yellow and brown, and just where the stair begins or ends or where a figure human or otherwise is intended to be shown is beyond all conjecture to any but the initiated."[39]

Anna Belle Crocker saw no sharp division. She has been credited with educating conservative Portland and with advocating modernism. Indeed she wrote proudly in her autobiography of her part in helping Portland appreciate twentieth-century art, yet she refused to join the battle. In the spring of 1928, just two months after A. E. Doyle had died, Crocker served on a jury for an exhibition in Seattle of local artists where, some felt, modernists had been favored. When she was questioned about it, she insisted the jury had been fair. She did not disagree that some jurors, artists with modern interests, had perhaps shown preferences for modernists. "As a rule," she wrote, "painters cannot judge honestly against what they really think and feel is the better method of approach." As for herself, she had no such preference: "I do not feel that my opinions were based upon modernistic tendencies. I enjoy works of art in every style of painting that I know of from early primitive things to present day paintings in the new ways of seeing. I have never felt because one could enjoy Cezanne and Picasso, for example, and their contemporary followers that

that prevented one from enjoying good works prevalent in the 19th century in America." She explained that the Portland Art Association discontinued juried exhibitions: "on account of similar troubles and you have my experienced sympathies."[40]

This was the artistic community that nurtured Pietro Belluschi. A. E. Doyle gave him a job and promoted him rapidly. He learned from Doyle's friends, Purcell and Willcox.[41] Belluschi especially credited Harry Wentz: "He was good with artists, and he had the gift of teaching, although he wasn't very vocal, but he made us aware—that was John Yeon, myself, and others—what were the basic rules of composition and the relationship of forms, rules that can be applied to architecture as well as to art. He was very sensitive and very nice and we loved him." Wentz invited Belluschi to Neahkahnie to stay in his cottage, which more than anything else Doyle had done, Belluschi admired: "It has function, appropriateness, harmony, materials, setting, orientation; it is modern, emotional beautiful."[42] Belluschi also had a good relationship with Anna Belle Crocker, "a very wonderful person," he said, with "an instinctive sense of what was good. She was intuitive and with an unusual artistic sense began to make purchases which showed her great gifts."[43]

Crocker gave Belluschi his first important opportunity because, according to Belluschi, she had faith in him; she turned over to him a project that she and Doyle had worked on together. Belluschi's Art Museum, which he did in 1931 and 1932, caused a stir in Portland. In designing it, he said, he disdained styles because "that standard mask called 'style,' whether that be Georgian, Italian or English is just a bad formula and only our lack of imagination has tolerated its application." Rather than "twist the body to fit the suit ... let us build a new suit consistent with the body." His design was influenced by the need for light in the galleries, as was the Harvard Fogg Museum, which Doyle had studied at Bernard Berenson's suggestion. Belluschi explained that the windows were "of a certain peculiar shape placed at a certain location" for light. There was no attempt "to disguise, cut, or change them in any way in order to conform to any rule of style." The building is low to the ground with high horizontal windows on two wings adjoined to a large open entryway made bright by tall glass doors. Belluschi made the exterior "consistent with the interior" by "eliminating the more transitory qualities of style."[44] The Art Museum, he said, should "serve its high educative purpose" and "reinstate the artist to his main role of prophet," rather than "a vapid maker of ornamental artiness." Architecture must be logical, and it must come from "study and deep understanding of the peculiar problem at hand" rather than out of "preconceived aesthetic theories" which can be no more than "artificial, tricky, or just fashionable."[45]

There was resistance to his ideas. Some believed that the Art Museum should be in the Colonial style. Belluschi wrote Frank Lloyd Wright and complained of being "kicked between fashion and dead tradition." He asked Wright to send a letter in support. Wright complied and endorsed Belluschi's plan and its "sensible modern exterior" which "would mark an advance in culture for Portland." He denounced "Georgian" as "reactionary" and "fake" to posterity although it "will continue in the backwater a long time."[46]

⟡⟡⟡

The slump that began in 1927 extended into the Depression. Several important jobs in these years were legacies from Doyle's time. One of Belluschi's important early jobs in this period was a West Hills mansion that Hamilton Corbett had discussed with Dave Jack while Doyle was in Europe. Another was the Reed Library, which Doyle had been thinking about for years. A remodel of Union Station, which Belluschi did, had been on Doyle's mind as he toured the East Coast with his family in the late spring of

Pietro Belluschi's Portland Art Museum. (Author's photograph)

Belluschi's Reed College Library. (RC)

1927. In the depths of the Depression, when there was no work, Belluschi went home to live with his family in Italy. When he returned, he built interesting, innovative houses, in the Northwest Regional style. Here too Doyle had an influence, because the Neahkahnie Wentz cottage was an inspiration for both Belluschi and John Yeon.[47]

A. E. Doyle nurtured the early years of Belluschi's remarkable career; Doyle's remained the only name on the firm for fifteen years after he died. Even in 1936 when the Oregon Legislature amended the statute on the certification of architects and required that architectural firms' names represent the names of the member architects an exception was made.[48] In 1943 Belluschi bought out the other partners and began practicing under his own name. Doyle was too ill and too removed from the business when Belluschi joined the firm for Belluschi to have learned everything from him. Yet throughout his life he maintained a loyalty to A. E. Doyle and a respect for his modest and retiring demeanor. While architects elsewhere were posing as heroic, social reformers and revolutionaries, Belluschi emulated Doyle's example of "a professional whose first obligation was to the client."[49]

Portland has an unusual, perhaps a unique history. For three quarters of a century, three interrelated and succeeding generations of architects did much of the building: Whidden & Lewis, Doyle, and Belluschi. Emphases changed. Whidden & Lewis brought historicism and flourished because of their training in the East and Europe. Doyle prospered from his New York experience and his European study. His elegant old buildings and houses in classical and Renaissance styles grace Portland, but his more lasting contribution may be his beach cottages, which influenced Pietro Belluschi and others, who developed the Northwest Regional style. In A. E. Doyle's short career, of just twenty-one years, Portland matured. When he began his career, he gave

Portland sophistication in studied imitations from New York and Europe. His successors eschewed his copies of Roman temples and Renaissance palaces in terra-cotta and his replicas of English manor houses and cottages in ersatz thatch and plaster. They admired his simple beach cottages, Oregon originals, unlike anything in Europe, frame structures, low lying, simple shapes of farm houses and barns, in cedar, spruce, and fir, unadorned by ancient artifice and weathered by ocean winds and rain.

Afterward

In 1943 Pietro Belluschi bought out the other partners in A. E. Doyle and Associates, renamed the firm Pietro Belluschi, Architect, and moved the office from the Pacific Building to the outskirts of downtown, to 2040 SW Jefferson Street. His buildings in Portland include the Oregonian Building, the Art Museum, and, of course, the Commonwealth Building (originally the Equitable Building), which won him national recognition and was responsible in part for his appointment as Dean of the MIT School of Architecture from 1951 to 1965. When he left Portland for Cambridge, he sold the firm to Skidmore, Owings, & Merrill. The office furniture that Charlie and Doyle had selected to match Henry Bacon's went to SOM's San Francisco office. Among his many achievements after he left Portland, Belluschi participated in the Pan American Building, the Julliard School of Music, and Alice Tully Hall, to name only a few. In 1973 he returned to Portland, where he continued to work almost to his death in 1994.[1] His remarkable internationally recognized career was responsible for the unusually detailed record of A. E. Doyle's life and work, because Syracuse University Library acquired Belluschi's papers and with them Doyle's, which might otherwise have been lost.

Dave Jack withdrew from the firm with its reorganization. He moved in 1946 to Laguna Beach, where he died in 1950.[2] Sid Lister stayed on with Belluschi but had another career as a sales representative for W. H. Cress & Co. He died in 1973.[3] W. H. Crowell, who was sixty-five in 1943, when the firm was reorganized, continued part time in the Belluschi office. He died in 1962. Donald Stewart and Wyman Bear both eventually returned to Portland. Stewart had left New York first for Seattle, then Yakima and Vancouver. When he settled in Portland, his office was on the second floor of the Bishop's House, just below where the Portland Architectural Club met, and one of his partners was George McMath, A. E. Doyle's grandson. He lived to 1996, when he died at one hundred and one. Wyman Bear died in 1973. William Whidden resided in his last years in the Mallory Hotel, where he died in 1929; he was seventy-two. Ion Lewis lived to seventy-five;

he died in 1933 in the Arlington Club, which had long been his home. Morris Whitehouse and Ellis Lawrence died in 1944 and 1946, respectively.[4]

Portland treasures Doyle's houses and buildings. He has thirty-seven entries on the National Register of Historic Places. They include nineteen of his Portland buildings, nine of his Portland houses, three of his Neahkahnie cottages, and six others: the Oregon Electric Station in Eugene, a house and a bank in Hood River, Multnomah Falls Lodge, the public library in Goldendale, Washington, and a former department store building now named for him as the A. E. Doyle Building at 1st and Pine in Seattle. By way of comparison, William Whidden and Ion Lewis have between them twenty-eight, and Pietro Belluschi has four. Many old houses and buildings in Portland are said to be by him. While these attributions are usually expressed with reverence, they can be, perhaps often are, wrong.

Mrs. Corbett lived into her nineties in her mansion at the base of Doyle's Pacific Building. She died there peacefully in her sleep, July 4, 1936. A private memorial service was held in the house, and her remains were interred in the Corbett mausoleum in River View Cemetery. Within three months, the house was razed.[5] For many years Portland's bus depot occupied the half block, where now there is a Hilton hotel. A few of the plaster casts that H. W. Corbett had W. B. Ayer collect can still be seen in the Art Museum, but most are gone. When the new museum was completed in 1932, some were displayed in a temporary gallery. In 1938 they found a home for a few years in the sculpture garden. The museum prefers originals to copies, and most of the casts have been loaned to area colleges for art students to observe and sketch as did the members of the Sketch Club.[6] Lochoff's copies of Piero della Francesca's portraits, which the family gave the museum, were sold at auction in 1953.

Lucie Doyle lived on in the house at NE 23rd and Tillamook in a long widowhood of twenty-five years, four years longer than her marriage. She died May 27, 1953.[7] George McMath and Marjorie Newhouse recalled their grandmother as an intimidating, somewhat authoritarian, Victorian granddame, a proud descendant of pioneers. The obituaries contributed to her claim to breeding by reporting that she was the daughter of a merchant in Albany, Oregon. No one, even her family, knew, I discovered in talking to them about her, that this fearsome little lady, ever Mrs. Doyle, was the daughter of a Chehalis plumber.

Kathleen did three years at the Boston School of Design. After Boston she moved to San Francisco, where she became a designer for a department store and married. Helen was considered the beauty of the three daughters; she had a large and fashionable wedding. She and Kathleen were both widowed young and both remarried. Helen died in 1977, Kathleen in 1995. Jean remained for five years in Florence. After the Ramberg school she continued her study of the violin at the Conservatorio Cherubini and the University of Florence. After seven years in Italy, she returned to Portland to join the Portland Symphony, but she gave up on music as a career and developed an interest in teaching. At Northwestern University, where she went to do a degree in primary education, she became reacquainted with the youngest son of Thomas Lamb Eliot, Thomas D. Eliot, whom she married, then divorced; she continued to live in the Midwest and eventually remarried. She died in 2000. Bill never became an architect as his father had wanted. He was a meat cutter. He owned a locker plant in Oak Grove, south of Milwaukie. When home freezers closed locker plants, he had another career as a butcher with Safeway. He died in 1984.

After Mrs. Doyle died, the house was sold and divided into apartments. The earlier Doyle home at NE 8th is also an apartment house. The Neahkahnie cottage, which the Doyles sold in preparation for their European tour eighty years ago, has belonged to three different families and has been used alternately as a summer and a permanent home. Jean, alone of the children, tried to return to Neahkahnie. She bought the lot across 2nd Street from the Doyle cottage. She intended to build there, but she never did. Late in life she decided to sell. When a buyer was found, she returned to Neahkahnie and stayed briefly in one of the cottages near her family's. Coincidentally the purchaser was Kathleen MacNaughton, granddaughter of E. B. MacNaughton. The Isom Cottage was willed to the Multnomah County Library. It is known today as the Library Cottage at Neahkahnie and as Spindrift among the library staff who yearly hold a lottery to vacation in it. Anna Belle Crocker sold her cottage to a Portland State professor when she could no longer care for it. Harry Wentz's cottage is now owned by Peter Belluschi, the son of Pietro Belluschi.

Anna Belle Crocker retired from the Portland Art Museum in 1936; Harry Wentz, in 1941. They were jointly honored in 1959 during the Oregon State Centennial for "their contributions to the cultural life of Oregon." Crocker died in 1961 at age ninety-four.

Wentz died in 1965 at age eighty-nine; his long life contradicted the prognosis of his doctor who had said he would not survive childhood.[8] He spent the last months in a care facility, then the Gard Convalescent Home, at NW 25th and Johnson, where he was on August 17, 1964, when he watched the burning of the Forestry Building of the Lewis and Clark Exposition. Flames rose high above the city; cinders rained down on it; and smoke filled the valley. A. E. Doyle had been dead for thirty-six years. His daughter Kathleen was fifty-six and twice widowed. Yet Harry Wentz was crying when he telephoned to tell her: "My best friend's building is burning."[9]

APPENDIX

A. E. Doyle Major Jobs

All addresses are in Portland unless otherwise stated.

PUBLIC BUILDINGS

Building	Year	Address
Bank of California (most recently Bidwell & Company, NRHP)	1924	330 SW 6th Ave.
Bedell Company (Cascade Building) (designed by G. A. Shonewald, A. E. Doyle, Associate Architect)	1925	520 SW 6th Ave
Brewster Apartments (NRHP)	1909	2161 SW Yamhill
Butler Bank (NRHP)	1924	301 Oak Ave., Hood River
Central Library (NRHP)	1913	801 SW 10th Ave.
Corbett Brothers' Garage (Broadway Garage, NRHP)	1926	630 SW Pine
East Portland Branch Library (NRHP)	1911	1110 SE Alder
Eliot Building (plans drawn 1906)	1909	116 Oak Ave., Hood River
Ford Motor Assembly Plant	1914	2505 SE 11th
Glencoe School	1924	825 SE 51st Ave.
Graham, J. S., Store (A. E. Doyle Building, NRHP)	1919	119 Pine St., Seattle
Holtz Department Store (Mead Building)	1912	421 SW 5th
Lipman Wolfe & Co. (Hotel Monaco, NRHP)	1912	506 SW Washington
Martha Washington (Montgomery Hall)	1916	SW 10th and Montgomery
Meier & Frank (Macy's, NRHP)	1909, 1915	621 SW 5th Ave.
Morgan Building (NRHP)	1913	720 SW Washington
Multnomah Falls Lodge (NRHP)	1925	I-84, 33 miles east of Portland

Multnomah Stadium (PGE Park)	1926	1844 SW Morrison St.
Neighborhood House (NRHP) (Cedarwood School)	1910	3030 SW 2nd Ave
Nehalem Union High School	1925	Nehalem, Oregon
Northwestern National Bank Building (American Bank Building, NRHP)	1913	621 SW Morrison St.
Olds, Wortman, & King (designed by C. R. Aldrich. Doyle & Patterson, Associate architects; later Rhodes, the Galleria)	1912	921 SW Morrison St.
Oregon Electric Station (NRHP)	1912	27 East 5th Ave. Eugene
Oregon Hotel (Benson Hotel, NRHP)	1912	309 SW Broadway
Pacific Building (NRHP)	1925	520 SW Yamhill St.
Pittock Block (NRHP)	1914, 1923	921 SW Washington St.
Public Service Building (NRHP)	1927	920 SW 6th Ave.
Public Service Garage (also Hoffman Garage, now Metropolitan Garage, NRHP)	1926	919 SW 5th Ave.
Reed College		3203 SE Woodstock Ave.
Arts Building (Eliot Hall)	1912	
Dormitory (Old Dorm Block)	1912	
Gymnasium	1914 (razed)	
President's House	1916	
Faculty houses (various uses)	1920	
Anna Mann	1920	
Commons (Student Union)	1923	
Ritz Hotel (Whitmarsh Bldg.)	1912	623 SW Park
Selling Building (Oregon National Building, NRHP)	1920	610 SW Alder
Terminal Sales Building (NRHP)	1926	1220 SW Morrison

U. S. National Bank (U. S. Bank, NRHP)	1917, 1925	321 SW 6th Ave.
Wemme (Henry) Home for Wayward Girls (White Shield Center)	1916	2640 NW Alexandra
Westminster Presbyterian Church	1907	Chehalis, Washington
Woodlark Building	1913	813 SW Alder

HOUSES

Albee, H. R. (Colonial Revival, NRHP)	1912	3360 SE Ankeny St.
Ball, Bert C. (English Cottage, NRHP)	1921	2040 SW Laurel St.
Bell, James F. (Arts & Crafts)	1908	2470 NW Westover Rd.
Biddle, Spencer (Colonial Revival)	1923	356 SW Kingston Ave.
Bingham, Alfred (Colonial Revival)	1907	2037 NW Lovejoy St.
Bowles, Joseph (Mediterranean, NRHP)	1924-26	1934 SW Vista Ave.
Burke, Lewis (Colonial Revival, NRHP)	1908	2610 NW Cornell Rd.
Cobbs, Frank J. (Jacobethan)	1917	2424 SW Montgomery Dr.
Collins, George W. (Colonial Revival)	1908	1863 SW Montgomery Dr.
Crocker, Anna Belle		
(Beach Cottage)	1916	Southwest corner of 4th and Neahkahnie Mountain Road, Neahkahnie
(Shingle Style)	1927	4217 SW Kelly Ave.
Curry, C. E. (Craftsman/Colonial Revival)	1909	1725 SW Prospect
De Hart, Edward J. (Shingle Style, NRHP)	1907	Westcliff Drive, Hood River

Doyle, A. E.		
(Arts & Crafts remodel)	1907-09	2136 NE 8th Ave.
(Beach Cottage, NRHP)	1915	37480 2nd, Neahkahnie
(Arts & Crafts remodel)	1920	2111 NE 23rd Ave.
Edwards, J. G. (Norman Farmhouse, NRHP)	1925	2645 Alta Vista Place
Ehrman, Edward (English Cottage)	1915	Corbett, Oregon
Eliot, Thomas Lamb (Beach Cottage Remodel)	1917-1921	37475 3rd, Neahkahnie
Harmon, Edward L. (Craftsman/Colonial, NRHP)	1909	2642 NW Lovejoy St.
Holtz, Aaron (Jacobethan)	1925	2370 SW Park Place
Isom, Mary Frances (Beach Cottage, NRHP)	1912	37465 Beulah Reed Rd, Neahkahnie
Kennicott, G. W. (Remodel)	1907	Chehalis, Washington
Lynch, Matthew (Colonial Revival)	1925	337 SW Kingston Ave.
Malarkey, Daniel (Arts & Crafts Bungalow)	1907	2611 SW Ravensview Drive
Nichols, Herbert S. (Craftsman/Colonial, NRHP)	1907	1925 SW Vista Ave.
Oberdorfer, Augustus (Colonial Revival)	1917	2010 SW Carter Lane
Parker, Leroy (Colonial Revival)	1911	2210 SW Main St.
Ransom, Frank (Colonial Revival)	1922	2885 Shenandoah Terrace
Strong, Frederick H. (Arts & Crafts Remodel, NRHP)	1911	1130 SW King Ave.
Wentz, Harry (Beach Cottage, NRHP)	1916	38070 Beulah Reed Rd, Neahkahnie
Wheeler, Cora (English Cottage, NRHP)	1923	1841 SW Montgomery Dr.
Williams, C. K. (Colonial Revival)	1908	2168 SW Main St
Winfree, A. B. (English Cottage)	1922	2174 NE Clackamas
Wolverton, C. E. (Craftsman)	1912	1808 SW Laurel
Wuest, Esther (English Cottage)	1925	6320 SE Yamhill

Notes

Preface

1. The use of white terra-cotta was "part of a nationwide trend," and A. E. Doyle designed or was associated with many of the white buildings in the center of Portland in the early twentieth century. He is usually credited with Portland's "White City" because he dominated construction in the city in the second and third decades of the twentieth century. (Ritz, "A. E. Doyle's White City," in Ritz, *An Architect Looks at Downtown Portland*, pp. 27-33.)
2. Graf, "A. E. Doyle," p. 7.
3. Pell, *The Architecture of Albert Ernest Doyle.*
4. Snyder, *Portland Names and Neighborhood*, p. 67.

Chapter 1: Growing Up

1. Unless otherwise indicated the information in this chapter is drawn from the *Portland City Directory*. These directories provide detailed information about the residence and employment of Portland people. Complete series of these directories are available at the Multnomah County Library, Central Library, and the OHS.
2. Letter, A. E. Doyle to S. D. Lynd, Mar. 1, 1919, SUPBP, Box 221, File, 1919.
3. Wilbur, *Thomas Lamb Eliot,* pp. 19-20.
4. I have drawn these examples from *The Oregonian* in the early 1880s, especially from Sep. 10 and 11, 1883.
5. Carey, *History of Oregon*, vol. 2, p. 110.
6. After Porter, James Doyle worked on his own for a year. In 1885 he was a carpenter with Nicolai Brothers, who made sashes, doors, and blinds. In 1888 and for the next decade he was self-employed. In 1898 he worked for Charles Freedner and James Killgreen, carpenters and contractors. He was listed two more times in the directories in 1900-01 and again in 1903 as a contractor and builder working out of his home. He died March 4, 1904.
7. Wollner, *The City Builder*, especially p. 10.
8. Interview Marjorie Newhouse, Nov. 14, 2002.
9. Here and elsewhere the descriptions of houses occupied by the Doyle family are from the Sanborn maps, Sanborn Map Company, Sanborn Maps, Portland, Oregon. Maps were prepared in 1889, 1901, 1905, 1908-1909, and 1924-1928.
10. Glazer, *Neighborhood House,* pp. 20-22.

11. In 1907 it is first possible to establish with certainty the ownership of these houses in *The Portland Block Book* (the Portland Block Book Company), which that year published the names of the owners of all city lots.
12. Multnomah County. Deed Records. Book 319, p. 66. Book 343, p. 60. Interestingly, James gave this address to the canvassers of the 1900-01 *City Directory*; the directory also listed separately Mrs. Mary A. Doyle at that address. The Polk Company's normal practice was to list women only when there was no husband present.
13. 1900 Oregon Census, Enumeration District 38, Sheet 9.
14. Death Certificate, March 4, 1904, State of Oregon, Department of Human Services, Health Services, Center for Health Statistics.
15. In 1893-1894, when Albert was sixteen and would have been in his third year of high school if he had gone, there were 475 students in the Portland High School or about 119 in each of the four high school grades. The same year there were 7,327 in the eight grades of primary and grammar school and another 6,419 children under fourteen who did not attend school or on average 1718 appropriately aged children for each grade. *Oreg.*, Jan. 1, 1895, Sec. 3, p. 29.
16. McMath SB.
17. His brothers followed him. Arthur was working by age fifteen and Edward by sixteen. Both started as messengers with Lipman Wolfe and became clerks or stenographers with a variety of employers. Daisy the youngest and only girl first appears in 1905 when she was twenty and a seamstress in the prominent ladies' dressmaking establishment of the Shogren sisters.
18. The policy of the Polk Company was to enumerate heads of household and employed people. Therefore when A. E. Doyle appears as boarding at home with his parents, he was, in the view of the enumerator, employed and working from home.
19. Letter, A. E. Doyle to R. W. Montague, Dec. 29, 1927, SUPBP, Box 219, File: 1927-28.
20. Allen and Klevit, *Oregon Painters*.
21. *The Pacific Coast Architect*, 4 (Oct. 1912-Mar. 1913), p. 10.
22. Wentz, "The Portland Sketch Club."
23. Letter, A. E. Doyle to Miss H. H. Failing, 18 January 1905, PAM, Record Group II, Series 1, Box 2.
24. *Oreg.*, May 28, 1895, p. 5.
25. Wentz, "The Portland Sketch Club."
26. Corbett, *Oral History Interview*.
27. Crocker, *It Goes Deeper*, p. 8.
28. Woods, *From Craft to Profession*, p. 64.
29. "Portland Sketch Club Exhibition of 1900, Nov. 22, 23, 24,." PAM, Record Group VI; Flat Storage Boxes, Box 43, vol. 1.

30. Letter, A. E. Doyle to Kathleen Doyle, Oct. 25, 1927. Newhouse.
31. Gunselman, "Pioneering Free Library Service," 320-37.
32. Letter, A. B. Crocker to F. Lockley, Aug. 11, 1927, PAM, Record Group II, Series 1, Box 25.
33. OHS, SB, 211, p. 26.
34. DeWolfe, *Old Portland*, p. 20. Hawkins and Willingham, *Classic Houses of Portland*, pp. 101-12. NRHP, "Public Service Building," (nomination form) NRHP, sec. 8, p. 3.
35. Crocker, *It Goes Deeper*, pp. 5-7.
36. Gretchen Hoyt Corbett, interview.
37. Crocker, *It Goes Deeper*, pp. 6, 8.
38. Letter, A. E. Doyle to Burt L. Fenner, office of McKim Mead & White, NYC, Sep. 22, 1916, SUPBP, Box 221, File, 1916.
39. While he was in New York, he wrote his address under his name on the fly leaves of his new books and the year in which he acquired them. He bought his first book in New York in January 1902 and his last in 1903.
40. Letter, A. E. Doyle to W. Whidden, Dec. 27, 1927. SUPBP, Box 219, File: 1927-28.
41. Letter, Jocelyn S. Bagley, River View Cemetery to author, Jan. 23, 2007. The application, which would have been signed by one of them, if they had been there, was signed by J. P. Finley & Son, the "undertaker."
42. Belluschi, interview with Meredith Clausen.
43. Multnomah County, *Deed Record Book*, Book 324, p. 304.
44. *Albany City Directory for 1878*, Albany, 1878. (OHS)
45. The card is in the possession of Marjorie Newhouse, who related the family story about it.
46. Gohs, *Portland Reporter*, p. 10.
47. Interview Marjorie Newhouse, Dec. 10, 2002. She heard this from Harry Wentz.
48. *Oreg.*, Mar. 20, 1905, p. 12.
49. Brindley, *Pacific Monthly*, 287-90.
50. See for example a letter of Lillian Bain to H. H. Failing, May 22, 1905, PAM, Record Group II, Series 1, Box 2.
52. Letter, A. E. Doyle to Kathleen Doyle, Sep. 20, 1927, Newhouse.
53. Wentz, "The Portland Sketch Club."

Chapter 2: Preparation

1. Crocker, *It Goes Deeper* , especially pp. 9-11.
2. Joan Draper, "The Ecole des Beaux-Arts and the Architectural Profession in the United States: The Case of John Galen Howard," in Kostof, *The Architect: Chapters in the History of the Profession*, especially pp. 231-33.

3. Letter, A. E. Doyle to D. M. Jack, Nov. 21, 1926, SUPBP, Box 226, File: Mr. Doyle Abroad.
4. Fussell, *The Norton Book of Travel*, p. 459.
5. Baedeker, *Italy from the Alps to Naples*, p. xiii.
6. Photo and message undated but autumn of 1927, A. E. Doyle to Kathleen Doyle. Newhouse.
7. His physical description for his passport, issued 10th of April, 1906, is "5 feet 7 inches. Forehead, low. Eyes, gray. Nose, large. Mouth, large. Chin, square. Hair, brown. Complexion, dark. Face, thin." Newhouse.
8. Letter, A. E. Doyle to Lucie Godley, June 17, 1906, Newhouse.
9. The travel diary he kept belongs to Marjorie Newhouse. He did not title it and he did not number the pages. Entries are usually dated, and they are in chronological order. Throughout this chapter, except when specific citation indicates otherwise, all quotes from Doyle are from this diary. For each section of the tour, I cite the guide book I have compared to his travels; and when I quote a guide book to explain what he saw, I cite it within the text as Baedeker or Murray when the subject discussed indicates which guidebook is appropriate.
10. I have compared Doyle's diary to Baedeker, *Spain and Portugal*.
11. Doyle's Italian travels I have compared to Baedeker, *Italy from the Alps to Naples*.
12. Letter, A. E. Doyle to K. Doyle, Feb. 3, 1927, Newhouse.
13. Doyle's Sicilian visit has been compared with Baedeker, *The Mediterranean*.
14. For Greece I have used Baedeker, *Greece*.
15. Penrose, *An Investigation of the Principles of Athenian Architecture*, p. 108.
16. Letter, A. E. Doyle to Lucie Godley, June 14, 1906, Newhouse. His drawing has been published on a number of occasions; the original has been lost.
17. Murray, *Handbook for Travellers in Constantinople*.
18. Letter, A. E. Doyle to Lucie Godley, June 15, 1906, Newhouse.
19. Letter, A. E. Doyle to Lucie Godley, June 25, 1906, Newhouse.
20. Letter, A. E. Doyle to Lucie Godley, July 1, 1906. Newhouse.
21. Letter, A. E. Doyle to Donald J. Stewart, July 20, 1925, SUPBP, Box 192, File: July to December 1925.
22. Letter A. E. Doyle to Lucie Godley, June 14, 1906, Newhouse.
23. Ibid.
24. Letter, A. E. Doyle to Lucie Godley, June 15, 1906, Newhouse.
25. Letter, A. E. Doyle to Lucie Godley, June 17, 1906, Newhouse.
26. Letter, A. E. Doyle to Charles K. Greene, April 27, 1921, SUPBP, Box 222, File: 1920-22, Folder I.
27. Letter of December 14, 1925 to Donald J. Stewart. In Musick, *The Development of the Pacific Building*, appendix.

28. Letter, Donald J. Stewart to A. E. Doyle, June 7, 1926, SUPBP, Box, 192, Box 192, File: Jan.-Jun. 1926.
29. Baedeker, *Northern France*.
30. Ritz, *Central Library*, p. 14.
31. Ward, Lock and Company, *Pictorial and Descriptive Guide*.
32. Letter, A. E. Doyle to W. H. Crowell, Oct., 8, 1926, SUPBP, Box 226, File: Mr. Doyle Abroad,
33. Letter, A. E. Doyle, to D. M. Jack, Sept. 3, 1926, SUPBP, Box 226, File: "Mr. Doyle Abroad,"
34. Letter, A. E. Doyle to Anna Belle Crocker, Oct. 5, 1926, PAM, Record Group II, Series 1, Box 23.
35. I spoke by telephone with Jocelyn Wilk of the Archives of Columbia University and emailed Bill Santin of the Registrar's Office at Columbia. Neither could find a record of Albert Doyle. Even in the early twentieth century, the university kept records of all students, even those who were not seeking degrees.
36. Email from Janet S. Parks, Archivist Avery Archives, Columbia University.
37. David G. De Long, "William R. Ware and the Pursuit of Suitability," in Oliver (ed.), *The Making of an Architect*, pp. 13-22.
38. Letter, A. E. Doyle to O. Wenderoth, April 2, 1913, SUPBP, Box 221, File, Post Office Competition 1913.
39. Letter, A. E. Doyle to Charles H. Cheney, May 12, 1919, SUPBP, Box 221, File: 1919.
40. Cheney, "The Work of Albert E. Doyle," p. 38.
41. Carey, *History of Oregon*, vol. 2, p. 110.
42. (A. E. Doyle obituary), SUPBP, Box 220, File: Jan.-Jun. 1928.
43. *Oreg.*, Jan. 24, 1928 p. 1.
44. *Jour.*, Jan. 24, 1928, p. 5.
45. Withey and Withey, *Biographical Dictionary*, p. 181.
46. McMath, "Albert E. Doyle," in Placzek, pp. 597-98.
47. Ritz, *Architects of Oregon*, pp. 111-15.
48. Cheney, "The Work of Albert E. Doyle," p. 38.
49. Carey, *History of Oregon*, vol. 2, p. 110.
50. McMath, "After the Fair," in Vaughan and Ferriday (ed.), *Space, Style and Structure*, , vol. 1, p. 324.
51. I wrote Dr. Natalia Vogeikoff-Brogan, Archives, American School of Classical Studies at Athens about the claims made for Doyle's association with them. She replied 17 January 2002, "Doyle does not appear anywhere in the list of members and fellows published in the Annual Report of 1906-07, which included all the fellows and students of ASCSA from 1882 to 1908."
52. Larson, *The Rise of Professionalism*, p. 136.
53. Boyl, "Architectural Practice in America, 1865-1965—Ideal and Reality," in Kostof (ed.), *The Architect*, ed. Kostof, p. 309.
54. Eliot, "Albert Ernest Doyle," *Reed College Bulletin*.

55. Sheldon, *History of University of Oregon.*
56. Bedford and Strauss, "History II 1881-1912," in Oliver (ed.) *The Making of an Architect,* pp. 23-48.

Chapter 3: Starting

1. Wedding invitation and wedding program, Newhouse. Certificate of marriage, December 19, 1906, Lewis County, Washington, Office of the Auditor. *Chehalis Bee Nugget,* Dec. 21, 1907 (available in the Lewis County Historical Museum, Chehalis, WA.).
2. R. A. Paulson, "Early Irvington as a Boy Saw It," *Community Press,* Aug. 28, 1974. OHS, Vertical File: Irvington.
3. (A promotional flyer) *Roundtree and Diamond,* OHS, Vertical File: Irvington. *Oreg.,* Apr. 3, 1910, sec. 7.
4. *Portland City Directory,* 1902, 1903, 1904. Multnomah County, *Deed Records Book,* Book 324, p. 304.
5. Roos, *The History and Development,* p. 86.
6. "Alterations to Mr. Doyle's E. 8th Street House," SUPBP, Safe Drawer 2.
7. U.S. Census, 1910 Oregon, Enumeration District 226.
8. Letter with personal accounts enclosed, D. M. Jack to A. E. Doyle, Sep. 7, 1926, SUPBP, Box 226, File: "Mr. Doyle Abroad."
9. (Henry Godley's obituary), *Jour.,* Nov. 8, 1916, p. 7. (Sarah Godley's obituary), *Jour.,* Nov. 10, 1927, p. 19. For their residences and work in Portland from 1909, when they first appear, see City Directory.
10. SUPBP Box 1: Job 9. *Chehalis Bee Nugget* commented often on the planning and construction of the church.
11. Letter, A. E. Doyle to C. T. Hurd, Dec. 4, 1916, SUPBP, Box 221, File: 1916.
12. James F. Bell, physician; George W. Collins, vice-president of the George Ainslie & Co., sash and doors; Frank Bruhn, Bruhn & Rudeen Meats; Herbert S. Nichols, physician; K. G. Lundstrom, general contractor, concrete and cement; Arthur H. Breyman, vice-president, Pacific Title & Trust Co and secretary, Breyman Leather Co.; Alfred J. Bingham, Bingham & McClelland, brick contractors; Charles E. Curry, manager, Northwest Warehouse Co.; Louis Burke, live stock broker, and Leroy H. Parker, manager, John Roeblings Sons Co. (wire cloth, wire netting, wire rope & industrial wire); Charles K. Williams, manager Morris Brothers, Bankers, Municipal bonds, investments.
13. Six of the Craftsman/Colonial houses are still standing: George W. Collins (1863 SW Montgomery Drive), Herbert Nichols (1925 SW Vista), Edward Harmon (2642 NW Lovejoy), C. E. Curry (1725 SW Prospect Drive), L. H. Parker (2210 SW Main Street), and A. H. Breyman (1910 S. W. Myrtle). J. F. Bell (2470 NW Westover Road) is Arts and Crafts and well preserved. Two in Colonial Revival have

been altered: Knut G. Lundstrom (2215 NE 19th Street) and Alfred J. Bingham (2037 NW Lovejoy).

14. NRHP, Lakecliff.
15. McMath, "Footnote to Doyle's White City," in Ritz (ed.), *An Architect Looks at Downtown Portland*, p. 33.
16. *Oreg.*, Mar. 29, 1908, sec. 3, p. 9. *Jour.*, Mar. 29 1908.
17. Lowenstein, *The Jews of Oregon*, pp. 26-29. OHS, SB, 52, p. 217.
18. Letter, A. E. Doyle to Miss V. P. Cooley, undated, SUPBP, Box 219, File: 1927-28.
19. Letter, A. E. Doyle to Kathleen Doyle, Apr. 2, 1923, Newhouse.
20. *Oreg.*, July 4, 1914, sec. 1, p. 16.
21. Interview with George McMath, December 5, 2002.
22. Wilbur, *Thomas Lamb Eliot*.
23. There are several letters to T. L. Eliot about an art school and the Sketch Club in the archives of the Portland Art Museum. See for example Letter, A. W. Walcott to Thomas L. Eliot, Sep. 3, 1901, PAM. Record Group II, Series 1, Box 1.
24. "Some notes from the Misses Crocker on the members of the first Board of Trustees of the Portland Art Association … Notes taken by Rachael Griffin from conversations with the Misses Crocker probably sometime in the 1940s"), PAM, Record Group II, Series 1, Box 1.
25. Thomas Lamb Eliot, Diary 1906. RC. A copy of Doyle's drawing is at the Hood River County Historical Museum, Unit 2B, Drawer 1. Job 47, SUPBP, Box 3.
26. Job 29. SUPBP, Box 1.
27. Gaston, *Portland Oregon*, vol. 2, p. 192. *Oreg.*, Jan. 24, 1932, sec. 2, p. 2.
28. Bosker and Lencek, *Frozen Music*, p. 44.
29. McMath SB. Job 26, SUPBP, Box 1.
30. Doyle's job list was assembled by George McMath and is an appendix in Pell, *The Architecture of Albert Ernest Doyle*. "Work of Whidden and Lewis," compiled by Herb Fredericks, is in the OHS, Vertical File: Whidden & Lewis.
31. Bosker and Lencek, *Frozen Music*, p.38.
32. Ferriday, *Last of the Handmade Buildings*, p. 28.
33. Ritz, *Central Library*, p. 36.
34. "Architectural League of the Pacific Coast," *Pacific Builder and Engineer*, 16 (Jul.-Dec. 1913), pp. 99-100.
35. *Arlington Club and the Men who Built It*, p. 44. *Jour.*, Aug. 23, 1960, Sec. 1, p. 3.
36. Interview with George McMath. December 5, 2002.
37. Letter A. E. Doyle to F. Bacon, Dec. 6, 1927, SUPBP, Box 219, File: 1927-28.
38. William Hawkins suggested this distinction.

39. See for example the foreword to the first issue. Other national publications helped to encourage the Craftsman movement, like *The Architectural Record, Ladies' Home Journal,* and *The American Home.*
40. OHS, Vertical File: Arts and Crafts Society. See especially a clipping from *Oreg.*, Nov. 13, 1910.
41. Clark, *Oregon Style*, p. 106.
42. OHS, SB, 52, p. 211.
43. There are brief biographies of the important architects of the period in Ferriday, *Last of the Handmade Buildings*, pp. 133-36, and also in Ritz, *Architects of Oregon.*
44. Ritz, *Architects of Oregon*, pp. 251-52.
45. MacColl, *The Shaping of a City*, pp. 26-29
46. *Arlington Club and the Men Who Built It*, p. 109.
47. *The Blue Book*, 1913, p. 168.
48. Ellis Lawrence, "Foreword," Portland Architectural Club, *Year Book*, 1910. *The Pacific Coast Architect*, 2 (1911), p. 109.
49. "Annual Dinner and Meeting of the Portland Architectural Club," *The Pacific Coast Architect*, 1 (Apr.-Sep. 1911), pp. 49-50.
50. *The Pacific Coast Architect*, 2 (Oct. 1911-March 1912), p. 108.
51. *The Pacific Coast Arcitect*, vol. 4 (Oct. 1912-Mar. 1913), p. 10.
52. *The Pacific Coast Architect*, 1 (Apr.-Sep. 1911), p. 50.
53. Haskell, *The Emergence of Professional Social Science*, especially pp. 27-36.
54. Thomas Bender, "The Erosion of Public Cultures, Cities, Discourses and Professional Disciplines," in Haskell (ed.), *The Authority of Experts*, pp. 84-106.
55. *General Laws of Oregon*, 1919, Chapter 418, pp. 788-92.
56. These contrary opinions were expressed in editorials in the two West Coast trade journals then published in Portland: *The Pacific Builder and Engineer* (August 27, 1910) and *The Pacific Coast Architect* 1(Apr.-Sep. 1911).
57. Downs (ed.), *Encyclopedia of Northwest Biography*, pp. 121-123. *Jour.*, Apr. 5, 1944, p. 4; April 6, 1944, sec. 2, p. 3. *Oreg.*, Apr. 5, 1944, sec. 5, p. 6 and April 6, 1944, sec 1, p. 8.
58. Michael Shellenbarger, "Ellis F. Lawrence (1879-1946): A Brief Biography," in Shellenbarger (ed.), *Harmony in Diversity*, pp. 9-24.
59. Watson, *Westminster Presbyterian Church*, pp. 99-100.
60. Michael Shellenbarger, "Ellis F. Lawrence," especially pp. 12, 14, 18.
61. *Pacific Builder and Engineer*, 16 (Jul.-Dec. 1913), pp. 99-100.
62. A transcript of this paper and discussion is provided in "Architectural League of the Pacific Coast: Teaching of Architecture on the Pacific Coast," *Pacific Builder and Engineer*, 16 (Jul.-Dec. 1913), pp. 92-104.

63. Ibid.
64. Hall, "Portland the Spinster," pp. 30-38.
65. Crocker, *It Goes Deeper*. p. 10.
66. *Oreg.*, Mar. 18, 1965, Sec. 2, p. 17.

Chapter 4: In Partnership

1. Doyle always said it was in his second year, which would mean in 1908, but he was imprecise about dates. I have found correspondence and contracts of Doyle & Patterson in the late spring of 1907. And I have found some of Doyle without mention of Patterson, even in the letterhead, in the early summer. Certainly by the second half of 1907, if not before, they were working together.
2. Ritz, *Architects of Oregon*, pp 309-10.
3. Ibid., pp. 266-67.
4. Fryer, "Skeleton Construction," 228-35.
5. *Oreg.*, Jan. 1, 1906. Table "Portland's Progress in Building Summarized."
6. *Oreg.*, Jan. 1, 1908, sec. 2, p. 5; Jan 1, 1909, sec. 3, pp. 1-12; Jan 1, 1910, sec. 2, p. 3.
7. *Oreg.*, Jan. 1, 1908. sec. 1, p. 6.
8. McMath SB.
9. O'Donnell and Vaughan, *Portland, an Informal Guide*, p. 62.
10. *Oreg.*, Jan 1, 1904, p. 43. *Oreg.*, Jan. 1, 1913, sec. 3, pp. 3, 6.
11. *City Directory*, 1891, p. 54. When Portland was incorporated in 1851, there were probably about one thousand inhabitants. In 1860 there were 2874, in 1870, 8293. By 1880 the population was 17,577. In 1890 it had nearly tripled to 46,385. Reaching 90,426 in 1900 was achieved in part because of the consolidation of Portland, East Portland, and Albina in 1891 and the annexation of Sellwood two years later. At least fourteen thousand of the 1900 Census total were due to expansion of the city rather than births or immigration.
12. *City Directory*, 1910, p. 18.
13. NRHP, H. R. Albee House. OHS, Vertical File: Laurelhurst.
14. E. B. MacNaughton, Autobiography, taped interview with Dorothy Johansen, RC.
15. *Oreg.*, Jan. 1, 1910, sec. 1, pp. 2, 11.
16. *Oreg.*, Jan. 1, 1912, sec. 2, p. 7.
17. Lansing, *Portland*, pp. 201-6.
18. *Oreg.*, Jan. 1, 1909, sec. 3, p. 6.
19. *Oreg.*, Jan. 1, 1909, sec. 2, p. 12.
20. *Oreg.*, Jan. 1, 1917, sec. 3, p. 12.
21. Ferriday, *Last of the Handmade Buildings*, p. 13.
22. *Oreg.*, Jan. 1, 1909, sec. 3, p. 10.
23. *Oreg.*, Jan. 1, 1913, sec. 3, p.6.

24. Abbott, *The Great Extravaganza,* p. 74.
25. Leach, *Land of Desire,* p. 32.
26. Abbott, *The Great Extravaganza,* p. 74.
27. Lowenstein, *The Jews of Oregon,* p. 217.
28. SUPBP, Box 6, Job #90 .
29. Leach, *Land of Desire,* esp. pp. 22, 40, 64.
30. McMath SB. *Oreg.* clipping.
31. Ibid. On the second floor was the fabrics department for "silks, yard goods, patterns, woolen goods and a department for millinery and art needle work." On the fourth floor were the juvenile and underwear and corset departments. The fifth floor was for rugs, carpets, and draperies. On the sixth were imported art goods, cut-glass, pottery, and chinaware. On the seventh floor were restrooms, a lounge area, and a lunch room for employees. On the eighth floor were an "octagonal room for fitting of evening gowns" and the firm's general office. The ninth floor was for workshops and the tenth was storage.
32. *Oreg.,* May 26, 1912, sec.1, p. 14.
33. *Jour.,* Apr. 3, 1912, Sec. 4, p. 5. Ferriday, *Last of the Handmade Buildings,* p. 111.
34. Lowenstein, *The Jews of Oregon,* pp. 80-82. Selling was born in San Francisco in 1852 and as a boy moved with his family to Portland, where his father, Philip Selling, opened a general merchandise store at SW 1st and Yamhill. After completing school, Ben worked in the family store. In 1881 at twenty-nine he went out on his own to open a boot and shoe wholesale business. He prospered, and in 1892 he sold the store and traveled to Europe and to Palestine with his wife. When he returned, he had another successful business, a men's clothing store with his name at SW 4th and Morrison.
35. Mcmath SB.
36. Ibid. NRHP, The Selling Building.
37. Glazer, *Neighborhood House,* pp. 20-22. Lowenstein, *The Jews of Oregon,* p. 75.
38. Glazer, *Neighborhood House,* pp. 20-22. Lowenstein, *The Jews of Oregon,* p. 138.
39. NRHP, Neighborhood House. SUPBP, Box 5, Job #84.
40. Nicoll, "The Rise and Fall of the Portland Hotel," pp. 298-335.
41. *Oreg.,* Apr. 9, 1911 p. 10.
42. *The Portland Telegram,* Nov. 11, 1911. McMath SB. NRHP, Oregon Hotel.
43. Letter, A. E. Doyle to C. H. Cheney, May 12, 1919, SUPBP, Box 221, File: 1919.
44. Telegram, A. E. Doyle to John Parkinson, Jun. 21, 1918. SUPBP, Box 221, File: 1918.
45. Letter, A. E. Doyle to S. Benson, Dec. 28, 1916, SUPBP Box 221, File: 1916.

46. Letter, Simon Benson to A. E. Doyle, Jan. 1, 1917, SUPBP, Box 222, File: 1920-22, Folder I.
47. NRHP, Oregon Hotel.
48. Wilbur, *Thomas Lamb Eliot*, pp. 91-93. MacColl, *The Shaping of a City*, pp. 19-20. *Oreg.*, Jan. 1, 1909, sec. 3, p. 4.
49. Turner, *Campus*, p. 167.
50. Eliot, "Albert Ernest Doyle."
51. Letter, John Calvin Stevens to George T. Files, Jul. 19, 1910. RC, File: Thomas Lamb Eliot: Architects, Notes Concerning c. 1910. Professor Files sent the letter to Foster, Aug. 5, 1910.
52. Dorothy Johansen identified the ballots. RC, File: Thomas Lamb Eliot: Architects, Notes Concerning c. 1910.
53. McMath SB.
54. Turner, *Campus*, p. 220.
55. McMath, SB.
56. Letter, A. E. Doyle to P. Morgan, Jun. 13, 1916, SUPBP, File: 1916.
57. *Reed College Quest*, Jan 30, 1913.
58. Olson, "Under the Green Tiles," 11, 13-16.
59. Letter, A. E. Doyle to C. H. Cheney. May 12, 1919, SUPBP, Box 221, File: 1919.
60. *Oreg.*, Jan. 1, 1913, sec. 3, p. 10.
61. *Reed College Quest*, Feb. 13, 1913.
62. W. T. Foster, "Significance of Reed College, Institution of Highest Order," *Jour.*, sect 4, p. 11.
63. Gunselman, "Pioneering Free Library Service," p. 320.
64. Public Library of Multnomah County, *Central Building Portland Oregon*, Portland Library Association, 1913. Ritz, *Central Library*, appendix, p. 15.
65. NRHP, the East Portland Branch Library.
66. Letter A. E. Doyle to C. H. Cheney, May 12, 1919, SUPBP, Box 222, File: 1919.
67. Mary Frances Isom, in Ritz, *Central Library*, appendix 1, p. 16.
68. Cheney, "The Work of Albert E. Doyle," pp. 46, 50.
69. Doyle, "The Building," pp. 27-28. Ritz, *Central Library*, appendix, 93-113.
70. Letter, A. E. Doyle to Chalmers Hadley, May 5, 1915, SUPBP, Box 221, File: 1915.
71. Letter, A. E. Doyle to Anne M. Mulheron, Jun. 14, 1922, Box 224, File: Jul. to Dec. 1923.
72. Abbott, *Portland Gateway to the Northwest*, p.71. E. B. MacNaughton, taped interview with D. Johansen, RC. McMath, "After the Fair," in Vaughan and Ferriday (eds.), *Space Style and Structure*, p. 330.
73. NRHP, the Northwestern National Bank Building.
74. *Oreg.*, Sept. 6, 1913, McMath SB.
75. McMath SB.
76. NRHP, the Northwestern National Bank Building.

77. McMath SB.
78. *Oreg.*, Oct. 8, 1913. p. 2.
79. McMath SB. *Oreg.*, Mar. 14 1913. *The Morrison Street Bulletin*, Vol 1, no. 6. May 1913.
80. *Oreg.*, Nov 1, 1914. McMath SB.
81. Shellenberger, "Ellis F. Lawrence," 43.
82. Quoted by Clausen, *Pietro Belluschi*, pp. 55-56.
83. *Oreg.*, Jan. 1, 1914, sec. 1, p. 16. McMath SB.
84. NRHP, Pittock Block.
85. McMath, SB. *Oreg.*, Mar. 1, 1914, Sec. 1, p. 16.
86. *Oreg.*, Feb. 13, 1915, sec. 1, p. 16.
87. MacColl, *The Shaping of a City*, pp. 445-46, 477.
88. NRHP, The H. R. Albee House. Hawkins and Willingham, *Classic Houses of Portland*, pp. 235-36. The symmetrical façade faces north with the entry at a portico of Doric columns and pilasters. A large central hallway is entered from a vestibule and extends through the house. To the left the living room opens on a solarium. To the right is first the library and then the dining room. The kitchen beyond is in a wing that balances the solarium. Upstairs, a master suite with bedroom, bath, sitting room, and sleeping porch is to the east. On the west side of the hall are two bedrooms and a bath. Over the kitchen is a maid's room with bath and service stairs to the first floor.
89. HRI, Ford Motor Plant.
90. Letter A. E. Doyle to C. H. Cheney, May 12, 1919, SUPBP, Box 222, File: 1919.
91. SUPBP, Box 221, File: 1915.
92. Letter, A. E. Doyle to W. C. Miller, Nov. 2, 1915, SUPBP, Box 221, File: 1915.
93. Letter, A. E. Doyle to W. B. Patterson, Dec. 31 1915 (misfiled), SUPBP, Box 221, File: 1916.
94. Letter, A. E. Doyle to J. G. Beach, Los Angeles, CA, June 21 1918, SUPBP, Box 221, File: 1918.
95. Letter, W. B. Patterson to A. E. Doyle, Jan 18,1928, SUPBP, Box 219, File: 1927-28.

Chapter 5: Alone

1. *Oreg.*, Jan. 1, 1912, sec. 3, p. 8.
2. Letter, A. E. Doyle to Oscar Wenderoth, Supervising Architect, Treasury Department, April 2, 1913, SUPBS, Box 221, File: Post Office Competition 1913.
3. Letter, A. E. Doyle to R. H. Strong, Jul. 8, 1914, SUPBP, Box 221, File: 1914.
4. Gordon Voorhies' house is sometimes incorrectly attributed to Doyle.

5. Letter, A. E. Doyle to Ellis F. Lawrence, Nov. 25, 1914, SUPBP, Box 221, File: 1914.
6. "Report of Committee on Government Architecture—AIA," *The Pacific Coast Architect*, 4 (October 1912-March 1913), p. 202.
7. Edgar M. Lazarus, "Ethics Governing the Professional Practice of Architects," *The Pacific Coast Architect*, 3 (April-September 1912), p. 311.
8. Letter, A. E. Doyle to Julia Spooner, Oct. 30, 1919, SUPBP, Box 221, File: 1919.
9. Letter, W. G. MacAdoo to Senator Geo. W. Chamberlain, Oct. 2, 1913, SUPBP, Box 221, File: Post Office Competition 1913.
10. Letter, A. E. Doyle to Senator Geo. W. Chamberlain, Oct. 15, 1913, SUPBP, Box 221, File: Post Office Competition 1913.
11. The children ranged in age from about three (Billy) to about nine (Kathleen).
12. Letter August 17, 1914, A. E. Doyle to Mrs. A. E. Doyle, Newhouse.
13. (Drawings for the West Hills House), Newhouse. The entry is a large, central hallway. To the right is the living room, 18 x 32. Straight ahead is the library, 16 x 18. To the left is a dining room, 18 x 22. Beyond the living room is a piazza 14 feet wide the full width of the house. Upstairs there is a guest room 16 x 18 and four bedrooms for the children. Billy and Jean, the youngest, have rooms 12 x 14. Kathleen and Helen have rooms 12 x 16. The master bedroom is 18 x 22 with a bath, a dressing room, and several closets. Beyond the master suite there is a second floor sleeping balcony. Behind the main house is a service wing with a servants' hall, a butler's pantry, a kitchen, 14 x16, with a large pantry and service stairs to the second floor. Beyond the service wing, are an arched drive-through, a workshop, a tool house and a double garage. The grounds have a large formal flower garden and a kitchen garden.
14. Letter, A. E. Doyle to H. MacDonald, Apr. 25, 1921, SUPBP, Box 222, Folder, II, 1920-22.
15. Plans, "Summer Cottage at Neahkahnie Mt for Mrs. A. E. Doyle," SUPBP, Drawer #4.
16. NRHP, The Doyle Cottage, sec. 8, p. 5. McMath, "Emerging Regional Style," in Vaughan and Ferriday (eds.), *Space, Style, and Structure*, pp. 341-49.
17. Kadas, *In the Shadow of Neahkahnie*.
18. Head, *Neah-kah-nie Mountain*. Comerford, *At the Foot of the Mountain*, pp. 65-85.
19. Stewart Holbrook, *Far Corner: A Personal View of the Pacific Northwest* (1952), quoted by Schwantes, *Railroad Signatures across the Pacific Northwest*, p. 222.
20. Advertisement. *Oreg.*, Jan. 1, 1912, sec. 2, p. 6.

21. Head, *Neahk-Kah-Nie Mountain.*
22. McMath, "After the Fair," in Vaughan and Ferriday (eds.), *Space Style and Structure*, p. 343. NRHP, Mary Frances Isom Cottage. "Shore Cottage at Neahkahnie Mountain for Miss Isom April 1912," SUPBP, Drawer #25. Specifications, SUPBP, Box 2, Job #37.
23. NRHP, A. E. Doyle Cottage, sec. 8, p. 8.
24. "Seaside Cottage for A. B. Crocker Job #241," SUPBP, Drawer #38.
25. A copy of the Wentz Cottage plans is at OHS, photofile #1109.
26. Helen L. Mershon, "Cottage by the Sea," *Oreg*, Oct. 16, 1987, sec. D, p. 6.
27. McMath, "Emerging Regional Style," in Vaughan and Ferriday (eds.), *Space, Style, and Structure*, p. 345.
28. Hawkins and Willingham, *Classic Houses*, p. 520.
29. McMath, "After the Fair," in Vaughan and Ferriday (eds.), *Space, Style, and Structure*, p. 343.
30. Letter, A. E. Doyle to Mrs. L. Ferguson, Dec. 14, 1925, SUPBP, Box 192, File : July-Dec. 1925.
31. The plans for the Eliot cottage are incorrectly filed as "T. L. Eliot Building at Hood River." SUPBP, Drawer 6.
32. The letters between Mr. and Mrs. Madden and A. E. Doyle are filed in SUPBP, Box 221, File: 1917.
33. *Oreg.*, Jan 1, 1920, sec. 4, p. 3. Jan 1, 1921, sec. 4, p. 2.
34. Letter, A. E. Doyle to R. W. Charles, Apr. 22, 1926, SUPBP, Box 219, File: 1926.
35. Letter, A. E. Doyle to D. M. Jack, Mar. 8, 1926, SUPBP, File: 1926.
36. Letter A. E. Doyle to D. M. Jack, Aug. 4, 1926, SUPBP, Box 226, File: Mr. Doyle Abroad.
37. Letter, A. E. Doyle to Wilfred Higgins, Nov. 1, 1915, SUPBP, Box 221, File: 1915.
38. Letter, A. E. Doyle to C. C. Overmire, President, Portland Auto Club, Nov. 2, 1915, SUPBP, Box 221, File: 1915.
39. Letter, A. E. Doyle to Northwestern Fidelity Company, Dec. 29, 1915, SUPBP, Box 221, File: 1915.
40. Letter, A. E. Doyle to Morgan, Fliedner & Boyce, Dec. 29, 1915, SUPBP, Box 221, File: 1915.
41. Letter, A. E. Doyle to W. B. Patterson, Dec. 31, 1915 (misfiled), SUPBP, Box 221, File: 1916.
42. McMath SB. *Jour.*, May 21, 1916.
43. Letter, A. E. Doyle to W. T. Foster, Nov. 2, 1915, Box 221, File: 1915.
44. *Oreg.*, January 1, 1918, sec. 4, p. 14. There were 5959 building permits in 1914 for a total value of $8,335, 000. In 1915 they fell to 4623 for $4,895,000. In 1916 there were 4467 permits for $6,361,000.
45. Letter, A. E. Doyle to L. E. Macomber, May 18, 1916, RC, Arlington Club File, hereafter ACF.
46. Letter, unsigned, to Miss M. A. Rockwell, May 22, 1916, SUPBP, Box 221 File: 1916.

47. Lowenstein, *The Jews of Oregon*, p. 184. *Jour.*, Oct. 15, 1916, sec. 3, p. 9. McMath, SB. Wemme's will was drawn by George Joseph, a lawyer who practiced with Julius Meier, the younger son of Aaron Meier, before Julius became the director of Meier & Frank. George Joseph was the legal advisor to Meier & Frank. One of the executors of Wemme's estate was Ben Selling.
48. OHS, SB, 122:249.
49. Letter, A. E. Doyle to Mr. Myron Hunt, Nov. 22, 1923, SUPBP, Box 224, Miscellaneous Correspondence, File: Jul.-Dec. 1923.
50. Letter, M. Hunt to A.E. Doyle, December 13, 1923, SUPBP, Box 224, File: Jul. to Dec. 1923.
51. Hawkins and Willingham, *Classic Houses*, pp. 296, 304-7.
52. HRI, Frank J. Cobbs House.
53. *Jour.*, April 19, 1951, p. 10. *Oreg.*, April 10, 1951, p. 17.
54. Letter, A. E. Doyle to S. D. Lynd, Mar. 1, 1919, SUPBP, Box 221, File: 1919.
55. "Living Warmth," *Oregon Voter*, vol 10 (July-Sept. 1917), p. 201.
56. Letter, A. E. Doyle to C. C. Chapman, Aug. 20, 1917, SUPBP, Box 221, File: 1917.
57. Letter, F. Logan to A. E. Doyle, Jan. 5, 1917, SUPBP, Box 221, File: 1917.
58. Letter, A. E. Doyle to J. Parker, May 31, 1916, SUPBP, Box 221, File: 1916.
59. Letter, A. E. Doyle to B. L. Fenner, Sep. 22, 1916. SUPBP, Box 221, File: 1916.
60. Letter, A. E. Doyle to A. McBean, Sep. 7, 1916, SUPBP, Box 221, File: 1916.
61. Letter, A. E. Doyle to J. A. Zittel, May 4, 1917, SUPBP, Box 221, File: 1917. Reeves found work first with the National Cash Register Company and then as a salesman for H. W. Johns-Manville Co. Later he moved to Hawaii and worked for a cold storage company.
62. "Commissions received since June 1, 1915 to Nov. 13, 1916" and "Money paid out to A.E. Doyle from June 1st 1915 to Nov 13, 1916," SUPBP, Box 222. File: Correspondence 1916.
63. Letter, F. Logan to A. E. Doyle, Jan 5, 1917; Letter, A. E. Doyle to F. Logan, Jan 15, 1915, SUPBP, Box 221, File:1917.
64. From newspaper reviews quoted in *Arlington Club and the Men Who Built It*, pp. 43-44.
65. This correspondence was part of the Doyle Library, and it went with the library to Reed College, where it is now in Special Collections.
66. Letter, A. E. Doyle to Francis H. Bacon Co., Jun. 13, 1916, RC, ACF.
67. Letter, A. E. Doyle to Francis H. Bacon to attention of Mr. R. W. Jackson, Jun. 27, 1916. RC, ACF.
68. Letter, Francis Bacon to A. E. Doyle, Jul. 11, 1916. RC, ACF.
69. Letter, A. E. Doyle to G. Walter Gates, April 17, 1916, RC, ACF.

70. Letter, A. E. Doyle to L. E. Macomber , May 31, 1916, RC, ACF.
71. Letter, A. E. Doyle to G. W. Gates, April 17, 1916. RC, ACF.
72. Letter, A. E. Doyle to L. E. Macomber, May 18, 1916, RC, ACF.
73. A. E. Doyle, "Report of the Arlington Club Decorating and Furnishing Committee," Dec. 1916. RC, ACF.
74. Letter, A. E. Doyle to L. E. Macomber, May 18, 1916, RC, ACF.
75. "Report From the House Committee and the Committee on Art and Literature," Feb. 1921, RC, ACF.
76. Letter, F. W. Jones to A. E. Doyle, Feb. 9, 1917, SUPBP, Box 221, File: 1917.
77. Letter, A. E. Doyle to F. W. Jones, Feb. 14, 1917, SUPBP, Box 221, File: 1917.
78. Letter, A. E. Doyle to C. H. Cheney, May 12, 1919, SUPBP, Box 222, File: 1919.
79. Cheney, "The Work of Albert E. Doyle," *The Architect and Engineer*, pp. 39-86.
80. Letter, A. E. Doyle to C. H. Cheney, Jul. 16, 1919, SUPBP, Box 221, File: 1919.
81. Letter, A. E Doyle to R. C. McLean, Apr. 23, 1917. SUPBP, Box 221, File: 1918.
82. *Oreg.*, Jan. 1, 1918, sec. 4, pp. 4, 14.
83. *Oreg.*, Jan. 1, 1919, sec, 1, p. 1.
84. *Oreg.*, Jan. 1, 1919, p. 10.
85. Letter, A. E. Doyle to Francis Dykes, Jan. 4, 1918, SUPBP, Box 221, File: 1918.
86. Letter, A. E. Doyle to G. L. Baker, Aug. 5, 1919, SUPBP, Box 221, File: 1919.
87. Letter, A. E. Doyle to J. G. Beach, June 21 1918, SUPBP, Box 221, File: 1918.
88. Letter, A. E. Doyle to C. H. Kirk, Dec. 17, 1918, SUPBP, Box 221, File: 1918.

Chapter 6: After War

1. Letter, A. E. Doyle to A. McBean, Dec. 12, 1918. SUPBP, Box 221, File: 1918.
2. Letter, A. E. Doyle to C. K. Greene, Dec. 30, 1918, , Box 224, File: Chas K. Greene.
3. *Oreg.*, Jan. 1, 1922, sec. 5, p. 3.
4. The AIA jury results were published in *The Architect and Engineer*, March 1919. Cheney's article appeared in the July issue.
5. Letter, A. E. Doyle to C. A. Merriam, Aug. 5, 1919, SUPBP, Box 222, File: Doyle & Merriam 1919.
6. Letter, A. E. Doyle to G. H. Jones, Nov. 28, 1919, SUPBP, Box 221, File: 1919.

7. Letter, A. E. Doyle to S. D. Lynd, Mar. 1, 1919, SUPBP, Box 221, File: 1919.
8. Letter, A. E. Doyle to G. L. Baker, Aug. 5, 1919, SUPBP, Box 221, File: 1919.
9. Letter, A. E. Doyle to Julius Meier, Aug. 25, 1919, SUPBP, Box 221, File: 1919.
10. Letter, A. E. Doyle to L. Welton, Aug. 25, 1921, SUPBP, Box 222, Folder II.
11. Letter, A. E. Doyle to Frederick & Nelson, Jul. 21, 1914, SUPBP, Box 222, Folder II.
12. Letter, A. E. Doyle to H. M. Reeves, Feb. 18, 1916, SUPBP, Box 221, File: 1916.
13. Letter A. E. Doyle to H. C. Reese, Sept. 4, 1920. SUPBP, Box 224, File: (untitled).
14. Letter, A. E. Doyle to H. C. Reese, September 30, 1920, SUPBP, Box 224, File: (untitled).
15. Letter, A. E. Doyle to C. A. Merriam, Jul. 9, 1919, SUPBP, Box 222, File: Doyle & Merriam 1919.
16. Letter, A. E. Doyle to W. Pollman, Oct. 8, 1919, SUPBP, Box 221, File: 1919.
17. Letter, A. E. Doyle to C. A. Merriam, Dec. 13, 1919, SUPBP, Box 222, File: Doyle & Merriam 1919.
18. Letter, C. A. Merriam to A. E. Doyle, May 25, 1920, SUPBP, Box 222, File: Doyle & Merriam 1919.
19. Multnomah County Deeds, Book 803, p. 83.
20. Letter, A. E. Doyle to Nelly Fox, Dec. 13, 1921, SUPBP, Box 222, File: 1920-2, Folder I.
21. SUPBP, Box 226, File: A. E. Doyle Correspondence and Bills on House.
22. "House for A. E. Doyle 755 Tillamook," SUPBP, Safe Drawer #2.
23. Letter, A. E. Doyle to Mrs. C. B. Lucas, Feb. 11, 1920, SUPBP, Box 222, Folder II.
24. Greene's biography is from an application for a veterans' bonus or loan, SUPBP, Box 224, File: Chas K. Greene. See also Ritz, *Architects of Oregon*, p. 156.
25. Letter, A. E. Doyle to Miss Cornelia Marvin, Aug. 11, 1919, SUPBP, Box 221, File: 1919.
26. Tax Returns, SUPBP, Box 224, File: Chas K. Greene.
27. Letter, A. E. Doyle to C. K. Greene, Apr. 25, 1921, SUPBP, Box 222, File: Folder I.
28. Letter, A. E. Doyle to C. K. Greene, Apr. 27, 1921, SUPBP, Box 222, File: Folder I.
29. C. K. Greene's frequent letters were filed together. SUPBP, Box 224, File: C. K. Greene 1926 and Back.
30. Letter, C. K. Greene to Buddies, undated but end of May 1921, SUPBP. Box 224, File: Chas K. Greene.

31. Letter, C. K. Greene to C. A. Merriam, undated but end of May 1921, SUPBP, Box 224, File: Chas K. Greene.
32. Letter, R. Weaver to A. E. Doyle, Sept. 21, 1922, SUPBP, Box 222, Folder II.
33. Letter, D. J. Stewart to A. E. Doyle, Sep. 30, 1922, SUPBP, Box 222, Folder II.
34. *Oreg.*, Jan. 1, 1924, sec. 5, pp. 1-22.
35. Letter, A. E. Doyle to C. A. Merriam, Feb. 21, 1923, SUPBP, Box 223, File: Doyle & Merriam 1923.
36. NRHP, The Butler Bank.
37. *Oreg.*, Jan. 1, 1922, sec. 5. Letter, A. E. Doyle to Miss Anne M. Mulheron, SUPBP, Box 222, Folder II.
38. Letter, A. E. Doyle to J. McComb, Dec. 21, 1922, SUPBP, Box 222, Folder II.
39. Letter, A. E. Doyle to A. G. Lindley, April 25, 1923, SUPBP, Box 219, A. E. Doyle Correspondence Personal, File: 1923.
40. Letter, A. E. Doyle to C. A. Merriam, May 27, 1923, SUPBP, Box 223, File: Doyle & Merriam 1923.
41. Greene's tax returns are in SUPBP, Box 224, File: Greene 1926 and Back.
42. Letter, A. E. Doyle to M. Fleishhacker, Sep.. 4, 1923. SUPBP, Box, 219, File: 1923.
43. Letter, A. E. Doyle to P. E. Denivelle, Jul. 20, 1925, SUPBP, Box 192, File: Jul.-Dec. 1925.
44. *Oreg*. Jan 1, 1926, sec. 2, p. 2.
45. A. E. Doyle to F. O. Gladding, Jun. 25, 1926, SUPBP, Box 192, File Jan.-Jun. 1926.
46. *Oreg*. Jan 1, 1925, sec 5, p. 3.
47. NRHP, Bank of California, p. 2.
48. Letter, A. E. Doyle to J. W. Psangler, June 9, 1925, SUPBP, Box 192,. File: Jan.-Jun. 1925.
49. NRHP, Coleman H. Wheeler House. Hawkins and Willingham, *Classic Houses*, pp. 363-4. Letter, A. E. Doyle to Mrs. C. H. Wheeler, Dec. 1, 1922, SUPBP, Box 222, Folder II. The estimates were $45,000 for construction and $4500 (10%) for his fees.
50. Letter, A. E. Doyle to T. L. Eliot, SUPBP, Box 219, File: 1926.
51. Hawkins and Willingham, *Classic Houses*, p. 462. NRHP, The J. G. Edwards Residence.
52. Hawkins and Willingham, *Classic Houses*, pp. 360-61. NRHP, Bert Ball House.
53. *Oreg.*, Apr. 6, 1953, sec. 1, p. 15.
54. Hawkins and Willingham, *Classic Houses*, pp. 308-9. HRI.
55. Letter, J. R. Bowles to A. E. Doyle, Feb. 2, 1923, SUPBP, Box 223, File: Jan. to Jun. 1923.
56. *Oreg.*,Jan. 1, 1927, sec. 1, p. 18. NRHP, J. R. Bowles Residence.
57. Hawkins and Willingham, *Classic Houses*, pp. 335-36.

58. MacColl, *The Growth of a City*, p. 29. As Doyle was beginning the plans for his house, Bowles became embroiled in a dispute with one of the Portland newspapers, *The News*, now defunct. The editor, Fred Boalt, claimed in a front-page editorial in 1922 that Joseph R. Bowles had offered his paper one thousand dollars in advertising if the newspaper would support the candidacy of I. L. Patterson for governor. Bowles vehemently denied this accusation and threatened to sue the paper for libel unless Boalt retracted. Bowles could prove that he had not been in Portland at the time. Boalt retracted but not to Bowles' liking. In another scathing and prominent editorial he admitted he was in error. Joseph R. Bowles had not offered the bribe; it was his brother Charles Bowles. There was a resemblance between the two, and they were close. Joseph was president and Charles was vice-president of the Northwest Steel Company. Other newspapers became involved. *The Oregon Voter* was sympathetic to business interests in general, admired Joseph R. Bowles, in particular, and attacked *The News* for not knowing Charles Bowles and for discrediting the candidacy of Senator Patterson. *The Journal*, which was more sympathetic to labor and sometimes suspicious of capitalists, sided with *The News*. (OHS, SB, 213:13.)
59. Letter, A. E. Doyle to P. E. Denivelle, Jul. 20, 1925, SUPBP, Box 192, File: Jul.-Dec. 1925.
60. Letter, A. E. Doyle to P. E. Denivelle, Jul. 11, 1925, SUPBP, Box 219, File: 1925.
61. Letter, A. E. Doyle to F. H. Bacon, Jul. 11, 1925, SUPBP, Box 219, File: 1925.
62. Letter D. M. Jack to A. E. Doyle, Aug. 12, 1926, SUPBP, Box 226, File: Mr. Doyle Abroad.
63. W. H. Crowell to A. E. Doyle, Aug 12, 1926, SUPBP, Box 226, File: Mr. Doyle Abroad.
64. Letter, W. H. Crowell to A. E. Doyle, Sept 7, 1926, SUPBP, Box 226, File: Mr. Doyle Abroad.
65. Letter, D. M. Jack to A. E. Doyle, Oct. 13, 1926, SUPBP, Box 226, File: Mr. Doyle Abroad.
66. There was much interest in the Ladd mansion's demolition. OHS, SB 258, pp. 113-17.
67. Hall, "Portland the Spinster," *Collier's*, p. 30.
68. NRHP, The Pacific Building. The Pacific Building front face is 200 feet wide by 130 feet high while, for example, the Farnese Palace in Rome is 185 feet wide by 97 feet high.
69. *Jour.*, May 16, 1926, sec. 2, p. 2.
70. Musick, *The Development of the Pacific Building*.
71. See for example, Bosker and Lencek, *Frozen Music*, pp. 77-79.
72. NRHP, Public Service Building and Garage. Ritz, *Architects of Oregon*, pp. 186-87.

73. NRHP, The Public Service Building and Garage.
74. NRHP, Corbett Brothers' Auto Storage Garage.
75. NRHP, Terminal Sales Building.
76. NRHP, Pacific Building, sec. 7, p. 3.
77. *Oreg.*, Jan. 1, 1912, sec. 2. *Oreg.*, Jan. 1, 1920, sec. 4, p. 4.
78. NRHP, Multnomah Falls Lodge.
79. *Oreg.*, Jan. 1, 1923, sec. 5, p. 3.
80. *Oreg.*, Jan. 1, 1917, sec. 3, p. 12.
81. Ferriday, *Last of the Handmade Buildings*, p. 15.
82. Hegemann and Peets, *The American Vitruvius,* especially pp. 6, 29, 150, 187.
83. Ritz, *An Architect Looks at Downtown Portland*, pp. 47-52.

Chapter 7: To Avoid as Much Worry as Possible

1. Belluschi, interview with Meredith Clausen. transcript, p. 12.
2. Letter, D. M. Jack to A. E. Doyle, Oct. 5, 1926, SUPBP, Box 226, File: Mr. Doyle Abroad.
3. The Pacific Building (plans), OHS, MS 3022-76, folder 3. NRHP, Pacific Building Nomination Form, sec. 7, p. 10.
4. Letter, A. E. Doyle to F. Bacon, Nov. 21, 1925, SUPBP, Box 192, File: Jul.-Dec. 1925.
5. Letter, A. E. Doyle to D. M. Jack, Sep. 21, 1926. SUPBP, Box 226, File: Mr. Doyle Abroad.
6. Letter, A. E. Doyle to D. M. Jack, Oct. 3, 1926, SUPBP, Box 226, File: Mr. Doyle Abroad.
7. Letter, A. E. Doyle to F. H. Ransom, Feb. 19, 1925, SUPBP, Box 192, File: Jan.-Jun. 1925.
8. Letter, E. F. Lawrence to A. E. Doyle, Dec. 13, 1924, SUPBP, Box 192, File: Jul.-Dec. 1924.
9. Letter, A. E. Doyle to E. F. Lawrence, Dec. 16, 1924, SUPBP, Box 192, File: Jul.-Dec. 1924.
10. Letter, A. E. Doyle to Mrs. G. B. McLeod, Feb. 19, 1925, SUPBP, Box 192, File: Jan.-Jun. 1925.
11. Letter, A. E. Doyle to E. F. Lawrence, Feb. 6, 1925, Box 192, File: Jan.-Jun. 1925.
12. Letter, A. E. Doyle, to D. M. Jack, Sept. 21, 1926, SUPBP, Box 226, File: Mr. Doyle Abroad.
13. Letter, A. E. Doyle to A. McBean, May 29, 1926, SUPBP, Box 192, File: Jan.-Jun. 1926.
14. Letter, A. E. Doyle to R. H. Tanner, Dec. 28, 1925, SUPBP, Box 192, File: Jul.-Dec. 1925
15. Letter, A. E. Doyle to St. Helena Sanitarium, Feb. 8, 1926, Box 219, File: 1926.
16. Letter, A. E. Doyle to D. M. Jack, Mar. 5, 1926, Box 219, File: 1926.

17. Letter, A. E. Doyle to D. M. Jack, Mar. 12, 1926, SUPBP, Box 219, File: 1926.
18. Letter, D. M. Jack to D. J. Stewart, Apr. 13, 1926, SUPBP, Box 192, File: Jan.-Jun. 1926.
19. Letter, A. E. Doyle to Dr. H. C. and Eva J. Fixott, July 14, 1926, SUPBP Box 219, File: 1926.
20. Letter, A. E. Doyle to T. L. Eliot, Jul. 12, 1926, SUPBP, Box 219, File: 1926.
21. Letter, A. E. Doyle to C. A. Merriam, Feb. 2, 1926, SUPBP, Box 224, File: Doyle & Merriam 1925.
22. Letter, D. M. Jack to A. E. Doyle, March 10, 1926, SUPBP, Box 219, File: 1926.
23. Letter, A. E. Doyle to C. A. Merriam, Jun. 8, 1926. Box 224, File: Doyle & Merriam 1926.
24. Ritz, *Architects of Oregon*, p. 91.
25. Entry for Polk City Directory compiled by office of A. E. Doyle, Dec. 19, 1925, SUPBP, Box 193, File: Jul.-Dec. 1926.
26. Letter, D. M. Jack to C. K. Greene, Dec. 16, 1921, SUPBP, Box 224, File: C. K. Greene 1926 & Back
27. Letter, C. K. Greene to IRS, July 16, 1923, SUPBP, Box 224, File: Chas. K. Greene.
28. Letter, W. H. Crowell to D. M. Jack, undated but spring of 1926, SUPBP, Box 192, File: Jan-Jun. 1926.
29. Letter, C. K. Greene to A. E. Doyle, Aug. 10, 1926, SUPBP, Box 226, File: Mr. Doyle Abroad.
30. Letter, Mrs. A. C. Shives to C. K. Greene, Jul. 17, 1926, SUPBP, Box 224, File: Chas K. Greene.
31. Belluschi, interview with Meredith L. Clausen, transcript, pp. 6-10.
32. Letter, Whitehouse & Price Architects, Spokane, Washington, to A. E. Doyle, April 6, 1925, SUPBP, Box 192, File: Jan.-June 1925.
33. Letter, A. E. Doyle to W. H. Crowell, Oct. 28, 1926, SUPBP, Box 226, File: Mr. Doyle Abroad.
34. Letter, D. M. Jack to A. E. Doyle, Sep. 27, 1926, SUPBP, Box 226, File: Mr. Doyle Abroad.
35. Letter, D. M. Jack to A. E. Doyle, Oct. 21, 1926, SUPBP, Box 226, File: Mr. Doyle Abroad.
36. This is from an unsigned memorandum, written by D. M. Jack, Dec. 30, 1927, and quotes Doyle's narrative of how J. G. Beach returned to the Doyle firm. SUPBP, Box 220, File: Jun. to Dec. 1927
37. There are two very complete accounts of the Doyles' tour abroad. Lucie Godley (Mrs A. E.) Doyle kept a journal with frequent, often daily, entries. There are no page numbers. The journal now belongs to Lisa Holzgang. When I cite Mrs. Doyle, I refer to this diary. A. E. Doyle wrote D. M. Jack and his office frequently. His letters were often typed and distributed then filed with the originals and with correspondence too sensitive for general circulation in a file called

"Mr. Doyle Abroad" which is in SUPBP, Box 226. Almost all the correspondence between Doyle and his office during his European tour is in that file. Therefore any letter or telegram cited hereafter in that file will for brevity appear without box number and file name.

38. Letter, A. E. Doyle to D. M. Jack, Jul. 20, 1926.
39. Letter, A. E. Doyle to D. M. Jack, Jul. 25, 1926.
40. Letter, A. E. Doyle to D. M. Jack, Aug. 4, 1926.
41. Letter, A. E. Doyle to D. M. Jack, Aug. 13, 1926. A retired sea captain hated the English, Mrs. Doyle wrote, and "came to England to verify his already formed bad opinion of them," while Doyle said, he "hates the British and is going to England to confirm his views." A retired English farmer from Vancouver, Mrs. Doyle said "liked the ladies." Mr. Doyle said he "regales us with stories of his affairs with women." There was a lapsed nun who had married a priest and written a book about it. A music teacher from Los Angeles who had made $40,000 in real estate was going to Germany for a year with his wife and two small sons. A charming English colonel and his wife from Scotland, Mrs. Doyle said, were "delightful" while he said, "nothing queer about them." There were two Dutch women. An old one spent her life visiting her children, and a young one with a five-months-old baby had been deported "because of a technicality in her passport." The twelfth was "a lovely old English lady" sharing a cabin with the escaped nun; she was a "very positive person, but [she] is not quite happy." The six Doyles were, Mr. Doyle wrote, "the hungry six [who] never miss a meal. … [They are] on the whole a happy and agreeable family very little discontented in our own crowd."
42. Letter, A. E. Doyle to D. M. Jack, Aug. 19, 1926.
43. Letter, D. M. Jack to A. E. Doyle, Aug. 12, 1926.
44. Letter, A. E. Doyle to H. C. Reese, August 27, 1926.
45. Letter, A. E. Doyle to D. M. Jack, Aug. 24, 1926.
46. This Scotland travelogue was written over several days on several different hotel stationeries before they were gathered together and sent off to D. A. Jack sometime in early September 1926.
47. Postcard, Bill Doyle to D. M. Jack, Aug. 30, 1926.
48. Letter, A. E. Doyle to D. M. Jack, Sep. 16, 1926.
49. Letter, D. M. Jack to A. E. Doyle, Sep. 11, 1926.
50. Letter, A. E. Doyle to D. M. Jack, Sep. 21, 1926.
51. Telegram, D. M. Jack to A. E. Doyle, Sep. 29, 1926.
52. Letter, A. E. Doyle to D.M. Jack, Oct. 18, 1926.
53. Letter, D. M. Jack to A. E. Doyle, Sep. 7, 1926.
54. Letters, D. M. Jack to Mrs. Mary Mallory Roberts, Sep. 2, 1926 and Oct. 19, 1926, SUPBP, Box 224, File: Chas K. Greene.
55. Hawkins and Willingham, *Classic Houses*, pp. 465-66.
56. This account is untitled. SUPBP, Box 224, File: Chas K. Greene.
57. Letter, D. M. Jack to A. E. Doyle, Oct. 5, 1926.

58. A. E. Doyle's postcard collection, RCA.
59. In several letters during the Autumn of 1926 Doyle wrote Crocker and she him about problems of the old museum and ideas about a new one. PAM, Record Group II, Series 1, Box 23.
60. Letter, D. M. Jack to A. E. Doyle, Sept. 27, 1926.
61. Letter, A. E. Doyle to D. M. Jack, Oct. 14, 1926.
62. Letter, W. F. Higgins to A. E. Doyle, Oct. 14, 1926, SUPBP, Box 226,.
63. Letter, D. M. Jack to A. E. Doyle, Oct. 16, 1926, SUPBP, Box 226.
64. Letter, A. E. Doyle to D. M. Jack, Oct. 28, 1926, SUPBP, Box 226.
65. Ibid.
66. Letter, R. Strong to A. E. Doyle, Oct. 30, 1926, Box 219, File: 1927-28.
67. Letter, D. M. Jack to A. E. Doyle, Oct. 13, 1926, SUPBP, Box 226.
68. Letter, A. E. Doyle to D. M. Jack, Nov. 12, 1926, SUPBP, Box 226.
69. Letter, A. E. Doyle to D. M. Jack, Sep. 6, 1926, SUPBP.
70. Letter, A. E. Doyle to D. M. Jack, Oct. 3, 1926, SUPBP, Box 226.
71. This is a recurring theme in Doyle's October letters.
72. Letter, A. E. Doyle to D. M. Jack, Sep. 21, 1926.
73. Letter, A. E. Doyle to D. M. Jack, Nov. 12, 1926.
74. Letter, D. M. Jack to A. E. Doyle, Oct. 21, 1926, Box 226.
75. Letter, A. E. Doyle to D. M. Jack, Oct. 2, 1926, SUPBP, Box 226.
76. Letter, A. E. Doyle to D. M. Jack, Oct. 3, 1926, SUPBP, Box 226.
77. Letter, A. E. Doyle to D. M. Jack, Oct. 18, 1926, SUPBP, Box 226.
78. Postcard, A. E. Doyle to D. M. Jack, Oct. 24, 1926, SUPBP, Box 226.
79. Letter, C. K. Greene to A. E. Doyle, Oct. 5, 1926, SUPBP, Box 226.
80. Letter, D. M. Jack to A. E. Doyle, Oct. 5, 1926.
81. Letter, Dorothy Longmuire (the office secretary) to A. E. Doyle, Nov. 15, 1926.
82. Letter, C. K. Greene to D. M. Jack, undated but postmarked Nov. 10, 1926, SUPBP, Box 193, File: Jul. to Dec. 1926.
83. Letter, A. E. Doyle to D. M. Jack, Nov. 12, 1926.
84. Telegram, D. M. Jack to A. E. Doyle, Nov. 6, 1926.
85. A. E. Doyle's sketches: "A Floor Plan of Our Apartment, Dec. 1, 1926" and "Our Sitting Room, Dec. 8, 1926," Newhouse.
86. *The Lucy Dodd School 1927-28. An American School for Girls* (a school catalog), SUPBP, Box 219, File: 1927-28. OHS, SB 122, p. 219. *Oreg.* July 11, 1926, sec. 5. p. 2.
87. Telegram, A. E. Doyle to D. M. Jack, Dec. 23, 1926.
88. Letter, A. E. Doyle to Kathleen Doyle, Dec. 30, 1926, Newhouse.
89. Marjorie Newhouse has four letters from A. E. Doyle in Portland to his daughter, Kathleen (Marjorie's mother). They are dated Jan. 15, Jan. 26, Feb. 3, and Feb. 9, 1927.
90. Letter, A. E. Doyle to D. M. Jack, Mar. 1, 1927.
91. Letter, A. E. Doyle to D. M. Jack, Mar. 8, 1927.
92. Letter, A. E. Doyle to A. B. Crocker, Mar. 28, 1927, PAM, Record Group II, Series 1, Box 24.

93. Letter, A. E. Doyle to Kathleen Doyle, April 13, 1927, Newhouse. Letter, A. E. Doyle to A. B. Crocker, Apr. 14, 1927, PAM, Record Group II, Series 1, Box 24. See also Weaver, *A Legacy of Excellence*.
94. Letter, A. E. Doyle to B. Berenson, Aug. 17, 1927, SUPBP, Box 219, File: 1927-28.
95. Letter, A. B. Crocker to B. Berenson, no date, PAM, Box 24.
96. Samuels, *The Making of a Connoisseur*. Samuels, *Bernard Berenson, the Making of a Legend*. For Isabella Stewart Gardner, Berenson collected much of what is now in the museum that bears her name. He worked for other American millionaires like P. A. B. Widener, Carl W. Hamilton, and Samuel H. Kress.
97. *The American Renaissance, 1876-1917*, Brooklyn: Brooklyn Institute of Arts and Sciences, 1979, p. 2.
98. http:urcoll.f.a.pitt.edu
99. Brown, *Berenson and the Connoisseurship of Italian Painting*, p. 25.
100. Letter, A. E. Doyle to D. M. Jack, Apr. 30, 1927.
101. Letter, A. E. Doyle to A. B. Crocker, Mar. 28, 1927, PAM, Record Group II, Series 1, Box 24.

Chapter 8: Dwindling

1. Letter, A. E. Doyle to D. M. Jack, May 26, 1927; Letter, A. E. Doyle to D. M. Jack, May 28, 1927; Telegram, A. E. Doyle to D. M. Jack, May 19, 1927, SUPBP, Box 226, File: Mr. Doyle Abroad.
2. Belluschi, interview with Clausen, transcript, p. 10.
3. Greene's name is misspelled *Green* in the 1927 City Directory.
4. "Special Report," Portland Operating #5161, Portland Investigator X-1 Reports, April 25, 1927., SUPBP, Box 220, File: Jan.-Jun. 1927.
5. Letter, C. K. Greene to D. M. Jack, undated, SUPBP,. Box 220, File: Jan-June 1927.
6. Letter D. M. Jack to C. K. Greene, May 20, 1927, SUPBP, Box 220, File: Jan-Jun. 1927.
7. Boag, *Same-Sex Affairs*. The coverage of the investigation in the *Portland News* was front page and daily from November 15, 1912.
8. "Albert Ernest Doyle," *Reed College Bulletin*, vol. 7, #2 (Jan. 1928), no pagination.
9. Letter, S. Murray to A. E. Doyle, Nov. 15, 1923, SUPBP, Box 224, File: Jul.-Dec. 1923. See Ritz, *Architects of Oregon* for Tucker and Bear.
10. Letter D. M. Jack to C. K. Greene, May 20, 1927, SUPBP, Box 220, File Jan.-Jun. 1927.
11. Letter D. M. Jack to C. K. Greene, Aug. 8, 1927, SUPBP, Box 220, File: Jun.-Dec. 1927.
12. Letter, D. M. Jack to F. H. Greene, Aug. 8, 1927, SUPBP, Box 220, File: Jun.-Dec. 1927.
13. Letter, D. J. Stewart to D. M. Jack, Jun. 12, 1927, SUPBP, Box 220, File: Jun.-Dec. 1927.

14. Letter, D. M. Jack, to D. J. Stewart, Jul. 1, 1927, SUPBP, Box 220, File: Jun.-Dec. 1927
15. Letter, D. M. Jack to C. A. Merriam, July 29, 1927, SUPBP, Box 224, File: Doyle and Merriam 1927.
16. Letter, W. G. Doyle to D. M. Jack, Aug. 29, 1927, SUPBP, Box 220, File: Jun.-Dec. 1927.
17. Carey, *History of Oregon*, p. 110.
18. Clausen, *Pietro Belluschi*, especially, pp. 31 and 43.
19. Letter, Elizabeth R. Stewart to D. M. Jack, August 24, 1927, SUPBP, Box 220, File: Jun.-Dec. 1927.
20. Letter, D. M. Jack to D. J. Stewart, Oct. 24, 1927, SUPBP, Box 220, File: Jun.-Dec. 1927.
21. Letter, A. E. Doyle to L. A. Hobart, Sept. 15, 1927, SUPBP, Box 220, File: Jun.-Dec. 1927.
22. Letter, W. Bear to D. M. Jack. Sept. 28, 1927, SUPBP, Box 220 File: Jun.-Dec. 1927.
23. Letter, S. Gould to D. M. Jack, Oct. 11, 1927, SUPB, Box 220, File: Jun.-Dec. 1927.
24. Letter, S. Gould to D. M. Jack, Oct. 27, 1927, SUPBP, Box 220, File: Jun.-Dec. 1927.
25. Letter, S. Gould to A. E. Doyle, Jan 2, 1928 and letter, D. M. Jack to S. Gould, Jan. 6, 1928, SUPBP, Box 220, File: Jun.-Dec. 1927.
26. Letter, A. E. Doyle to Kathleen Doyle, Sep. 20, 1927, Newhouse.
27. Letter, A. E. Doyle to Kathleen Doyle, Oct. 1927, Newhouse.
28. Letter, A. E. Doyle to V. Macchioro, undated, SUPBP, Box 219, File: 1927-28.
29. Letter, A. E. Doyle, to Kathleen Doyle, Oct. 25, 1927, Newhouse.
30. Letter, A. E. Doyle to Mrs. Lucy Dodd Ramberg, undated, SUPBP, Box 219, File: 1927-28.
31. Letter, A. E. Doyle to B. Berenson, Aug. 17, 1927, SUPBP, Box 219, File: 1927-28.
32. Letter, A. E. Doyle to A. B. Crocker, undated, PAM, Record Group II, Series 1, Box 25.
33. Letter, A. E. Doyle to Kathleen Doyle, Oct. 25, 1927, Newhouse.
34. Doyle wrote Kathleen on Nov. 3, Nov. 7, and Nov. 13, Newhouse.
35. Letter, D. M. Jack to Mrs. Vera H. Pooler, Dec. 13, 1927. SUPBP, Box 220, File: Jun.-Dec. 1927.
36. Letter, Vera H. Pooler to D. M. Jack, December 13, 1927, SUPBP, Box 220, File: Jun.-Dec. 1927.
37. Telegram, Mrs. A. E. (Lucie) Doyle to Mrs. Lucy Ramberg, Dec. 15, 1927, SUPBP, Box 220, File: Jun.-Dec. 1927.
38. Telegram, Jean Doyle to D. M. Jack, Dec. 16, 1927, SUPBP, Box 220, File: Jun.-Dec. 1927.
39. Telegram, D. M. Jack to Jean Doyle, Dec. 16, 1927, SUPBP, Box 220, File: Jun.-Dec. 1927.

40. Telegram, D. M. Jack to A. J. McComb, Dec. 23, 1927, SUPBP, Box 220, File: Jun.-Dec. 1927.
41. Deposition (undated), SUPBP, Box 220, File: Jun.-Dec. 1927.
42. Letter, J. G. Beach to A. E. Doyle, Dec. 22, 1927, SUPBP, Box 220, File: Jun.-Dec. 1927.
43. Memorandum, December 30, 1927, SUPBP, Box 220, File: Jun.-Dec. 1927.
44. Letter, A. E. Doyle to W. Whidden, Dec. 27, 1927. SUPBP, Box 219, File: 1927-28.
45. Letter, A. E. Doyle to H. L. Corbett, Jan. 9, 1928, Box 219, File: 1927-28.
46. Letter, D. M. Jack to R. Charles, Jan. 9, 1928, SUPBP, Box 220, File: Jan.-Jun. 1928.
47. Letter, D. M. Jack to Mrs. Vera H. Pooler, Jan. 10, 1928, SUPBP, Box 220, File: Jan.-Jun, 1928.
48. Letter, D. M. Jack to Mrs. Vera H. Pooler, Jan. 12, 1928 (this letter is misfiled), SUPBP, Box 221, File: Jul.-Dec. 1928.
49. Letter, A. E. Doyle to C. A. Merriam, Jan. 16, 1928, SUPBP, Box 224, File: Doyle and Merriam 1927.
50. Letter, D. J. Stewart to A. E. Doyle, Jan 10, 1928, SUPBP, Box 220, File: Jun.-Dec. 1927.
51. A. E. Doyle to Hugh Hume, Jan. 21, 1928, SUPBP, Box 219, File: 1927-28.
52. Letter, D. M. Jack to W. Clist, Jan. 24, 1928, SUPBP, Box 220, File: Jan-June 1928.

Chapter 9: Carrying On

1. *Oreg.*, Jan. 24, 1928, p. 1. *Jour.*, Jan. 24, 1928, p. 5. *Oreg.*, Jan. 25, 1928, p. 8. *The Spectator*, Jan. 28, 1928, p. 5.
2. SUPBP, Safe Drawer #2, "Headstones for Mr. Doyle & Family."
3. Letter, Pacific Telephone and Telegraph to A. E. Doyle & Associate, Feb. 8, 1928, SUPBP, Box 220, File: Jan.-Jun. 1928.
4. Letter, D. M. Jack to Arlington Club, Mar. 7, 1928, SUPBP, Box 220, File: Jan-Jun. 1928.
5. Letter, A. B. Crocker to Henrietta E. Failing, May 8th 1928, PAM, Record Group II, Series I, Box 28.
6. *The Spectator*, Saturday, February 9, 1929.
7. Clausen, *Pietro Belluschi*, pp. 29-31.
8. Letter, P. Belluschi to Pacific Telephone & Telegraph Co., Dec. 17, 1928, Box 221, File: Jul.-Dec. 1928.
9. Pommer and Otto, *Weissenhof 1927 and The Modern Movement in Architecture*, p. 1.
10. Le Corbusier, *Towards A New Architecture*, p. 286. On the significance of 1927 and 1928 to the development of modern architecture see Kidney, *The Architecture of Choice*, p. 52.

11. Frank Lloyd Wright, "In the Cause of Architecture," *The Architectural Record*, 63 (Jan-June 1928), p. 57.
12. Postcard, A. E. Doyle to D. M. Jack, Oct. 22, 1926, SUPBP, Box 226, File: Mr. Doyle Abroad.
13. Postcard, A. E. Doyle to D. M. Jack, Oct. 24, 1926, SUPBP, Box 226, File: Mr. Doyle Abroad.
14. Letter, R. Strong to A. E. Doyle, Oct. 30, 1926, SUPBP, Box 219, File: 1927-28.
15. Ritz, *An Architect*, p. 9. Ferriday, *Last of the Handmade Buildings*, p. 20.
16. Letter, A. E. Doyle to D. M. Jack, Mar. 8, 1926, SUPBP, Box 219, File: 1926.
17. Sullivan, *The Autobiography of an Idea*, especially, pp. 257-58, 323-24. Andrew, *Louis Sullivan and the Polemics of Modern Architecture*, especially pp. xi, 39, and 104.
18. Clausen, *Pietro Belluschi*, especially, pp. 31 and 43.
19. Ibid., p. 42.
20. *Oreg.*, Jan. 14, 1968, "Northwest Magazine," p. 20.
21. *Oreg.*, Apr. 14, 1965, p. 21. *Oreg.*, Oct. 11, 1931, sec. 1, p. 1. Hawkins and Willingham, *Classic Houses*, pp. 384-86, 457-59.
22. Hawkins and Willingham, *Classic Houses*, pp. 384-86, 457-59.
23. Sullivan's *Autobiography of an Idea* is not now in the Doyle Library at Reed. It was listed in the 1927 catalog and disappeared sometime between then and 1994, when Reed acquired the library.
24. Letter, A. E. Doyle, to R. M. Bates, Nov. 2, 1923, SUPBP. , Box 219, File: 1923.
25. Letter, A. E. Doyle to J. W. Psangler, June 9, 1925, SUPBP, Box 192, File: Jan.-Jun. 1925.
26. Letter, A. E. Doyle to A. B. Crocker, Oct. 5, 1926, PAM, Record Group II, Series 1, Box 23.
27. Letter, D. M. Jack to A. E. Doyle, August 12, 1926, SUPBP, Box 226, File: Mr. Doyle Abroad.
28. Letter, A. E. Doyle to Mr. Arthur, London, Sep. 12, 1926, SUPBP, Box 226, File: Mr. Doyle Abroad.
29. Letter, M. Jack to A. E. Doyle, Sep. 7, 1926, SUPBP, Box 226, File: Mr. Doyle Abroad.
30. Ritz, *An Architect Looks*, p. 3.
31. Letter, A. E. Doyle to F. N. Clark & Company, July 24, 1916, SUPBP, Box 221, File: 1916.
32. Letter, A. E. Doyle to W. P. Polland, Sep. 10, 1919, SUPBP, Box 221, File: 1919.
33. NRHP, The Benson Hotel.
34. Ritz, *An Architect Looks*, p. 9.
35. Bosker and Lencek, *Frozen Music*, pp. 51, 77.
36. Letter, W. F. Higgins to A. E. Doyle, Oct. 14, 1926, SUPBP, Box 226, File: Mr. Doyle Abroad.

37. Letter, A. E. Doyle to D. M. Jack, Jul. 20, 1926, SUPBP, Box 226, File: Mr. Doyle Abroad.
38. Letter, A. E. Doyle to E. F. Lawrence, January 13, 1928, Box 219, File: 1927-28.39. The three modernist exhibitions of 1913, 1924, and 1927 are very well documented in the Portland Art Museum Scrapbooks. They include both reviews in the newspapers and exhibit programs. PAM, Record Group VI, PR Sub-Group: Scrapbooks Series News Clippings, Box 43, vol. 3.
40. Letter, A. B. Crocker to C. F. Gould, Apr. 5, 1928, PAM, Record Group II, Series 1, Box 28.
41. Clausen, *Pietro Belluschi*, p. 43.
42. Stubblebine (ed.), *The Northwest Architecture of Pietro Belluschi*, p. 5.
43. Belluschi, interview with Clausen, transcript, pp. 20-21.
44. Clausen discusses the Portland Art Museum and the controversy surrounding it with full citation of the important sources. See her *Pietro Belluschi*, pp. 54-64.
45. Belluschi, "On the Role of the Modern Museum in Our New Civilization," in Stubblebine (ed.), *The Northwest Architecture*, especially pp. 15, 22.
46. Wright, *Letters to Architects*, pp. 88-89.
47. For discussions of Doyle's contribution to the Northwest Regional style see McMath, "Emerging Regional Style," in Vaughan and Ferriday (eds.), *Space, Style, and Structure*, vol. 1, pp.344-45; Hawkins and Willingham, *Classic Houses*, pp. 520-21; and Clausen, *Pietro Belluschi*, pp. 48-49.
48. *Supplement of 1935 to the Oregon Code of 1930*, vol. 5, 68-304.
49. Clausen, *Pietro Belluschi*, p. 55-56.

Afterward

1. Ritz, *Architects of Oregon*, pp. 29-34. Clausen, *Pietro Belluschi*.
2. *Oreg.*, Mar. 10, 1950, p. 15.
3. *Oreg.*, May 8, 1973, p. 26.
4. Ritz, *Architects of Oregon*.
5. *Oreg.*, Oct. 4, 1936, sec. 1, p. 25. *Oreg.*, July 5, 1936, sec. 1. p. 1.
6. "Heritage in the Making Greek and Roman Casts from the Portland Art Museum December 8, 1987 – January 17, 1988," Portland: Oregon Art Institute. PAM, Vertifical File: Greek and Roman Casts.
7. *Jour.*, May 27, 1953, p. 10.
8. *Oreg.*, May 3, 1959, Sec. 3, p. 11. *Oreg.*, Feb. 4, 1961, p. 7. *Jour.*, Feb. 5, 1961, Sec. 1, p. 13, *Oreg.*, Feb. 12, 1961 sec. 3 p. 13, *Oreg.*, Mar. 21, 1965, Sec. 2, p. 13.
9. Interview, December 10, 2002, Marjorie Newhouse, who was then living with her mother and overheard the conversation.

Selected Bibliography

Manuscripts

The manuscript collections are described in the Preface.

Interviews

Belluschi, Pietro, Transcript of tape-recorded interview with Pietro Belluschi, Portland, Oregon, Aug. 22 & 23, Sep. 4, 1983, Meredith L. Clausen, interviewer, Archives of American Art Smithsonian Institution. Northwest Oral History Project.

Corbett, Gretchen Hoyt, *Oral History Interview with Gretchen Hoyt Corbett*, April 28, 1967, OHS.

Crocker, Anna Belle and Florence, with Rachael Griffin sometime in the 1940s. See "Some notes from the Misses Crocker on the members of the first Board of Trustees of the Portland Art Association … Notes taken by Rachael Griffin from conversations with the Misses Crocker probably sometime in the 1940s," PAM, Record Group II, Series 1, Box 1.

McMath, George, with author, December 5, 2002.

MacNaughton, E. B., with D. Johansen, RC. June 1960.

Newhouse, Marjorie, with author, November 14, 2002 and December 10, 2002.

Wentz, Harry, "The Portland Sketch Club," notes by Harry Wentz given to Rachael Griffin in 1957, PAM, Record Group II, Series 1, Box 1.

Newspapers, Contemporary Periodicals, and Annuals

The Blue Book and Social Register of Portland, published by The Blue Book Company Publishers.

Chehalis Bee Nugget

The Oregon Journal

The Oregonian

The Pacific Builder and Engineer

The Pacific Coast Architect

The Portland News

The Portland Telegram or *The Evening Telegram*

Portland Architectural Club, *Yearbook and Catalogue*

Oregon Voter: Magazine of Citizenship—for Busy Men and Women

The Reed College *Quest*

Spectator: Portland's Premier Weekly Review

Unpublished Studies and Sources

Crocker, Anna Belle, *It Goes Deeper Than We Think*, privately printed, 1946.

Glazer, Michele, *Neighborhood House: The History of a Portland, Oregon Settlement House, 1896-1929*, unpublished, OHS, 1982.

Head, Lewis M., *Neah-kah-nie Mountain, the Most Beautiful Spot on the Oregon Coast*, n.p., n.d., (c. 1910), OHS.

Kadas, Marianne Hakanson, *In the Shadow of Neahkahnie: Northwest Regional Style Beginnings*, unpublished M.A. Thesis, University of Oregon, 1991.

Musick, Felicity, *The Development of the Pacific Building and the Public Service Building*, unpublished final project for internship at OHS, June 10, 1976.

National Register of Historic Places, Nomination Forms, Oregon Parks and Recreation Department, State of Oregon Preservation Office, Salem, and at OHS.

Pell, Paul Timothy, *The Architecture of Albert Ernest Doyle*, unpublished Reed College B.A Thesis, 1976.

"Work of Whidden and Lewis," compiled by Herb Fredericks, OHS, Vertical File: Whidden & Lewis.

Published Books and Periodical Articles

Abbott, Carl, *Portland Gateway to the Northwest*, Northridge, California: Windsor Publications, 1985.

Abbott, Carl, *The Great Extravaganza*, Portland: OHS Press, 1996.

Allen, Ginny, and Jody Klevit, *Oregon Painters: The First Hundred Years (1859-1959)*, Portland: OHS Press, 1999.

Andrew, David S., *Louis Sullivan and the Polemics of Modern Architecture: The Present Against the Past*, Urbana and Chicago: University of Illinois Press, 1985.

Arlington Club and the Men Who Built It, Portland: Arlington Club, 1968.

Boag, Peter, *Same-Sex Affairs: Constructing and Controlling Homosexuality in the Pacific Northwest*, Berkeley, University of California Press, 2003.

Bosker, Gideon, and Lena Lencek, *Frozen Music: A History of Portland Architecture*, Portland; OHS Press, 1985.

Brindley, W. E., "Originality of the Lewis and Clark Exposition," *Pacific Monthly*, 13 (1905), 287-90.

Brown, David Alan, *Berenson and the Connoisseurship of Italian Painting*, Washington: National Gallery of Art, 1979.

Brooklyn Museum, *The American Renaissance, 1876-1917*, Brooklyn: Brooklyn Institute of Arts and Sciences, 1979.

Carey, Charles Henry, *History of Oregon*, Chicago and Portland: Pioneer Historical Publishing Co., 1922, 3 vols.

Cheney, Charles H., "The Work of Albert E. Doyle, Architect of Portland, Oregon," *The Architect and Engineer*, 58 (1919), pp. 39-86.

Clark, Rosalind, *Oregon Style, Architecture from 1840 to the 1950s*, Portland: Western Imprints, 1984.

Clausen, Meredith L., *Pietro Belluschi: Modern American Architect*, Cambridge, MA: MIT Press, 1994.

Clock, Paul, *The Saga of Pacific Railway & Navigation Co.: Punk Rotten & Nasty*, Portland: Corbett Press, c. 2000.

Comerford, Jane Ann, *At the Foot of the Mountain*, Portland: Dragonfly Press, 2004.

DeWolfe, Fred, *Old Portland*, Portland: Portland Press – 22, 1976.

Downs, Winfield Scott (ed.), *Encyclopedia of Northwest Biography*, New York: American Historical Company, 1943.

Edwards, G. Thomas, and C. A. Schwantes, *Experiences in a Promised Land: Essays in Pacific Northwest History*, Seattle: University of Washington Press, 1986.

Eliot, Thomas Lamb, "Albert Ernest Doyle 1877-1928," Reed *College Bulletin*, Vol. 7, Number 2 (January 1928).

Ferriday, Virginia G., *Last of the Handmade Buildings*, Portland: Mark Pub. Co., 1984.

Fryer, W. J. Jr., "Skeleton Construction: The New Method of Constructing High Buildings," *Architectural Record*, 1 (1891-1892), 228-35.

Fussell, Paul, *The Norton Book of Trave*l, New York and London: Norton, 1987.

Gaston, Joseph, *Portland Oregon, Its History and Builders: In Connection with the Antecedent Explorations, Discoveries, and Movements of the Pioneers that Selected the Site for the Great City of the Pacific*, Chicago: S. J. Clarke Pub. Co., 1911.

Gohs, Carl, "Forestry Building First Big Job for Young Architect A. E. Doyle," *Portland Reporter*, Sep. 5, 1964, p. 10.

Graf, Victor, "A. E. Doyle: He set the Trend of Portland Architecture in the 1920s," *Northwest Magazine*, February 5, 1978.

Gunselman, Cheryl, "Pioneering Free Library Service for the City, 1864-1902: The Library Association of Portland and the Portland Public Library," *OHQ*, 103 (2002), 320-37.

Hall, Wilbur, "Portland the Spinster," *Collier's* May 19, 1917, pp. 30-38.

Haskell, Thomas, ed., *The Authority of Experts: Studies in History and Theory*, Bloomington: Indiana University Press, 1984.

Haskell, Thomas, *The Emergence of Professional Social Science: The American Social Science Association and the Nineteenth-Century Crisis of Authority*, Urbana: University of Illinois Press, 1977.

Hawkins, William J., and W. F. Willingham, *Classic Houses of Portland, Oregon, 1850-1950*, Portland: Timber Press, 1999.

Hegemann, Werner, and Elbert Peets, *The American Vitruvius, An Architects' Handbook of Civic Art*, New York: The Architectural Book Pub., Co., 1922.

Historic Resource Inventory, City of Portland, Oregon: Identified Properties. Portland: Bureau of Planning, 1984.

Johansen, Dorothy O., and C. M Gates, *Empire of the Columbia: A History of the Pacific Northwest,* New York: Harper & Row, 1967.

Karl Baedeker (firm), *Belgium and Holland,* Leipsic: K. Baedeker and New York: C. Scribner's Sons, 1905.

Karl Baedeker (firm), *Greece,* Leipsic: Karl Baedeker and New York: C. Scribner's Sons, 1905.

Karl Baedeker (firm), *Italy from the Alps to Naples,* Leipsic: Karl Baedeker and New York: C. Scribner's Sons, 1904.

Karl Baedeker (firm), *The Mediterranean: Seaports and Sea Routes,* Leipsic: Karl Baedeker and New York: C. Scribner's Sons, 1911.

Karl Baedeker (firm), *Northern France from Belgium and the English Channel to the Loire,* Leipsic, K. Baedeker; New York: C. Scribner's Sons, 1899.

Karl Baedeker (firm), *Spain and Portugal,* Leipsic and New York: 2nd edition, Leipsic: Karl Baedeker, 1901.

Kidney, Walter C., *The Architecture of Choice: Eclecticism in America 1880-1930,* New York: Braziller, 1974.

King, Bart, *An Architectural Guidebook to Portland,* Corvallis: Oregon State University Press, 2007.

Kostof, Spiro, ed., *The Architect: Chapters in the History of the Profession,* New York: Oxford University Press, 1977.

Lansing, Jewel, *Portland, People, Politics, and Power, 1851-2001,* Corvallis: Oregon State University Press, 2003.

Larson, Magali Sarfatti, *The Rise of Professionalism: A Sociological Analysis,* Berkeley: University of California Press, 1977.

Le Corbusier, *Towards A New Architecture,* New York: Brewer & Warren, 1927, trans. by F. Etchells.

Leach, William R., *Land of Desire: Merchants, Power, and the Rise of a New American Culture,* New York: Patheon Books, 1993.

Lowenstein, Steven, *The Jews of Oregon, 1850-1950,* Portland: Jewish Historical Society of Oregon, 1987.

MacColl, E. Kimbark, *The Growth of a City: Power and Politics in Portland, Oregon, 1915-1950,* Portland: Georgian Press, 1979.

MacColl, E. Kimbark, with Harry Stein, *Merchants, Money, and Power: The Portland Establishment, 1843-1913,* Portland: Georgian Press, 1988.

MacColl, E. Kimbark, *The Shaping of a City: Business and Politics in Portland, Oregon 1885 -1915,* Portland: Georgian Press, 1976.

Marlitt, Richard, *Matters of Proportion: The Portland Residential Architecture of Whidden & Lewis,* Portland: OHS Press, 1989.

Meissner, Daniel J., "Theodor B. Wilcox, Captain of Industry and Magnate of the China Flour Trade, 1884-1918," *OHQ,* 104 (Winter, 2003), pp. 518-41.

Murray, Richard N., "Painting and Sculpture," *The American Renaissance, 1876-1917*, Brooklyn: Brooklyn Institute of Arts and Sciences, 1979.

Nicoll, G. Douglas, "The Rise and Fall of the Portland Hotel," *OHQ*, 99 (1998-99), pp. 298-335.

O'Donnell, Terrence, and Thomas Vaughan, *Portland, an Informal Guide*, Portland: Western Imprints, 1984.

Oliver, Richard, ed., *The Making of an Architect 1881-1981: Columbia University in the City of New York*, New York: Rizzoli, 1981.

Penrose, Francis Cranmer, *An Investigation of the Principles of Athenian Architecture: or, the results of a Survey Conducted Chiefly with Reference to the Optical Refinements Exhibited in the Construction of the Ancient Buildings at Athens*, London and New York, MacMillan, 1888.

Placzek, Adolf H., ed., *Macmillan Encyclopedia of Architects*, New York, Free Press, 1982.

Pommer, Richard, and Christian F. Otto, *Weissenhof 1927 and the Modern Movement in Architecture*, Chicago: University of Chicago Press, 1991.

(Portland) *City Directory*. Portland, R. L. Polk & Co. (Before the Polk Company City Directories were by by S. J. McCormick & Sons and J. K. Gill & Co.)

The Portland Block Book, Portland, The Portland Block Book Company, 1907.

Ritz, Richard E., *An Architect Looks at Downtown Portland*, Portland: Greenhills Press, 1991.

Ritz, Richard E., *Architects of Oregon*, Portland: Lair Hill Pub., 2002.

Ritz, Richard E., *Central Library: Portland's Crown Jewel*, Portland: Library Foundation, 2000.

Ritz, Richard E., *A History of the Reed College Campus and its Buildings*, Portland: The Trustees of the Reed Institute, 1990.

Roos, Roy E., *The History and Development of Portland's Irvington Neighborhood*, Portland: R. E. Roos, 1997.

Samuels, Ernest, *Bernard Berenson, The Making of a Legend*, Cambridge, MA.: Belknap Press, 1987.

Samuels, Ernest, *Bernard Berenson, The Making of a Connoisseur*, Cambridge, MA.: Belknap Press, 1979.

Schwantes, Carlos A., *Railroad Signatures Across the Pacific Northwest*, Seattle: University of Washington Press, 1993.

Schwantes, Carlos A., *Columbia River: Gateway to the West*, Moscow, ID.: University of Idaho Press, 2000.

Scott, Harvey, W., *History of Portland Oregon*, Syracuse: D. Mason, 1890.

Sheldon, Edmund P., "Oregon's Log Palace," *Pacific Monthly*, 13 (1905), 221-29.

Sheldon, Henry D., *History of University of Oregon*, Portland: Binford & Mort, 1940.

Shellenbarger, Michael (ed.), *Harmony in Diversity: The Architecture and Teaching of Elis F. Lawrence*, Eugene: Museum of Art and the Historic Preservation Program, School of Architecture and Allied Arts, University of Oregon, 1989.

Snyder, Eugene E., *Portland Names and Neighborhoods: Their Historic Origins*, Portland: Binford & Mort, 1979.

Stubblebine, Jo, ed., *The Northwest Architecture of Pietro Belluschi*, New York: F. W. Dodge Corp., 1953.

Sullivan, Louis H., *The Autobiography of an Idea*, New York: Norton, 1926 (first published 1922).

Vaughan, Thomas, and V. G. Ferriday (ed.), *Space, Style and Structure: Building in Northwest America*, Portland: OHS Press, 1974.

Tallmadge, Thomas E., *The Story of Architecture in America*, New York: W. W. Norton & Co., 1927.

Turner, Paul Venable, *Campus: An American Planning Tradition*, Cambridge, MA.: MIT Press, 1987.

Ward, Lock and Company, *Pictorial and Descriptive Guide to London and Its Environs*, London: Ward, 1906.

Watson, Esther Kelly, *Westminster Presbyterian Church*, Portland: Irwin Hodson Co., 1981.

Wilbur, Earl Morse, *Thomas Lamb Eliot, 1841-1936*, Portland: privately printed, 1937.

Withey, Lynne, *Grand Tours and Cook's Tours: A History of Leisure Travel, 1750-1915*, New York: W. Morrow, 1997.

Withey, Henry F., and Elsie R. Withey, *Biographical Dictionary of American Architects (Deceased)*, Los Angeles: New Age Publishing Co., 1956.

Wollner, Craig, *The City Builders: One Hundred Years of Union Carpentry in Portland, Oregon*, Portland: OHS Press, 1990.

Wood, Erskine, *Life of Charles Erskine Scott Wood, a Renaissance Man*, Vancouver, WA.: privately printed, 1991.

Woods, Mary N., *From Craft to Profession: The Practice of Architecture in Nineteenth-Century America*, Berkeley: University of California Press, 1999.

Index